*Simon Peter was
bound by fear*

*What changed him
can change you*

THE CAPTIVE
and the King's Will

John R Cross

Published by GoodSeed® International

II ❖

The Captive and the King's Will
Edition 1a

Copyright © 2018 by John R. Cross

Printed 2018, 2021

Published by GoodSeed International
Email: info@goodseed.com

ISBN 978-1-77304-084-4

CONTENTS

To remain consistent with the Bible texts chosen, in most cases I have used small initial letters for pronouns and nouns that relate to God.

Where Scripture text is boldfaced, an emphasis has been added. Square brackets indicate additions for explanatory purposes.

The Captive and the King's Will introduces the reader to seven different translations of the Bible. None of the translations differ in content communicated or affect the accompanying commentary.

PREFACE

This book is written for those who are new believers in the Lord Jesus Christ. It is a book of next steps—steps that a person takes in walking with God day by day. It is a book that is best read slowly, giving time to "chew" on the subject matter.

As you read, I trust you will gain comfort in identifying with the lives of those you find within these pages. I certainly do. Take for example Simon Peter. He was a close friend and disciple of Jesus and yet over and over, Peter blundered badly in life. But God used Peter in spite of himself. God seems to delight in doing that.

So if you are one of those who is looking for some basic Bible ABCs, then this may be the book for you. You can join me on my journey as I continue to learn what it means to do the will of the King, one step at a time, one day at a time.

Let me also convey my sincere thanks to Matt Almy, Ian Mastin and Don Dolton for their helpful illustrations; to John Peek, Troy Johnstone, Jessica Graf, Po Kwai Ko and Terry Ratcliff for the cover; and to those many unnamed souls who gave input on the content. A special thanks to those who provided lodging while I wrote and then encouraged me in immeasurable ways.

It is to my adult children: Andrew, Naomi and her husband, Troy, that I dedicate this book. Their own personal, quiet but faithful walks with God have been an inspiration to me. May the Lord of all creation be pleased to use this book to draw many closer to himself.

John R. Cross

Dungannon, N. Ireland   May 2018

The words of Jesus:

> "Everyone then who hears these words of mine and does them will be like a wise man who built his house on the rock. And the rain fell, and the floods came, and the winds blew and beat on that house, but it did not fall, because it had been founded on the rock." *Matthew 7:24-25 ESV*

CHAPTER ONE

1 THE STARTING POINT

The Scriptures speak of those who, once coming to believe in the Bible as true and putting their faith in the Lord Jesus Christ, then make the decision to…

> … not live the rest of [their earthly lives] for evil human desires, but rather for the will of God. *1 Peter 4:2 NIV*

But what is God's will?

This book follows the life of Simon Peter, a disciple of Jesus. He found himself captive to two kings: one by choice, the other against his will. King Herod arrested Peter and threw him in jail. Herod's will was that Peter be beheaded.

But Peter, by choice, found himself captivated by another King, who speaking in spiritual terms said:

> *This is the will of God, your sanctification.* 1 Thessalonians 4:3 ESV

But what is that? What is sanctification?

It is understandable that new believers don't know what sanctification is all about, but the truth is, many people have read the Bible for years and still struggle with the implications of this word.

OVER THE HEAD

Jenna grew up in a home where her parents taught her the Bible. As a child, she attended a private school where the Bible was part of the curriculum. As a young adult, Jenna graduated from a college where Scripture was taught. But as she jumped into the middle of a class I was teaching on sanctification, she confessed, "All of this is going right over my head."

Now this surprised the rest of the class, because none of them had grown up with as much exposure to the Bible as Jenna. Most of them came from a background of zero Bible knowledge and yet they were absorbing the content just fine. What made the difference?

Simply put, Jenna was missing critical foundations in her mind. Without those foundations, she was having difficulty in understanding concepts the rest of the class was absorbing without problem. She felt like a kindergartner in algebra class. Jenna needed to start where they had—with the basics—before moving on.

So where does one start?

We will start with some foundational realities that are important to know. This and the next section are a little technical, but they are important, so read carefully and make sure you understand them.

OUR WORLDVIEW

We will start with the beliefs we already hold in our minds, something we call a *worldview*. A worldview is the way we think—a reflection of how we answer certain key questions about life, questions like these:

1. Where did we come from? Where did this entire universe come from? This is the question of *origins*.

2. Now that we are here, how should we live? What is the right way and the wrong way to live? This is the question of *values*.

3. Since there is a right and wrong way to live, where do we get the information that tells us what is right and wrong? This is the question of *truth*.

4. And since we know that we will not live forever, what happens to us after we die? Is there a life after death and if so, what might that life be like? This is the question of *destiny*.

Our answers to these questions reflect what is known as our worldview. Whether our answers have been well thought out or not does not matter. Even the answer, "I've never really believed anything," reflects a worldview. We all have a worldview.

Now the Bible speaks with authority on these questions. It talks about origins, the purpose of life, what meaning it can hold, why we die, and what happens to us after death. This is not without significance. The information contained in the Bible is too momentous to ignore, too critical to misunderstand.

It is with that belief in mind that I wrote three books, each book addressing a different worldview. *The Stranger on the Road to Emmaus* was written for those coming from a Christianized worldview—whether Protestant, Roman Catholic or Orthodox. Since many people from these backgrounds know little about the Bible, I wrote *The Stranger* to bring clarity to their thinking.

All that the Prophets have Spoken was written for those coming from an Islamic worldview. Although very different, Christianized and

Islamic worldviews have a few things in common, therefore *The Stranger* and *All the Prophets* are similar books, being 25% different.

But a third book was needed. It was a book for those with a non-religious, secular*, postmodern, New Age or Eastern worldview. This resulted in *By This Name*, a book that is about 60% different than the preceding two books. (*See glossary.)

Each one of these products, though similar, was written to answer questions that arise out of specific worldviews. I wanted to explain as clearly as possible the biblical worldview and to do so without a crust of religiosity.

These books are a starting point. They contain the needed foundations that Jenna was missing.

SOME ASSUMPTIONS

The book you are now reading assumes you have read one of these three books. It assumes you have accepted the biblical worldview as true and that you have come to a point of placing your confidence in the Lord Jesus Christ as your God and your Saviour. In short, you are now a believer. If that is true, then this sequel is a book for you. If you have not read any of the preceding foundational books, then you may find the content "going over your head," as did Jenna. This may be true even if you have been exposed to the Bible for many years.

In this book, I will include brief reviews of the content in the first books to add greater depth to those foundations. At times I will be introducing terms that Bible students use to describe complex subjects. In teaching new believers, I have found these terms helpful, to give labels to what they are learning. You are embarking on a deeper understanding of the Bible so be prepared to learn.

If you have not read any of the above three books, then start with *By This Name*. It is the most comprehensive of the three.

The above books focus on the subject of salvation, specifically as it relates to *justification*.

- Justification happens at a point in time—the moment you were born spiritually into God's family. It is a second birth.

- Justification occurs at the moment you are saved from the **penalty** of sin, the eternal consequence of sin.

- Justification is when God legally declared you as clothed in the righteousness of Christ. It is God's point of view. He now looks on you as possessing a perfect 10-out-of-10 righteousness, fully equipped to live in Heaven.

No illustration is perfect, but if we were to graph out a life on a timeline, this is what it might look like for a brand new believer.[1]

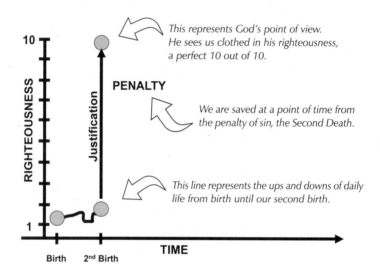

In the above chart, we see that, as believers, we've had a spiritual birth—a second birth. God views us as if we were already in Heaven, 100% righteous, a perfect 10 on the chart. This God-based view is what justification is all about. But hold it for a moment! From our point of view, we're still here on earth. Our sin **penalty** may have been paid, but as believers we still sin. How does that work?

This book answers that question. It focuses on the next chart, explaining how one is saved from the daily **power** of sin, right here on earth. It's a look at a major theme called *sanctification*.

Sanctification begins the moment you trust in Jesus and progresses through the ups and down of life until you exit this world. Sanctification is the King's will for your life.

It is important to understand that sanctification cannot be disconnected from justification. Everything that happens in sanctification is based on what happened in justification.

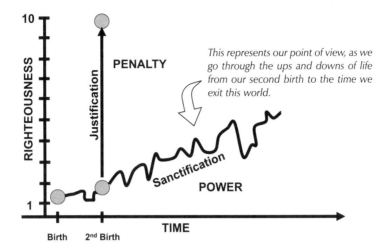

This book also touches on the third major theme in Scripture called *glorification*. Glorification relates to a future time when we are finally saved from the **presence** of sin. That will happen at death or when Jesus comes to take us to be with him.

It is good to study the graphs carefully. We will be coming back to them later on in the book and as we do so, they will make more and more sense.

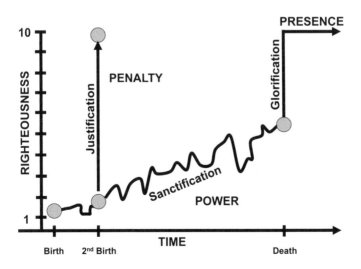

What does the Bible call those who trust in Jesus?

Disciples: When people put their trust in Christ, they are known as disciples—literally, "followers" of Christ. This is not a future stage in one's spiritual journey. Immediately upon believing in Christ, we are told that we...

> ... should follow His steps.   1 Peter 2:21 NKJV

Believers: This term emphasizes the way we are saved from the consequences of sin—it is by faith. We simply believe Jesus is God and that he took care of our sin problem in his death and resurrection. As such, we are "believers." We are now counted among those who...

> ...took Jesus at his word.   John 4:50 NIV

Christians: This label is found three times in the Bible and refers to those who have become "Christ-ones." In its true sense, the word "Christian" can only apply to an individual.

Biblically, there is no such thing as a Christian nation.

Some people identify themselves as "Christians" because they attend a Christian church. Or they may use the term to set themselves apart from a Muslim or Hindu. But in the Bible, the term *Christian* is only used of those who have personally put their trust in Christ to be saved from the penalty of sin.

Brothers or sisters in Christ: This recognizes that when people become Christians, they have joined a large family.

2 The Key to it All

As an author of books that answer people's questions about the Bible, I find myself in the privileged position of receiving letters from various parts of the world. This email came from Australia:

"I have finished your book, John, and have read the book of Romans, then I started on Acts, not sure why, just for fun I guess. I will re-read your book as you suggest and underline the verses as I go. However I am enjoying reading chapters of the Bible just as "books" not as verses thrown to me in church services. To get the flow of the story has been great, and I often find the time slipping by, the sort of - can't put it

down - kind of book! [Referring to the Bible.] *My main worry for myself is how to continue to grow spiritually and not stay the spiritual baby I have always been."*

That last sentence should be the echo of all our hearts. But how does a believer grow spiritually?

THE GOAL

First of all, in the ups and downs of life, we need to understand where we are headed. On a spiritual level, the goal is to become like Christ or what is called *Christlikeness*. (See first chart on page 13.) God's intended purpose for all believers is that they might be…

> *…conformed to the image of His Son.*   Romans 8:29 NKJV

God wants us to be just like Jesus. That sounds good, but is it even possible? How does Christlikeness happen?

WHAT IT IS NOT

First of all, to grow spiritually—to become like Christ—is *not* the process of learning how to act like a Christian. People may tell you that a real Christian lives a certain way—you must do this and not do that—that you must better yourself. But there is a problem. If you set out determined to live the life of a good Christian, you will find yourself falling flat on your face. Being a "good Christian" is outside of our ability to perform. We will see the truthfulness of that fact as we launch into our story and read about the life of the disciple Peter. He tried hard and failed miserably. We will too.

Secondly, to grow spiritually does not mean that we do nothing. Growth is not passive. There are things we need to do and not do.

So, if the key to becoming like Christ is not learning how to act, and yet there are things we do need to do and not do, then how does it work? What is the key?

Well, actually a case could be made for a number of "keys." Here are four with which to start.[2]

1. You become like the person you know.

The key to growing spiritually is not learning *how* to live, but rather learning to *know* Jesus as a person—to get acquainted with our Creator God. It is more than knowing about him, it is actually knowing him.

> *Yet indeed I also count all things loss for the excellence of the knowledge of Christ Jesus my Lord.*   Philippians 3:8 NKJV

This is significant as the next three points are based on knowing Jesus.

2. You become like the person you respect.

We've all witnessed the phenomenon where a person is so highly looked up to that the person begins to imitate the walk, the speech, even the accent of the one he respects. It is the way we are wired—we are all imitators of someone.

As we learn to know Jesus, we will begin to respect him. And the more we respect him, the more we will desire to live in a way that pleases him. Without really thinking about it, we begin to imitate him!

As we lift Jesus up high in our minds, we begin to "worship the ground he walks on," in the words of the popular idiom. In this case, it is entirely appropriate, as the words *honour, respect* and *worship* are all closely related and Jesus is worthy of all three.

3. You become like the person you trust.

> The idols of the nations are silver and gold,
> the work of human hands.
> They have mouths, but do not speak;
> they have eyes, but do not see;
> they have ears, but do not hear,
> nor is there any breath in their mouths.
> Those who make them become like them,
> so do all who trust in them.   Psalm 135:15–18 ESV

God was the one who wired our brains—he knows how we work. He knows that if we trust in a wooden or porcelain god, we will become dull and blind in our thinking. It is a principle of life that whether idol, money or our ego, we are conformed much by the object of our trust.

It is one reason we are told to trust the Lord Jesus. When we put our faith in him, we begin to become like him.

This brings us back to our first point. To trust Jesus we must also know him. We will not trust him as long as he is unknown to us. People don't trust strangers. So we must get acquainted—in depth.

4. You become like the person you love.

Finally, as we learn to know Jesus, we will begin to love him. And the more we love him the more we will desire to live in a way that pleases him. We won't want to do anything that will bring shame to his name. We will act in a way that brings him pleasure.

> *For the love of Christ controls us, because we have concluded this: that one has died for all, therefore all have died; and he died for all, that those who live might no longer live for themselves but for him who for their sake died and was raised.*
>
> 2 Corinthians 5:14-15 ESV

It is our love for him that motivates us to live good lives.

GOAL

As you can see, *respect, trust* and *love* are all built on the first key point—that of *knowing* God. To know Jesus is the supreme goal in sanctification.[3] It is not about keeping a list of rules or trying harder. Striving, persevering and discipline[4] are all biblical concepts that have a role in sanctification, but you can strive and persevere, and still not be conformed into the image of God.

It is only when those words are contextualized into the process of learning to know, respect, trust and love the Lord that they take on a biblical role. For example, it takes daily discipline and effort to read the Bible, but without reading the Bible you will never *know, respect, trust* and *love* the Lord. The process of growing in our faith cannot be separated from learning the Word of God—the Bible. The purpose of this book is to take you deeper in your understanding of God—to know him.

CLARITY

Now it is possible to learn a lot about the Bible and not understand the Bible at all. We don't want that. To help prevent that from happening, we are going to pay special attention to the architecture of Scripture. In the Bible, God teaches us about himself by using a *physical object* to illustrate a *spiritual truth*. For example, a physical object (a lamb) is used to illustrate a spiritual truth (the reality that Jesus is our Lamb, our sinless substitute). In my previous books, I used these physical-spiritual connections to help us understand how Jesus took care of our sin-penalty.

As we approach the subject of growing from a spiritual babe to a mature believer, we want to use the same architecture—the physical-spiritual connections—to give clarity. Early in this book we will learn physical illustrations that will help us understand spiritual lessons later in the book. My advice to you is this—persist in the process chapter by chapter—don't quit. Work to understand each lesson well, as later chapters will build on the previous ones.

As you understand the Bible more and more, your respect, trust and love for the Lord will grow as well, and in the process you will find yourself growing spiritually day by day. This is called *sanctification*. It is the King's will. It is what this book is all about.

Now to the story…the night before Jesus was crucified.

3 THE SHORT WALK

Circa AD 33

Simon Peter was one of the 12 disciples. For three years he had travelled with Jesus sharing in the joys and hardships of the Lord's ministry. Often Jesus spoke to his disciples about events yet to come. These things were not easy to understand. Lately, Jesus had been talking about death—his own death—giving specific details about what would happen. But how could this be? Peter believed with all his heart that Jesus was the Messiah, the one who was supposed to restore the realm that King David had once ruled—only one much better. He wasn't supposed to die!

In the preceding hours Peter had helped prepare the Passover meal. It was to be commemorated in the upper room of a house situated on Mount Zion.

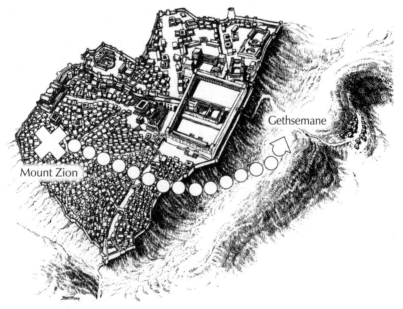

Even as they were partaking of the feast, Jesus had bewildered them with information. Judas Iscariot had gotten up right in the middle of it all and walked out. Finally, they had sung a hymn and then left the house to stretch their legs. It was obvious that their feet were taking them in the direction of an olive grove. The locals called the place Gethsemane, which literally meant "an olive press." This was familiar ground—a place where they often gathered. Peter felt better walking—the night air was crisp and it cleared his weary head.

As they walked, Jesus shared his thoughts with his 11 disciples (Judas Iscariot was still missing). Once again Jesus spoke with them about future things, but this time what he had to say seemed imminent—it would happen in the next few hours.

> *Jesus said to them, "You will all fall away, for it is written, 'I will strike the shepherd, and the sheep will be scattered.' But after I am raised up, I will go before you to Galilee."*
>
> *Mark 14:27-28 ESV*

What on earth did Jesus mean? Of course it was obvious that Jesus was the "shepherd," but were the disciples the "sheep" who would be scattered? Peter thought that unlikely! For three years he had stuck with Jesus through thick and thin. Besides, he was a fisherman. He'd been in storms before—real ones. Certainly there was no place Jesus was going that he couldn't go.

> *Simon Peter said to Him, "Lord, where are You going?" Jesus answered, "Where I go, you cannot follow Me now; but you will follow later."*
>
> *Peter said to Him, "Lord, why can I not follow You right now?… I am ready to go with You, both to prison and to death."*
>
> *John 13:36-37 NASB, Luke 22:33 NKJV*

Peter glanced around at the other disciples. Matching his pace to Jesus, he leaned over, his voice hoarse and forceful. He nodded back at the others.

> *"Even if all fall away, I will not."* Mark 14:29 NIV

Jesus halted and turned to Peter:

> *"I tell you the truth,… today—yes, tonight—before the rooster crows twice you yourself will disown me three times."*
>
> *But Peter insisted emphatically, "Even if I have to die with you, I will never disown you." And all the others said the same.*
>
> *Mark 14:30-31 NIV*

4 THE OLIVE PRESS

The journey from Mount Zion to Gethsemane is not long—only a 15-minute walk. It is mostly downhill, curving around the Temple Mount to the bottom of the Kidron valley.

> *On the other side there was an olive grove, and he and his disciples went into it.* John 18:1 NIV

> *Then they came to a place which was named Gethsemane; and He said to His disciples, "Sit here while I pray." And He took Peter, James, and John with Him, and He began to be troubled and deeply distressed. Then He said to them, "My soul is exceedingly sorrowful, even to death. Stay here and watch."* Mark 14:32-34 NKJV

> *He withdrew about a stone's throw beyond them, knelt down and prayed, "Father, if you are willing, take this cup from me; yet not my will, but yours be done." An angel from heaven appeared to him and strengthened him. And being in anguish, he prayed more earnestly, and his sweat was like drops of blood falling to the ground.* Luke 22:41-44 NIV

Gethsemane may have been a place for pressing olives, but on this night it was Jesus who was being crushed. Though the night was cold, his sweat was like great drops of blood.

> *When He rose from prayer, He came to the disciples…* Luke 22:45 NASB

> *…and found them sleeping, and said to Peter, "Simon, are you asleep? Could you not keep watch for one hour?"* Mark 14:37 NASB

Peter may have promised Jesus that he would follow him through thick and thin, but at this point he was having a hard time just staying awake. Jesus said:

> *"Keep watching and praying that you may not come into temptation; the spirit is willing, but the flesh is weak."*

> *Again He went away and prayed, saying the same words.*

> *And again He came and found them sleeping, for their eyes were very heavy; and they did not know what to answer Him.*

> *And He came the third time, and said to them, "Are you still sleeping and resting? It is enough; the hour has come; behold, the Son of Man is being betrayed into the hands of sinners."* Mark 14:38-41 NASB

THE ARREST

*Now Judas, who betrayed him, knew the place, because Jesus
had often met there with his disciples. So Judas came to the
grove, guiding a detachment of soldiers and some officials
from the chief priests and Pharisees. They were carrying
torches, lanterns and weapons.* John 18:2-3 NIV

Peter was wide awake now. The grove was filling with scores of
men—there must have been hundreds! And Judas had finally
shown up. What was going on?

*Jesus, knowing all that was going to happen to him, went
out and asked them, "Who is it you want?"*

"Jesus of Nazareth," they replied.

*"I am he," Jesus said. (And Judas the traitor was standing
there with them.) When Jesus said, "I am he," they drew
back and fell to the ground.*

*Again he asked them, "Who is it you want?" And they said,
"Jesus of Nazareth."*

*"I told you that I am he," Jesus answered. "If you are looking
for me, then let these men go."* John 18:4-8 NIV

But Peter would have none of it. No way was he going to leave
Jesus with these scoundrels! His blood was up and he was ready
to fight.

*Then Simon Peter, having a sword, drew it and struck the
high priest's servant and cut off his right ear. (The servant's
name was Malchus.)* John 18:10 ESV

*But Jesus said, "No more of this!" And he touched his ear
and healed him.* Luke 22:51 ESV

*Jesus said to Peter, "Put your sword into its sheath; shall I not
drink the cup that the Father has given me?"* John 18:11 ESV

FRIEND

*Now the betrayer had given them a sign, saying, "The one I
will kiss is the man; seize him." And he came up to Jesus at
once and said, "Greetings, Rabbi!" And he kissed him. Jesus
said to him, "Friend, do what you came to do." Then they
came up and laid hands on Jesus and seized him.*
Matthew 26:48-50 ESV

*Then Jesus said to the chief priests and officers of the temple
and elders who had come against Him, "Have you come out*

with swords and clubs as you would against a robber? While I was with you daily in the temple, you did not lay hands on Me; but this hour and the power of darkness are yours."

Luke 22:52-53 NASB

So the band of soldiers and their captain and the officers of the Jews arrested Jesus and bound him. John 18:12 ESV

Then all the disciples deserted him and fled. Matthew 26:56 NIV

5 THE SERVANT GIRL

Those who had arrested Jesus took him to Caiaphas, the high priest, where the teachers of the law and the elders had assembled. Matthew 26:57 NIV

If ever there was a lynch mob, this was it! Initially Peter had surged with courage—he had pulled his sword and gone for Malchus, but even that impetuous feat had gone awry. Fortunately Jesus had healed the terrified man so fast it is doubtful much of the crowd even knew what had happened.

And Judas Iscariot, what had he been thinking? It seemed quite clear that Judas had pointed out Jesus to the mob. How could he do that? Unbelievable! Well, Judas might betray Jesus but Peter wouldn't. He was afraid, but he had mastered his fear before. Many times he had faced tough situations as a fisherman and pulled through. The other disciples might run, but on that night…

…Peter followed at a distance. Luke 22:54 NKJV

Peter wasn't sure what they would do with Jesus, but if he could get close enough it might give him an opportunity to speak up in defence of his master. Peter braced himself for tough questions the religious leaders might ask.

In a short time the mob led Jesus to the official palace of the high priest—a residence not far from the "upper room." As the throng pushed into the courtyard, Peter became aware that both he…

... and another disciple were following Jesus. Because this disciple was known to the high priest, he went with Jesus into the high priest's courtyard, but Peter had to wait outside at the door. The other disciple, who was known to the high priest, came back, spoke to the girl on duty there and brought Peter in.

"You are not one of his disciples, are you?" the girl at the door asked Peter.   *John 18:15-17 NIV*

Peter had braced himself for questions from the religious leaders but he hadn't expected one from a servant girl at the door. It caught him off guard. It was helpful that the question had been asked somewhat in private.

He said, "I am not."   *John 18:17b NKJV*

Peter lied. It was just a little lie and to a servant girl, but he lied. But then again, who would know?

PESKY SERVANTS

From where Peter was standing, he could see Jesus being interrogated by the religious leaders. Keeping his eyes on Jesus, Peter did his best to melt into the courtyard crowd.

It was cold, and the servants and officials stood around a fire they had made to keep warm. Peter also was standing with them, warming himself.   *John 18:18 NIV*

...another servant girl saw him, and she said to the bystanders, "This man was with Jesus of Nazareth."   *Matthew 26:71 ESV*

The hum of conversation halted while those around the fire tried to fix their eyes on the person in question. Peter froze. The servants must have been talking! Quickly, Peter looked around the inquiring faces. Some looked curious, others hostile. If the servant girl said anything more...well. Abruptly, Peter...

...denied it with an oath: "I do not know the man."
Matthew 26:72 ESV

Momentarily satisfied, the fireside crowd picked up their thread of conversation. Casually Peter shifted to a different setting, one where servant girls were scarce. He found himself muttering under his breath. He hadn't meant to swear, but when he started to speak his voice had a tremor, and it didn't sound convincing. The oath had lent some reinforcement. Still, it bothered him.

Peter now found himself in a better situation with a clear view of Jesus, though at a distance. He felt a little rattled. Just looking at Jesus seemed to help. The Master was certainly composed—which didn't surprise Peter—but it was obvious that he had been roughed up. Jesus was in bad shape. Not sure what to do, Peter hunkered down to wait. With time moving slowly, Peter engaged in small talk with those standing near until…

> About an hour later another asserted, "Certainly this fellow was with him, for he is a Galilean."   *Luke 22:59 NIV*

Peter's mind jerked alert. He had become too relaxed. His eyes focused on his inquisitor.

> "Surely you too are one of them; for even the way you talk gives you away."   *Matthew 26:73 NASB*

> One of the high priest's servants, a relative of the man whose ear Peter had cut off, challenged him, "Didn't I see you with him in the olive grove?"   *John 18:26 NIV*

Those within hearing, and there were many, turned to look. Peter's accuser had been present when he pulled his sword on Malchus. Peter recognized the servant and the man obviously recognized Peter. What should he do?!

> Then he began to curse and swear, saying, "I do not know the Man!"   *Matthew 26:74 NKJV*

> And immediately, while he was still speaking, the rooster crowed.   *Luke 22:60 ESV*

It had only been a few hours since Jesus told Peter that he would deny him three times before the rooster crowed. "Cockcrow" was a general expression assigned to the time just before sunrise.[5] Well now, here it was, just before daylight and Peter had done exactly as Jesus said—he had denied his master three times. The words were still in Peter's mouth when…

> …the Lord turned and looked at Peter.   *Luke 22:61 ESV*

From Peter's vantage point across the courtyard crowd, it was clear that Jesus was looking at him. Peter could see his bruised and bloodied face clearly. But it was his eyes…no, maybe it was the expression on his face that cut to his heart. In a moment it all flooded back.

> And Peter remembered the saying of the Lord, how he had said to him, "Before the rooster crows today, you will deny me three times."   *Luke 22:61 ESV*

Peter had promised to follow Jesus to prison, to death, anywhere…
but he had not even succeeded in following him past the courtyard
door. The other disciples might leave Jesus, but no, not Peter! But
now he had utterly failed. What, oh what could he do? There
was no way that he could talk to Jesus now. With eyes pleading,
Peter turned away from Jesus…

And he went out and wept bitterly.   *Luke 22:62 ESV*

IDENTITY

In this story, we see Peter being asked three times if he belonged
to those who followed Jesus. Three times Peter denied it.
Three times Peter identified himself with the wrong crowd.
He linked himself with scoffers and mockers. As to the Lord…

…Peter followed at a distance.   *Luke 22:54 NKJV*

He didn't want to be identified too closely with Jesus. Take
note of this identity issue, as the Bible says our identity is
absolutely critical. It defines who we are and what we will
become. We will discuss identity later in the book.

It is inherent to our human hearts to be like Peter, to follow the
Lord at a distance. The Bible challenges us to do otherwise.
Jesus said:

*"Take My yoke upon you and learn from Me, for I am
gentle and lowly in heart, and you will find rest for your
souls. For My yoke is easy and My burden is light."*
Matthew 11:29-30 NKJV

---

6 THE NEED FOR HELP

Whether or not the events of Peter's denial unfolded exactly as
I have portrayed them is open to debate. What we do know, in
succinct, stark words, is that in his darkest hour, Peter denied he
knew Jesus—three times.

Undoubtedly, Peter was going against all he held dear, against his
own code of ethics, against the principles upon which he sought
to guide his life. And yet, he had failed miserably. Why?

Often, in daily life, we are like Peter. In our hearts we are willing
to follow the Lord to prison, even death…but when confronted

with the slightest opposition, we deny we even know him. In case we should put ourselves in a different category than Peter, the Bible says:

> The temptations in your life are no different from what others experience.
> 1 Corinthians 10:13 NLT

In other words, we are all made out of the same mud. That being so, we know from experience that in tough situations, it is helpful to have a good friend by our side—one who can steady our hearts, stiffen our resolve and help us know what to say and do. It is usually when we are alone or isolated from help that we take our biggest tumbles.

But that's the problem. Often we are alone. That is the simple truth. So is there help for our situation? What can we do?

Well, there is an answer, but often believers stumble through life with the solution in their reach and don't even know it.

It reminds me of an incident that happened a few years ago while I was showing some friends around our part of Canada. We live not far from the Rocky Mountains and a favourite place to visit is Banff National Park. I had pulled our vehicle over to the side of the road in order for us to stretch our legs. Hardly had I gotten out of the van when a car literally skidded to a halt directly behind my vehicle. An old man (OM), quite elderly, got out in a hustle and quickly came over to me (JRC). The conversation went like this:

- OM: "I am lost. Is this the road to North Battleford?"
- JRC: "Well sort of, in an indirect way. (All roads are connected somehow in Canada.) Do you have a map?"
- OM: "I do, but I'm not sure where it is."
- JRC: "I won't be able to direct you to North Battleford without a map."

He rummaged through the back seat of his car and eventually found his map, but when we started to look at it, he was actually looking at the wrong page. It soon became apparent that he needed help in reading the map. As we talked, it struck me that not only did he need a map, but he also needed a guide. Both were necessary if he was to get to where he was going.

We need help

There are some parallels here:

First, like the old man, we need to realize that we need help. This is where Peter went wrong. He felt he was strong enough within himself to follow the Lord without any help. But when the chips were down, it didn't take much to topple him from his pedestal. He failed when a servant girl unexpectedly asked him a simple question. We need to come to grips with reality.

We face a…

> … *strong enemy.* Psalm 18:17 KJV

This enemy will go to any length to trip us up. King David wrote that he faced people and situations that were…

> … *too mighty for [him].* Psalm 18:17 ESV

So right from the beginning, we must recognize that we need help for the journey.

MAP

Secondly, to get where we are going, we need a map. Life is complicated and though, as believers, we have chosen the road that leads to Heaven, the journey is still far from over. The map for our journey is the Holy Bible—the Word of God. In speaking of Scripture, one songwriter wrote:[6]

> *Your light and Your truth, let them lead me; Let them bring me to…Your dwelling places.* Psalm 43:3 NASB

GUIDE

In making provision for our journey, the Lord did not stop at giving us a Map. He also provided a guide—the Holy Spirit. But who or what is the Holy Spirit?

- One religious cult says the Holy Spirit is not an intelligent person, but an "it"—an active force.

- Another cult understood the Holy Spirit to be the unfolding of the thoughts and infinite mind of God.

- One major non-Christian religion that subscribes to parts of the Bible considers the Holy Spirit to be the angel Gabriel.

- Another false group has variously described the Holy Spirit as being like magnetism, electricity, a divine fluid, or an impersonal energy. Some make a distinction between the Holy Ghost and the Holy Spirit—the Holy Ghost being a person and the Holy Spirit an impersonal force.[7]

None of these are even close to correct. We need good answers to these false teachings if the Holy Spirit is to be our Guide—if we are to keep from imitating Peter's courtyard experience.

In this book I hope to provide a few pointers on the use of the Map and how to cooperate with the Guide. In the process, we will learn what made the difference in Peter's life, what took him from being a common coward to a man of immense courage. As believers, it is something we all need to know. We will start with a brief look at our Map.

THE HOLY BIBLE

The word *Bible* is derived from the Greek and Latin word for book—the word itself does not appear within the pages of the Bible. Instead the Bible refers to itself as *Scripture* or the *Word*. Depending on the context, it may also call itself *the Law and the Prophets* (referring to the entire Old Testament), *precepts, statutes, commands, decrees, prophecies* or *promises*. Using "picture language" Scripture is sometimes called a *sword*.

The word *holy* means "that which is set apart, that which is different." It has the idea of being unique, one-of-a-kind. When we speak of the Holy Bible, we are literally speaking of a unique, one-of-a-kind book.

---

7 THE CRUCIAL MAP

It is important for us to remember that our Map—the Holy Bible—is a message directly from God. When the Bible speaks, it is God speaking.

> *For prophecy never had its origin in the will of man, but men spoke from God as they were carried along by the Holy Spirit.*
>
> 2 Peter 1:21 NIV

It was the Holy Spirit who guided the prophets as they recorded God's Word. It would be quite accurate to say that our Guide wrote the Map. What better guide could one have?

It is also important to understand that both Map and Guide work together and are hindered without each other. The Scriptures are the only means whereby we can learn about the Holy Spirit, and the Holy Spirit always guides us according to Scripture. This is very significant.

Whether you are a brand new believer or have been a Christian for many years, I can guarantee that you will go nowhere spiritually if you leave your Map—the Holy Bible—"buried in the back seat of your car," unread. Even if you attend church regularly and read books about the Bible, you will move little beyond being a spiritual infant if you do not consistently consult Scripture. Why is this?

Well, to be a believer means that you have faith in God and his Word as being true. But your faith can remain weak or stagnant if you are not gaining greater confidence in the truthfulness of the Bible and your knowledge of God. There is only one way for your faith to grow strong.

> *Faith comes by hearing, and hearing by the word of God.*
> *Romans 10:17 NKJV*

If you're not reading or hearing the Bible read on a consistent basis, you will remain a spiritual infant—your faith will have no foundations to rest upon. In the process, the Holy Spirit will be limited in his means to guide you, since you lack knowledge of the Bible. So it is very important to not leave your Map in the back seat, unread.

RIGHT ROAD

Because the Bible is God's own Word, it does more than just pass on dry facts. It brings order to life and shows us what is proper and good. It takes us down the right road.

> *Your word is a lamp to my feet and a light to my path.*
> *Psalm 119:105 ESV*

> *Lead me, O LORD, in your righteousness because of my enemies; make your way straight before me.* *Psalm 5:8 ESV*

> *For the word of God is living and active. Sharper than any double-edged sword, it penetrates even to dividing soul and spirit, joints and marrow; it judges the thoughts and attitudes of the heart. Nothing in all creation is hidden from God's sight. Everything is uncovered and laid bare before the eyes of him to whom we must give account.* *Hebrews 4:12-13 NIV*

Wrong Road

The Bible is also the only tried and tested means for overcoming evil in the world and sin in our lives.

> *How can a young man keep his way pure? By guarding it according to your word.* Psalm 119:9 ESV

> *Your word I have treasured in my heart, That I may not sin against You.* Psalm 119:11 NASB

We all struggle with sin. To neglect this powerful resource is to ignore our only help—our faith will suffer deeply. Like Simon Peter, we go through tough times on our journey. God's Word gives strength and life to sustain us in these difficulties.

> *Those who live in the shelter of the Most High will find rest in the shadow of the Almighty. This I declare about the Lord: He alone is my refuge, my place of safety; He is my God, and I trust Him.* Psalm 91:1-2 NLT

Daily, Correctly

Centuries ago in Greece, there was a group of believers in a city called Berea. Their perspective on the Word provides us with an example for our own lives. It was said of the Bereans that when they heard the Bible taught…

> *…they received the word with great eagerness, examining the Scriptures daily to see whether these things were so.* Acts 17:11 NASB

Not only do we need to search the Scriptures daily but in so doing we must interpret our Map correctly.

Be diligent to present yourself approved to God as a workman who does not need to be ashamed, accurately handling the word of truth.   2 Timothy 2:15 NASB

We don't want to have a garbled perspective of the Bible. Reading the biblical map accurately is paramount to having a successful journey. This book is a start down that path.

SIMON PETER

We will be continuing with the life of Simon Peter, but before we do, we want to lay some foundations from the Old and New Testament so we can truly understand this man and what he wrote. Those foundations will bring clarity to our thinking and help us down the path of knowing God and his will for our lives, our sanctification. Read the next two to three chapters carefully and be patient in learning. There is much in these pages to process.

SUMMARY

I will use a simple parallel throughout this book:

Our Map　 = The Holy Bible

Our Guide = The Holy Spirit

BUYING A BIBLE

Even if you already own a Bible, it will be helpful to read the following, as you may pick up a few pointers on how to advise others.

One of the first decisions you must make regarding the choice of a Bible concerns the matter of translations. Here is some helpful background.

BACKGROUND

The prophets originally recorded the Scriptures in three languages. The entire Old Testament was written in *Hebrew* with the exception of a few chapters in the books of Ezra and Daniel and one verse in Jeremiah. These were written in a language called *Aramaic*. The New Testament was written in Koine *Greek* (common Greek).

These original documents—the ones that the prophets wrote—were called *autographs*. The Bible speaks of these autographs as being inspired, or literally, "God-breathed."

> *All Scripture is God-breathed and is useful for teaching, rebuking, correcting and training in righteousness, so that the man of God may be thoroughly equipped for every good work.* 2 Timothy 3:16-17 NIV

Obviously, the autographs are long gone. However, we have copies of the autographs—thousands of them, ranging from fragments to entire books. Though some minor discrepancies have crept into these copies, the variants are truly small and affect no significant teaching in the Bible.[8]

TRANSLATIONS

Centuries ago, scholars used these copies to translate the Bible into English as well as into other languages. This process continues to this day with no other book in the world having been translated into more languages than the Bible.

Autograph	Copies	Translations
One document only, handwritten by a prophet	Thousands of handwritten copies	Many languages
Written in	**Copied in**	**Printed in**
Hebrew Aramaic Greek	Hebrew Aramaic Greek	English, as well as thousands of other languages

In the English language, we are blessed with many translations of the Bible. Some of these translations follow the Hebrew and Greek grammar quite closely. They could be called *strict translations*. Though precise, they can be a little stiff to read. In an attempt to make the Bible more readable, less strict translations have also been done in English. Some call these loose translations *paraphrases* because to a certain extent, the "translators" have put the biblical text in their own words. These translations are easy to read, but are not as accurate as a strict translation. In the English language, we have a whole spectrum of translations ranging from strict to loose.

It is important for you to know that many Bible believers have strong feelings about translations. Some feel very strongly that only an early English translation called the King James Version (KJV) should be used. This strict translation was first done in AD 1611 and uses Shakespearean English. Though admired for its beautiful use of language, many find this translation difficult to understand.

Buy a translation that you find easy to read. I would suggest you lean towards the stricter translations. This book will help you understand the terminology typically found in those editions.

Chapter Two

1 The Age

The Bible is under attack, but then that's nothing new—it's been under attack for centuries. One thing that makes the Bible so unique is that not only has it consistently withstood these attacks, but it has come out shining. Historically, one area of attack has been directed at the nature of God.

We have discussed this in some detail in my previous books, however, we need to take a little deeper look as it applies directly to our Guide—the Holy Spirit. To do this we will return to the early pages of the Bible in order to gain some foundational information.

...ISMS

The first two-thirds of the Bible is called the Old Testament. It covers the history of the world, from creation to about 400 years before the arrival of the Messiah.

To understand the Old Testament, it is helpful to know the culture of the time it was written. We know that God used Moses to record the first five books of the Bible. Moses was educated in ancient Egypt. The Egyptian worldview—what they believed about life, death and life after death—was representative of the larger world at that time. The ancient nations believed a mixture of spiritism, animism, pantheism and polytheism.

Not much has changed. Today society has embraced the ancient world's mixture of "isms" and added to it various forms of disbelief—"isms" such as materialism, secularism, atheism and agnosticism. Moses may have written long ago, but what he wrote then could never be more relevant than today.

The following is a brief list of some of the most common "isms." Each one adversely corrupts the nature of God.

Animism: The belief that spirits inhabit certain structures, rooms (e.g., kitchens), rocks, trees, rivers and so on. These spirits may or may not be ancestors who have previously died.

Spiritism: The belief that the dead communicate with the living, usually through a person called a *medium*. Spiritism is connected to various forms of witchcraft or sorcery.

Polytheism: The belief in more than one god, usually many. This may include the idea that we humans can be or are gods.

Pantheism: The belief that "God" is an impersonal force, identical with all that we see in nature. God is in everything, and everything is god. Traditionally, this has been an eastern concept, but this idea of God is becoming dominant in the Western world.

Materialism: The belief that "feeling good" and having worldly possessions constitute all that is worthwhile in life.

Naturalism: The belief that everything, including our thoughts and feelings, is just part of our physical body and the world around us. This is typical of Darwinism.

Secularism: The belief that decisions about what is right and wrong should be made without the influence of religion.

Atheism: The belief that there is no God or gods.

Agnosticism: The belief that there can be no proof that God exists or does not exist. An agnostic will usually say he just "doesn't know" and "doesn't think anyone can know."

When the first words of the Bible were penned, it was to people who believed similar ideas. With this in mind we will review some key Old Testament stories.

2 The God Yahweh

Historically, in western societies we have referred to Deity simply by using the name *God*. We assumed that those around us also had the biblical God in mind—with biblical attributes. But in the society in which Moses lived, he would not have been able to make that assumption. For him, living in a world where people revered many gods, to use the name *God* would have solicited the question, "Which god?"

Referring to the biblical God with the name *Lord* is also problematic, since many gods carry that prefix. Neither does the name *Creator* work since every culture has the notion of a creator. A distinction needs to be made.

We see the Lord making that distinction when he first met with Moses at the burning bush.

> *The angel of the Lord appeared to [Moses] in a blazing fire from the midst of a bush...God called to him from the midst of the bush...He said, "Do not come near here; remove your sandals from your feet, for the place on which you are standing is holy ground."* Exodus 3:2,4-5 NASB

God declared himself holy—unique, one-of-a-kind. He was different from other gods.

Next, God gave Moses his personal name, the name *Yahweh*, the I AM—"the self-existent one." This name appears in the Old Testament over 6800 times and is usually translated in an English Bible with the word *LORD* (capitalized).[1]

Those two bits of information learned at the burning bush created the needed distinction to separate Yahweh from all the other gods—from all other "isms." Yahweh was holy—unique—and to that name the words *God*, *Lord*[1] and *Creator* could be attached without confusion.

> *No one is holy like the LORD [Yahweh], for there is none besides You.*
> 1 Samuel 2:2 NKJV

THE NAME

Just as we humans have personal names, such as John, Susan, Ravi, or Mohamed, so God has the personal name Yahweh.

God = Yahweh = LORD = Creator
(In the Bible, all refer to the same Deity.)

The Creator's personal name is not Allah, Brahma, Krishna, Gaia or for that matter, God. It is Yahweh. We must not think that all these gods are one and the same God. It should be noted that some translations of the Bible in English use the word *Jehovah* for the name *Yahweh*—they are synonymous.

A UNIQUE GOD

It is with this Deity in mind that Moses penned the first words of the Bible:

> *In the beginning God created…*
> Genesis 1:1 KJV

It was Yahweh who was there in the beginning. The Bible makes it clear that he is the eternal one—the one who has always existed.

From those first five words, Moses went on to record two full chapters on creation. In them he explained how the universe and the world in which we live came into existence. Through creation we gain a solid introduction to the attributes of God.

- The Lord Yahweh is a **person** or **being** with personality and character, not a universal force or an abstract divine mind.
- Yahweh is **all-powerful**, or what Bible scholars call *omnipotent*— *omni* meaning "all," and *potent* referring to "power."
- Yahweh is **all-knowing**, or *omniscient*—the latter half of the word is related to the word *science* meaning "knowledge."
- Yahweh is **everywhere present** at one time, or *omnipresent*.

It is not hard to see how all three of these attributes must be present in one being in order to create the universe in which we live. The creation story also reveals other aspects of God's character.

- The LORD is great, yet he **communicates** with man.
- Yahweh is the **source** of all life. Life did not begin on its own in a pond of scum.
- Yahweh is **separate** from his creation. The Creator-creation distinction should not be blurred. He is not part of his creation.
- The LORD is a God of **order**. He established both physical and spiritual laws that he faithfully maintains.
- Yahweh is a **perfect** God, morally pure without any sin.
- The LORD is a **just** God, absolutely fair in all his dealings. He's the Judge before whom everyone will give account.
- The LORD Yahweh is a caring God, one who **loves** us though we don't deserve it.
- Yahweh is a **faithful** God—a God with a dependable history. He makes promises and keeps them.
- Yahweh is **King**, the Most High, the sovereign Ruler of all.

We can summarize all these attributes with the phrase "God is great." Collectively, the *attributes* of God can be expressed as the *glory of God*—it is what he is like.

These attributes are important to understand because Scripture clearly teaches that Yahweh came to earth in the person of Jesus Christ. It was God who was nailed to the cross.

God = Yahweh = Jesus Christ
(All refer to the same Deity.)

Now to complicate things even more, Yahweh and the Holy Spirit are one and the same. Confused? Let's revisit the concept of the Trinity.

3 THE TRINITY

The Old Testament hammers the fact that Yahweh is one, and it does so by constantly comparing the true God with the many false gods that were prevalent in that day.

But the New Testament reveals to us that although God is one in nature, he is three in person:

- The Father = The Most High
- The Son   = Jesus Christ
- The Spirit   = The Holy Spirit

This is not the same as the Hindu concept of a trimurti. The Bible does not teach three individual "Gods" existing as one, but rather three persons who are inseparable, co-eternal, co-equal, united in one divine Being called Yahweh.

It seems that initially, in revealing himself to a polytheistic world, Yahweh obscured his triune nature so as to drive home the point that he is one God. It is only after the entire Old Testament is recorded and the nation of Israel has become firmly convinced of the "oneness" of God that Yahweh revealed further details of his nature.

THE OLD TESTAMENT

Though the concept of the Trinity may be somewhat obscure in the Old Testament, it is nonetheless there. The first words Moses wrote about God allow for the Trinity.

> In the beginning God created…   *Genesis 1:1 KJV*

The Hebrew word used for God—*Elohim*—is in the plural form (allowing for three persons), but the word itself is singular (one being). Grammatically, this allows for the existence of the three-in-one God. Elohim is the most common Hebrew word translated *God*.

THE SON

But the Old Testament also mentions the various members of the Trinity individually. For example, in the book of Proverbs there is a riddle with five questions centred on the Son. Here it is:

Who but God goes up to heaven and comes back down?
Who holds the wind in his fists?
Who wraps up the oceans in his cloak?
Who has created the whole wide world?
What is his name—and his son's name?
Tell me if you know!   Proverbs 30:4 NLT

This Old Testament riddle jars you into confronting the reality of the Son. That being said, the Son does not take centre stage until the New Testament part of the Bible.

The Exact Representation

In referring to the Son, we always need to remember that the word *Son* does not imply some sort of procreation by God (God did not have physical union with Mary), but rather...

> *The Son is the radiance of God's glory and the exact*
> *representation of his being.*   Hebrews 1:3 NIV

The Son is the mirror image of God—God on earth, revealed for all to see. In simple terms, the Son is God.

The Spirit

The Old Testament also specifically mentions the Spirit. The second sentence of the Bible reveals that the Holy Spirit was active in creation. While the earth was still without form and empty, Moses wrote:

> *The Spirit of God moved upon the face of the waters.*
> Genesis 1:2 KJV

From that point on we see the Spirit mentioned throughout the Old Testament. But once again, it is not until the New Testament that we begin to really understand the role of the Holy Spirit.

Who or What

Since the focus of this book is on the Holy Spirit, let me take a moment to address the confusion surrounding his identity.

In the Bible, the Holy Spirit is spoken of as a *being*—complete with personality, intellect and feelings.

As such, the Holy Spirit can be lied to, grieved and insulted. This presents a problem for those who believe he is some sort of force, similar to electricity or magnetism. It doesn't make sense to speak of grieving electricity or insulting magnetism. The same could be said of those who consider the Holy Spirit to be some sort of fluid. You don't tell lies to a fluid.

As to the confusion between the Holy Ghost and the Holy Spirit, it can be simply explained as the difference between two translations of the same text. When the Bible was translated into English in AD 1611, scholars used the phrase "the Holy Ghost." The newer translations use the word *Spirit* instead of Ghost, as the word *ghost* has taken on spooky connotations. They are one and the same.

So as we talk about our Guide—the Holy Spirit—we need to be thinking of a *person*, not a force or fluid.

It is also important to not confuse the Holy Spirit with "spirit guides" found in New Age, occultic or animistic religions. Those false "guides" are actually demons imitating the Holy Spirit, passing themselves off as serving mankind, but are, in fact, extremely dangerous. They are not to be believed or followed in any way. Only the Holy Spirit, God himself, should be our guide. Only he can be trusted. It is only him that we can know, respect, trust and love without fear.

> For You are my rock and my fortress; for Your name's sake
> You will lead me and guide me.   Psalm 31:3 NASB

MORE ON THE TRINITY

In ancient times vowels were not written, so Yahweh would have been spelled YHWH. This is called the *tetragrammaton*, which in the Greek language means "having four letters."

From the book of Genesis to the book of Revelation we see that Scripture reveals Yahweh as one God, yet three persons—the Father, the Son, and the Holy Spirit.

Bible scholars often speak of the Trinity using a numerical order. The *Father* is regarded as the first person of the Trinity, the *Son* is spoken of as the second person, and the *Holy Spirit* is the third person. In this book we will look at the third person, the Holy Spirit. Although you can never divide the Trinity, the Bible speaks of the Holy Spirit as being specifically assigned to us believers as our personal guide.

4 The Fall

The apex of God's creative handiwork was mankind. Man was unique in Yahweh's creation. This was because…

> …*God created man in his own image, in the image of God he created him; male and female he created them.* Genesis 1:27 ESV

Bible scholars generally agree that reference to "the image of God" applies to the non-physical side of man. As humans, we were created to reflect the nature of the true God, apart from a physical body. Now this leads us to something quite interesting. At the most basic level, the Bible defines humans as having both an *immaterial* and *material* side to our being.

The Material

The material side is the physical body, what we can see and touch. We can study the intricacies of the human body under the microscope and marvel at its abilities in the Olympics. Obviously, it's the easiest part to understand. The Bible speaks of the origin of this aspect of our being when…

> …*the LORD God formed the man of dust from the ground.*
> Genesis 2:7 ESV

The word *formed* is used elsewhere in the Bible to describe a potter shaping an earthen vessel from clay.[2] Simply put, God made the physical body out of the same elements that you find in the ground.

The Immaterial

The non-physical or immaterial side of us is not so easy to comprehend—it cannot be seen or handled. It is described using words like *heart, conscience, mind, spirit* and *soul*. We see the origin of this part of our being when Yahweh created Adam. God…

> …*breathed into his nostrils the breath of life; and man became a living being.* Genesis 2:7 NKJV

Something happened here beyond Adam taking his first breath of air. At creation when Adam stood on his feet, it could be said that there were three factors in his existence, all having part in this "breath of life."[3]

- There was the body, complete with physical eyes and ears, hands and feet. The "breath of life" would have provided the initial oxygen to the lungs.

- God also "breathed" the soul into the body. The soul cannot be seen, but it is obviously very real. It's what leaves the body when it dies. We would say the soul is the "real you," a part that exists forever. Everyone has a soul.

Now it may be that the imparting of the soul was all that was intended by the words "the breath of life," but some Bible scholars think there was something more.

- Since a *breath of air* or *wind* is sometimes used as evidence for the presence of the Holy Spirit, they suggest, "Could it be that the Holy Spirit was also the 'breath of life,' placed within man, joining man to God, giving Adam and Eve spiritual life?"

Now this brings us to what Bible scholars call "the fall" of mankind —when Adam and Eve sinned against God in the garden of Eden. If, as suggested above, it was the Holy Spirit who was breathed into Adam and Eve at their creation, then the tragedy of their fall is that the Holy Spirit moved out, leaving behind spiritually dead humans, subject to the impending reality of physical death.

How the above all unfolded may be open to discussion, but what is not debatable is that when Adam disobeyed Yahweh, man became separated from God—man died spiritually. It was then…

>…*sin entered the world, and death through sin.*
>
> *Romans 5:12 NKJV*

Adam and Eve were so profoundly aware of that separation, they hid from God who was seeking their presence.

Everywhere

Now here is a question. Is not Yahweh everywhere? How can we be separated from him? To answer these questions, we need to understand God's presence in two different ways:

His Universal Presence: God is everywhere—he is omnipresent. In that sense, he acts and speaks into the lives of all humans, whether they are believers or not. Scripture says:

> The eyes of the LORD are in every place, watching the evil and the good.   Proverbs 15:3 NASB

His "Family" Presence: God has reserved a special place in his presence for those who love him and are part of his family. Humans are only allowed into this space if they are in a right relationship with God.

> Surely the righteous will give thanks to Your name; The upright will dwell in Your presence.   Psalm 140:13 NASB

His "family" presence is a unique place where those whom God created can find friendship and fellowship with their Maker.

When Adam and Eve were first created, they enjoyed this "family" presence. But upon rejecting God, they removed themselves from this special relationship—they died spiritually—they were separated from God. We will learn more about this special relationship in the next section.

			At Creation	After the Fall
Material seen by eyes		**Physical Body**	Perfect Without blemish Perfect health	Dying Marred, subject to suffering and death
Immaterial unseen by eyes		**Soul**	Innocent but able to sin	Corrupted dominated by sin
		Spirit*	**Man spiritually alive by the sacred presence of God**	**Man spiritually dead having become separated from…**
*Some make a distinction between soul and spirit; others say they are the same, just different names.				**…God's "family" presence**

IT'S IMMATERIAL

The Darwinian worldview denies the immaterial aspect of man's being, stating that thoughts and emotions are just by-products of cells in our physical brains. But that leaves an awful lot to explain. For example, take the subject of information.

Information is non-material. You can write it with ink on paper using letters of the alphabet, but the actual information itself is not physical. For example, consider these "words."

Ni het .ninignebg oGd ..deretac

The letters are printed with ink on paper—they are physical. But rearrange those same letters and something more springs to life—something not physical. It is "information."

In the beginning God created...

The physical letters of the alphabet are not the information itself; they are just the vehicles used to transmit it. The actual information is not physical—it is non-material.

To deny the non-material is like walking into a massive library and denying the existence of authors. You might be able to give a credible explanation for pages and letters, but how do you explain the information encoded therein. You can only do so if you recognize that there are authors capable of organizing the letters into meaningful sentences and paragraphs that communicate a particular non-material thought.

It is intrinsic to the human sense of existence that there is something more to us than just our physical bodies. We see it reflected in the use of language, the universal existence of a conscience and the reality of our own feelings.

From the perspective of the biblical worldview, God is the author of all information that is true and perfect. In contrast, Satan is the author of all information that is false, for...

...there is no truth in him. When he speaketh a lie, he speaketh of his own: for he is a liar, and the father of it.
John 8:44 KJV

In the physical realm, information that has been corrupted, such as DNA, is a result of the curse that is on the whole earth.

5 The Family

When Adam and Eve rebelled in sin, they established a new race on earth—a rogue family. Now it is important to understand that from a biblical perspective, we are not Asian, African, European, Polynesian or any other "race." Long before the study of genetics proved the point, the Bible said that God...

> ...has made from one blood every nation of men to dwell on all the face of the earth.   Acts 17:26 NKJV

The Bible sees us all as simply belonging to the "human race," or in better terms, one big family.

But it's not a good family—it's a rebellious clan. Why is this? It was because...

> ... sin entered the world through one man.   Romans 5:12 NIV

It was Adam, the first man, who started the human family. Today that family has grown to encompass every living human on the globe. Everyone conceived by the union of a man and woman is related to Adam. We have all been born into what the Bible calls the "in Adam" family. This family is deeply troubled, stemming from the fact that...

> ...just as sin entered the world through one man, and death through sin, and in this way death came to all [people], because all sinned.   Romans 5:12 NIV

Death is the ultimate statement in sorrow and suffering. But it wasn't just physical death that we inherited from Adam. Every son and daughter of Adam is also born spiritually dead.

> ...death came through a man...as **in Adam** all die.
> 1 Corinthians 15:21-22 NET

IDENTITY IN ADAM

Being members of Adam's family creates an identity crisis. As humans we have a tendency to be proud of our birth heritage. Just have someone comment negatively about our ethnic origin—whether Aboriginal, African, Arab, Asian, European, Indian, Jew, Latino, Polynesian, Melanesian, Slav or any other—and we become very defensive. Why is this? It's because "ethnic put-downs" cut to the very core of who we are—our identity. We easily take offense to anything negative regarding our job, our looks, our family—us. Having an identity means everything.

The only problem is, being part of the "in Adam" family is nothing to be proud of. Overall, it has been and remains a dishonest, often cruel family. It may be our identity as humans, but it's a troubled family with deep irremediable problems.

SECOND FAMILY

But the Bible speaks of a second large "family" upon this earth.

> For as by a man came death, by a man has come also the resurrection of the dead. For as **in Adam** all die, so also **in Christ** shall all be made alive. 1 Corinthians 15:21-22 ESV

Jesus established a family called the "in Christ" family. (Remember, he was not born of the union of a man and a woman. His birth was by a virgin. Adam was not in his lineage.) The "in Christ" family is a grace-based family, the result of God's undeserved love.

> For if the many died by the trespass of the one man, how much more did God's grace and the gift that came by the grace of the one man, Jesus Christ, overflow to the many! Romans 5:15 NIV

Family A	Family B
"in Adam"	"in Christ"

The Bible is clear that there is no third family. So the question is this, "How can one move from Adam's family to the family of Christ?" Here is the answer. Just as one had a physical birth to enter Adam's family, so one needs a spiritual birth to enter God's family.

> Jesus answered, "...That which is born of the flesh is flesh, and that which is born of the Spirit is spirit. Do not marvel that I said to you, 'You must be born again.'" John 3:5-7 NKJV

To be born again, one must simply trust God, taking him at his word. For example, the Bible says that:

- Jesus Christ is the Creator God, Yahweh himself. Do you believe that is true?

- Jesus is the Lamb of God, the one who died in your place, paying your eternal death penalty. Do you believe that he did that for you?

- Jesus did not remain dead. He came back to life and he offers eternal life to all who wish to receive it. Have you taken him at his word?

If you affirm that these three points are true for you, then the Bible says you have been born again; you belong to his family, the "in Christ" family. As a family member, you can safely live in his special "family" presence. You are accepted because he has clothed you in his righteousness, as a gift.

> For if, by the trespass of the one man, death reigned through that one man, how much more will those who receive God's abundant provision of grace [or undeserved love] and of the gift of righteousness reign in life through the one man, Jesus Christ.

> For just as through the disobedience of the one man the many were made sinners, so also through the obedience of the one man the many will be made righteous.

> …just as sin reigned in death, so also grace might reign through righteousness to bring eternal life through Jesus Christ our Lord.
>
> Romans 5:17,19,21 NIV

IDENTITY IN CHRIST

As believers, we not only have a new family, but it comes with a new identity as well.

> So then you are no longer strangers and aliens, but you are fellow citizens with the saints and members of the household of God.
> Ephesians 2:19 ESV

No longer do we need to feel put down when someone insults our country, our job, our looks or our ethnicity. We are citizens of a new country.

> But our citizenship is in heaven, and from it we await a Savior, the Lord Jesus Christ.
> Philippians 3:20 ESV

Neither do we need to be defined by our past, whatever it may have been. Now we are defined by our Saviour, the Lord Jesus Christ. Being members of the "in Christ" family is rich in meaning. As we continue through the Bible, we will mention some of those riches. For now it is sufficient to say that we need to live and act in a way that is consistent with our new identity.

Unfortunately, we are often like the disciple Peter—we don't want to be identified with Christ. We are embarrassed; we are afraid of what others may think; we fear what someone may do to us—and so, like Peter, we lie. Peter identified with the wrong crowd and it got him into no end of trouble—and he regretted it deeply. So it will be for us. We need to be confident in our new identity. This is only possible as we learn to know, respect, trust and love the Lord.

	Only Two Families	
Name of family	"in Adam"	"in Christ"
Family head	Adam*	Jesus Christ
Joined by	Physical Birth	Spiritual Birth (born again)
Defined by	Sin, Physical Death, the Second Death	Righteousness, Life, Eternal Life
Sometimes called	"the first Adam"*	"the second Adam"

*the word *Adam* simply means "man" in Hebrew

6 THE FLOOD

When Adam and Eve rebelled in sin, mankind lost a close Guide—we were separated from God. When it came to the worldview question of how to live and not live, Adam and Eve as well as their immediate descendants had no written moral code to follow. They did, however, have a conscience. It was…

> …God's law…written in their hearts, for their own conscience
> and thoughts either accuse them or tell them they are doing right.
> Romans 2:15 NLT

The dictionary[4] defines the conscience as "the sense of right and wrong that governs a person's thoughts and actions." It is part of the immaterial side of our being. We often say, "Let your conscience be your guide." But is that good advice?

EVIL CONSCIENCE

No, it isn't. Here's why. For years I travelled and lived among people who had no exposure to the Bible. I remember one group who would bury their sick and elderly alive. It was their belief that if a person died above ground, then that person's spirit would haunt the rest of the village. They felt quite right about doing this, their consciences approving their actions.

That is only one example of many I could relate. The conscience is quite capable of making a person feel very good about horrific acts of injustice. Scripture speaks of those…

> …*whose consciences have been seared as with a hot iron.*
>
> 1 Timothy 4:2 NIV

If the conscience is seared, with time, the…

> …*mind and conscience is defiled.*   Titus 1:15 KJV

The conscience is retrained to approve evil deeds. It becomes…

> …*an evil conscience.*   Heb 10:22 KJV

GOOD CONSCIENCE

Since the conscience can be corrupted, it is not an adequate guide of what is right and wrong. We need something more, someone from outside ourselves, who can train and guide us into having…

> …*a good conscience.*   I Timothy 1:5 KJV

Only then can we be confident of….

> …*a clear conscience.*   2 Timothy 1:3 ESV

This is the role of the Bible and the Holy Spirit. Working together as Map and Guide, they…

> …*convict the world of its sin, and of God's righteousness, and of the coming judgment.*   John 16:8 NLT

Unlike the conscience, the Holy Spirit cannot be seared — he will never approve of evil actions. He has only one standard of right and wrong and that standard does not change. He brings guilt and shame where there is sin, pointing the way to righteousness and reminding mankind:

> *Be sure your sin will find you out.*   Numbers 32:23 KJV

Working in conjunction with the Scriptures, the Holy Spirit convicts the world of sin — it's his responsibility. People do not like it, and for that reason they…

> …*suppress the truth in unrighteousness.*   Romans 1:18 NASB

They want the world to be a safe place for their sin. They work hard to get rid of Scripture and the convicting voice of the Holy Spirit. What they don't realize is that these are the only barriers against society sliding into violent paganism.

The convicting voice of the Holy Spirit is necessary. It can be compared to an adult repeatedly warning a child not to play with bees. The child may not like the admonition, however, the nagging is for the child's protection. Of course, one can harden his heart and ignore the Holy Spirit, but...

> A man who remains stiff-necked after many rebukes will suddenly be destroyed—without remedy.   *Proverbs 29:1 NIV*

NOAH

In societies where there are no Scriptures, they have only their consciences, and so with time they can become corrupt just as in the days of Noah. During his lifetime:

> The LORD saw how great man's wickedness on the earth had become.   *Genesis 6:5 NIV*

> Every imagination of the thoughts of his heart was only evil continually.   *Genesis 6:5 KJV*

> God saw how corrupt the earth had become, for all the people on earth had corrupted their ways.   *Genesis 6:12 NIV*

But God's spiritual laws do not change. If you break a law, you reap the consequence.

> So God said to Noah, "I have decided that all living creatures must die, for the earth is filled with violence because of them. Now I am about to destroy them and the earth.   *Genesis 6:13 NET*

The world had become a cruel place to live. Because the people suppressed the knowledge of God, they reaped the consequence of their sin. It came as a global flood.

> Everything on dry land that had the breath of life in its nostrils died.   *Genesis 7:22 NET*

The wage for sin was paid.

As for Noah and his family, they escaped the flood, not because they were sinless, but because they listened to their Guide—the Lord himself. They trusted God and his Word as being true. They had faith in Yahweh.

What a Mess

If one could say that the wheels began to come off the human race shortly after creation, by the time of Noah 1500 years into the world's history, one could say the human race had fully crashed.

> *The earth was corrupt in God's sight and was full of violence.*
>
> Genesis 6:11 NIV

Now we need to ask ourselves a question. If Yahweh is King over the universe, sovereign over the earth, then how could he allow things to get into such a mess? Attempts by Bible believers to answer this question can vary greatly.

We do know that the Bible clearly teaches that God, as the sovereign King, is in control of the world. But that control cannot be compared to a cosmic computer programmer. God did not sit down in eternity past and program a heavenly computer, where he predetermined that on March 5th, at 12:53 p.m., John would have a chicken leg for lunch, followed by a 20-minute walk, and then push the enter key. Such a concept of God's control places him in the non-biblical role of programming those he created to be rapists and murderers—or to be raped and murdered. It removes the distinction between what God allows and what God determines.[5] Above all, it diminishes his greatness and ignores man's responsibility—also plainly taught in Scripture. He would just be that glorified computer programmer.

Although it is clear that Yahweh is in control of the universe, it is also evident that God, in his sovereignty, gave mankind the ability to choose. Indeed, the entire Bible from Genesis to Revelation is a book about choices—either stories of the choices mankind has made, or advice about how to make them.

When and Where

From a biblical standpoint, God did predetermine many things—just when and where each ethnic group should live.

> *The God who made the world and everything in it is the Lord of heaven and earth... From one man he made every nation of men, that they should inhabit the whole*

earth; and he determined the times set for them and the exact places where they should live.   *Acts 17:24,26 NIV*

To this we can safely add that God also decides an individual's gender, physique and engiftments. With these predetermined boundaries—fences as it were—God places us on the earth. But within these boundaries, he gives us tremendous room to roam—to make choices. How God is able to give us such freedom and yet control the events of the earth is hard for us to comprehend. It certainly takes his greatness—his sovereignty—to an astonishing magnitude.

7 THE TWO RESPONSES

After Noah left the ark, God gave him and his family a very specific command.

> *As for you, be fruitful and increase in number; multiply on the earth and increase upon it.*   *Genesis 9:7 NIV*

At this point Noah and his descendants had a choice.

1. They could go and multiply on the earth as God had instructed them, or…

2. They could ignore God and stay in one place.

BABEL

> *The whole earth had a common language and a common vocabulary. When the people moved eastward, they found a plain in Shinar and settled there. Then they said to one another, "Come, let's make bricks and bake them thoroughly." (They had brick instead of stone and tar instead of mortar.)*
>
> *Then they said, "Come, let's build ourselves a city and a tower with its top in the heavens so that we may make a name for ourselves. Otherwise we will be scattered across the face of the entire earth."*   *Genesis 11:1-4 NET*

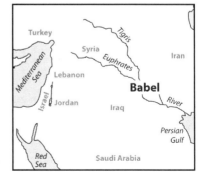

God said, "go" fill the earth; the people said "stay" so we won't be scattered. There was obviously no desire to obey the Lord. Instead, the focus was on what would please self and glorify man.

> The LORD said, "…Come, let us go down and confuse their language so they will not understand each other."
>
> So the LORD scattered them from there over all the earth, and they stopped building the city. That is why it was called Babel—because there the LORD confused the language of the whole world. From there the LORD scattered them over the face of the whole earth. *Genesis 11:6-9 NIV*

How it all worked out we don't know. Perhaps the people went to bed that night all speaking the same mother tongue, and woke up the next morning surrounded by "foreigners." Whatever the case, the people of Babel knew beyond a doubt that God had judged their rebellion. Throughout the Bible, the presence of a language you cannot understand was often used as a sign of God's judgment. Even to this day, the diversity of tongues on this globe should be an audible reminder of God's judgment on an ancient people who refused to trust him.

Abram

Not long after the events of Babel, God again said, "Go."

> The LORD had said to Abram, "Leave your country, your people and your father's household and go to the land I will show you." *Genesis 12:1 NIV*

Abram was faced with a choice:

1. He could leave his country and, taking a step of faith, believe the Lord would guide him to a new land he had never seen, or…

2. He could stay put, reminding the Lord that his instructions were short on details, without assurances of a better life…and, of course, he had a family for whom he was responsible.

What went through Abram's mind we do not know, but the Bible is clear about his choice.

> Abram left, as the LORD had told him… He took his wife Sarai…and they set out for the land of Canaan. *Genesis 12:4-5 NIV*

Abram went out by faith, believing God to guide him.

WALK BY FAITH

In the language of the Bible, *to believe* is the same as having *faith*. To believe means "to be convinced or persuaded that something is true or reliable."

> Now faith is being sure of what we hope for, being convinced of what we do not see. For by it the people of old received God's commendation. *Hebrews 11:1-2 NET*

One of those "people of old" was Abram who later became known as Abraham. He is used as an example of faith in the Bible. In that light, we as believers are told to…

> …walk by faith. *2 Corinthians 5:7 NJKV*

Spiritually, we walk one step at a time through the ups and downs of life. It's sanctification, a growing into spiritual maturity.

This is why when we hear Christians talk about "walking by faith" we need to think of Abraham. As he journeyed, each step he took was a step of faith in the right direction.

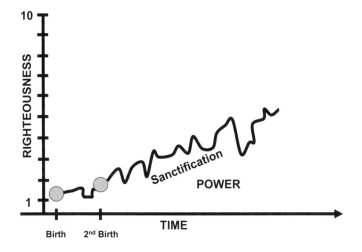

Abraham could have stayed home or gone the wrong way, but no, he went the right way.

That is the essence of walking by faith. It is the process of making wise choices—a long obedience in the right direction. Each wise choice we make is another step towards spiritual maturity.

Just like Abraham, we must trust the Lord to guide us—to make wise choices one day at a time. Scripture says we are to…

> …*walk by faith, not by sight.*   2 Corinthians 5:7 NJKV

If we walked by sight we would require miracles and visions before we would trust God. But that is not the way it is supposed to be. We believe, not because God shows us mighty miracles, but because we know Yahweh's character throughout the Bible.

In light of who he is, we trust him. We need to be like Abraham, fully persuaded, for…

> …*without faith it is impossible to please God.*   Hebrews 11:6 NIV

God honours those who walk by faith. We need to be convinced of this since it is natural to want to walk by sight.

A Choice

Both the people of Babel and Abraham were told the same thing, but their responses were quite different.

The People of Babel	Abraham
Told to fill the earth	Told to go to a new land
Stayed in one place	Went as told
Sought to exalt themselves	Sought to please the Lord
Trusted in own reasoning	Trusted in God
Example of rebellion	Example of faith
God judged	God blessed

Two Peoples

God promised Abraham that he and his descendants would be a special nation—the chosen people.

> "*I will make you into a great nation and I will bless you; I will make your name great, and you will be a blessing.*" Genesis 12:2 NIV

When God scrambled the languages at Babel, he created the nations of the world. But in so doing, only the descendants of Abraham—through Isaac and Jacob—were chosen to be a special nation. The day Abraham stepped out in faith, believing the promises of God, the world divided into two groups.

- There was the nation of Israel, also known as the Hebrews or the Jews, and...

- There were the Gentiles (sometimes called the Greeks), consisting of all the other nations of the world.

Understanding the existence of the Jewish-Gentile divide is an important aspect of our story. Yahweh promised Abraham:

"I will bless those who bless you, and whoever curses you I will curse; and all peoples on earth will be blessed through you."

Genesis 12:3 NIV

Through Jesus, a Jew, all nations of the earth have been truly blessed, for only in him do we find abundant life here on earth and eternal life in the world to come.

THE BASIS OF FAITH

The decision to be a Christian is not based on *unfounded* promises of forgiveness, abundant life, or an eternity in Heaven. Rather, it is decided on one simple reality. Is the Bible true?

Some need only a few biblical facts assembled for them and they find that quite sufficient in order to believe. Others have to think the Bible through from A to Z. They have many questions and demand many answers. Only after thinking it through deeply do they decide to trust it as true. Whether individuals require few facts or demand many, the Bible accommodates seekers from both ends of the spectrum. It only asks one thing: the seeker must be honestly seeking.

At some point in studying the Bible, a person is confronted with a decision—a faith decision. Will you believe it is true? Will you take God at his word?

8 The Theophany

After Abraham arrived in Canaan, God paid him a visit. He brought with him two angels.

> The LORD appeared to Abraham near the great trees of Mamre while he was sitting at the entrance to his tent in the heat of the day. Abraham looked up and saw three men standing nearby. When he saw them, he hurried from the entrance of his tent to meet them and bowed low to the ground.
>
> *Genesis 18:1-2 NIV*

Remember, when you see LORD spelled with all capital letters, it is a direct translation of God's personal name. This was Yahweh on earth! When this happened in the Old Testament, it was a *theophany*.

The word comes from the Greek language, where *theo* means "God "and *phan* means "to show" — as in *theophan* or *theophany*. Indications of a theophany are the words "the Lord came down," "the Lord appeared," or mention of "the Angel (or literally, 'the Messenger') of the Lord."

Some Bible scholars believe that when God appeared to Abraham, it was actually Jesus. While this can be disputed, every theophany in the Old Testament foreshadows the arrival of Jesus in human flesh, where God took the form of a man to live among us as *Immanuel* — literally, "God with us."

While They Ate

Abraham recognized that there was something significantly different about his three visitors. He invited them to dine.

> Abraham hurried into the tent to Sarah. "Quick," he said, "get three seahs of fine flour and knead it and bake some

bread." Then he ran to the herd and selected a choice, tender calf and gave it to a servant, who hurried to prepare it. He then brought some curds and milk and the calf that had been prepared, and set these before them. While they ate, he stood near them under a tree. Genesis 18:6-8 NIV

Abraham wasn't having a dream or vision. These weren't spirits eating his food. God and the angels had taken on tangible bodies. This is the nature of some theophanies.

"Where is your wife Sarah?" they asked him. "There, in the tent," he said.

Then the LORD said, "I will surely return to you about this time next year, and Sarah your wife will have a son." Genesis 18:9-10 NIV

Abraham and Sarah had heard this before—many years before. The only difference was that this time it was to happen within the next 12 months.

Now Sarah was listening at the entrance to the tent, which was behind him. Abraham and Sarah were already old and well advanced in years, and Sarah was past the age of childbearing. So Sarah laughed to herself as she thought, "After I am worn out and my master is old, will I now have this pleasure?"

Then the LORD said to Abraham, "Why did Sarah laugh and say, 'Will I really have a child, now that I am old?' Is anything too hard for the LORD? I will return to you at the appointed time next year and Sarah will have a son."

Sarah was afraid, so she lied and said, "I did not laugh." But he said, "Yes, you did laugh." Genesis 18:10-15 NIV

Like Abraham and Sarah, our faith can go through ups and downs. At times we may struggle with doubt. We must remember that it is *not the amount of faith* we have that is vital, but *in whom we are placing our faith*. It is the object of our faith that is important—not faith itself.

For example, when it comes to being saved from the eternal penalty for sin, it is not our faith that saves us; Jesus is the one who saves us. Faith is simply the *means* of salvation; it is not the *source* of our salvation. You may have very strong faith, but if you are trusting the moon god or your good deeds to save you, then that strong faith will be meaningless. But even weak faith placed solely in the Lord Jesus Christ will be honoured for salvation.

What applies to being saved from the eternal **penalty** of sin also applies to being saved from the daily **power** of sin. In our daily walk with the Lord we may at times doubt, but God remains faithful—we need to just keep believing. In simple terms, we just need to take God at his word.

We must be careful we don't fall into the trap of examining our faith apart from Christ. Our focus needs to be on the object of our trust: the Saviour. Is he worthy of trust? Examination of Christ will lead us to being fully persuaded that he has the power to do what he has promised!

Faith and Belief

> *Against all hope, Abraham in hope **believed** and so became the father of many nations, just as it had been said to him, "So shall your offspring be." Without weakening in his **faith**, he faced the fact that his body was as good as dead—since he was about a hundred years old—and that Sarah's womb was also dead. Yet he did not waver through **unbelief** regarding the promise of God, but was strengthened in his **faith** and gave glory to God, being **fully persuaded** that God had power to do what he had promised.*   Romans 4:18-21 NIV

Doubt loses its grip as we learn more about God and the Bible. This is why it is so important to study our Map. With time we gain confidence in it—we believe at a deeper level—and our faith grows in strength, just as it did for Abraham.

A Great Nation

As for Abraham and Sarah, God kept his word just as he had promised. Sarah, in her old age, had a son named Isaac. You may remember that it was Isaac who Abraham offered as a sacrifice, and it was Isaac who experienced God's provision of a substitute ram so he need not die that sacrificial death.

Isaac had a full life, a life recorded in the biblical book of Genesis. It was Isaac who fathered Jacob, a man whose name was later changed to Israel. Jacob had 12 sons and it was during his lifetime that the entire family moved to Egypt.

In Egypt and over the next four centuries, the descendants of Abraham, Isaac and Jacob grew into a large nation.

As the nation grew, it became a threat to the security of Egypt. This in turn led to them being enslaved by the Egyptians.

It is at this point in time that the stories of Moses occur, including his confrontation with Pharaoh, his demands to release the Israelites, Pharaoh's repeated refusals and the resulting ten plagues.

God used the events of the first Passover to thrust the Israelites out of Egypt. Then there followed the story of the Israelites escaping Pharaoh's army through the Red Sea. It is here that we pick up the story in the next chapter.

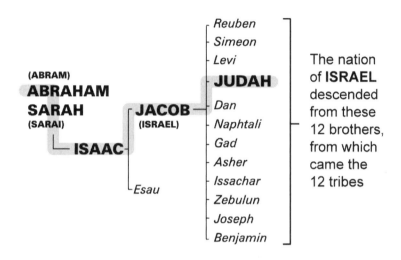

NEITHER AVATAR NOR DEMIGOD

Neither a theophany nor the arrival of Jesus in Bethlehem are the same as saying that Jesus was an avatar or demigod.

A demigod is said to be part god and part human. In contrast, Jesus was 100% God and 100% human—simultaneously.

Avatars are said to appear, disappear and reappear in different forms, sometimes as humans, but often as animals or part animal. In contrast, Jesus was born only once and truly became human flesh to live among us. Theologians call this the incarnation of Christ—the time when God became man and lived among us human beings.

So when we talk about a theophany or the incarnation of Christ, we must not confuse those concepts with the idea of an avatar or a demigod.

CHAPTER THREE

1 THE LAW

2 THE SACRED PLACE

3 THE TABERNACLE

4 THE CHOSEN PEOPLE

5 THE FEAST OF PASSOVER

6 THE FEAST OF UNLEAVENED BREAD

7 THE FEAST OF FIRSTFRUITS

8 THE FEAST OF PENTECOST

9 THE PROPHETS

10 THE VISUAL AID

1 THE LAW

Remember when Moses first met Yahweh?

> *The angel of the LORD appeared to him in flames of fire from within a bush. Moses saw that though the bush was on fire it did not burn up.*　　　　　Exodus 3:2 NIV

As we said in the last section, often when you see the phrase "the angel of the Lord," or "the messenger of the LORD," it is Yahweh showing his presence in some form here on earth. The "messenger of the LORD" who appeared at the burning bush was a theophany which included fire.

When we see the Israelites leaving Egypt, the Bible says:

> *The LORD went before them by day in a pillar of cloud to lead the way, and by night in a pillar of fire to give them light, so as to go by day and night.*　　　　　Exodus 13:21 NKJV

Once again we see fire indicating the presence of God.

Moving on in the story, when the Israelites arrived at Mount Sinai, God again showed his sacred presence.

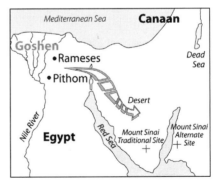

> *And to the eyes of the sons of Israel the appearance of the glory of the LORD was like a consuming fire on the mountaintop.*
> 　　　Exodus 24:17 NASB

This consuming fire was a profound statement to Jew and Gentile alike that the Creator God was present with the Israelites. It distinguished them from all other nations. The Gentile religions had their laws, priests and sacrifices, but only Israel could legitimately claim the sacred presence of the living God.

At one point Moses said to God:

> *"If your Presence does not go with us, do not send us up from here. How will anyone know that you are pleased with me and with your people unless you go with us? What else will distinguish me and your people from all the other people on the face of the earth?"*   *Exodus 33:15-16 NIV*

As we talk about our Map and Guide, we will see how God has provided every believer with a way for his sacred presence to be a constant companion, just as he did for the ancient Israelites. Keep this in mind as we continue the story.

Also keep in mind that fire is often used in Scripture to emphasize God's power and presence. This is not always the case, so one needs to read the context—the surrounding story—to determine if it is true for the given passage.

Moses

At Mount Sinai, God gave the Israelites the Ten Commandments. Actually the ten rules were part and parcel of 613 laws God gave to Moses. The rules are sometimes divided into three categories:[1]

- **The Moral Law** included the Ten Commandments and other rules such as:

  You shall love your neighbor as yourself.   *Leviticus 19:18 NKJV*

- **The Civil Law** comprised Israel's legal system, having to do with economic, land and criminal justice.

- **The Ceremonial Law** concerned the role of priests and sacrifices in the Tabernacle, as well as the celebration of certain festivals. Later we will look at this in greater depth.

Although for discussion purposes, it may be helpful to break the 613 laws into these sub-categories, don't get too hung up with trying to figure out which law fits where. The truth of the matter is, the Israelites made no such distinctions; they were to observe all 613 laws without exception.

Moral Law

In previous books, I focused our attention on the Ten Commandments—the Moral Law—since it captures the intent behind the whole Law. It helps us come to grips with the fact that...

*... Jews and Greeks [or Gentiles] alike are all under sin, just
as it is written: "There is no one righteous, not even one."*

Romans 3:9-10 NET

With the Moral Law hanging over our heads, it was of no use
saying, "I am better than so and so," or "I am not as bad as guys
like Hitler and Pol Pot." God does not accept us because we make
a better impression. Rather, the Law reveals that we will be judged
based on God's standard of absolute perfection.

*Now we know that whatever the law says, it says to those
who are under the law, so that every mouth may be silenced
and the whole world held accountable to God. Therefore no
one will be declared righteous in his sight by observing the
law; rather, through the law we become conscious of sin.*

Romans 3:19-20 NIV

The Law makes us aware that we are sinners. However, the Law
does not leave us condemned. It had a greater purpose.

The law was our schoolmaster to bring us unto Christ.

Galatians 3:24 KJV

The Moral Law actually protected, shepherded and led us to the
Lord Jesus. There we found the one who would save us from
our sin-debt.

WHAT ABOUT US?

One question often asked by new believers is this, "Do we need
to keep the Ten Commandments in order to be good Christians?"
This is a critical question and is better answered later in this book.
But keep in mind, strictly speaking, if you are going to try to follow
the laws of Moses, you must keep all 613 laws—the Moral, Civil
and Ceremonial laws.[2] That is a pretty heavy load to carry! But
keep reading. There is a good answer to this question.

THE COMMANDS, THE LAW

In Scripture you find many verses that refer to the Law or
commands of God, but these verses are not always referring
to the 613 laws found as given to Moses. Often these verses
are directed at the broad scope of Scripture and what God
desires to be done on earth and in the human heart.

2 THE SACRED PLACE

The Moral Law clearly showed mankind that he had a sin problem. But God didn't leave man in a lurch. He also gave the Ceremonial Law which pictured the coming solution. It had to do with the Tabernacle and its sacrifices. It, too, was...

> ...*our schoolmaster to bring us unto Christ.* Galatians 3:24 KJV

We see this clearly in the way the Ceremonial Law instructed an Israelite to...

> *... bring as your offering an animal from either the herd or the flock.*
>
> *If the offering is a burnt offering from the herd, he is to offer a male without defect. ...He is to lay his hand on the head of the burnt offering, and it will be accepted on his behalf to make atonement for him.* Leviticus 1:2-4 NIV

As the Israelite placed his hand on the head of the lamb, it pictured the day when our sins would be transferred from us on to Jesus, because...

> ...*the Lord has laid on him the iniquity of us all.* Isaiah 53:6 ESV

THE HOLY OF HOLIES

As a visual aid, probably the most intriguing part of the Tabernacle was the Holy of Holies. There is a reason for this. In a previous chapter we mentioned:

- God is everywhere present, in the sense of being omnipresent in his universe.

But we also saw that God has something we called:

- His family presence.

Our problem, of course, is that our eyes cannot see God—he is a Spirit. However, within the Tabernacle there was a physical room called the Holy of Holies. This was a sacred place where God symbolically dwelt among his people. One could not "see" God, but you could see his presence. By day there was that special cloud hovering over the Holy of Holies and by night there was the blazing pillar of fire.

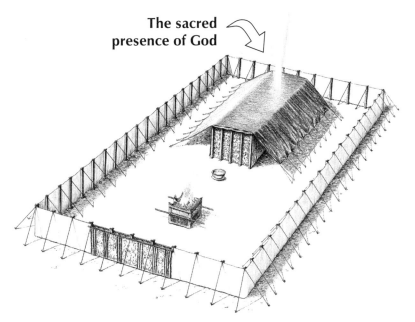

The sacred presence of God

NO ENTRY

No one had access to the Holy of Holies except the high priest, and then only once a year on the Day of Atonement. For one and for all, a heavy curtain barred access to this room. No one could enter God's presence. Even if one was willing to get down on his face and grovel his way in, the truth of the matter was that he would die. The problem was simple: God was holy and man was sinful and that was the end of all argument. And so that's the way it was for centuries, all through the life of the Old Testament.

But when Jesus came, something new happened. The Bible tells us that the heavy curtain represented Jesus—specifically his body. It says that when Jesus was on the cross, he shouted, "It is finished!" and the curtain was torn in two. This was a picture of his body being "torn" on our behalf. Now, to enter God's "family" presence, there is no need to grovel!

> *Therefore, brothers, since we have confidence to enter the Most Holy Place by the blood of Jesus, by a new and living way opened for us through the curtain, that is, his body, and since we have a great priest over the house of God, let us draw near to God with a sincere heart and with the full assurance that faith brings.*   Hebrews 10:19-22 NIV

With confidence, we now dwell in the sacred presence of Yahweh, secure in the fact we are accepted because of Jesus.

But there is a question we must ask ourselves. If Yahweh dwelt in a physical room, could he not indwell a physical body—a human body?

UPON

We know that in the Old Testament the Holy Spirit came upon individuals for special purposes. Such was the case when...

> The LORD said to Moses: "Bring me seventy of Israel's elders... Have them come to the Tent of Meeting... I will come down and speak with you there, and **I will take of the Spirit that is on you and put the Spirit on them**. They will help you carry the burden of the people so that you will not have to carry it alone.
> Numbers 11:16-17 NIV

Obviously, there were far more believers in Israel than these 70 men, but only they and a handful of others were so blessed.

FILLED

We also see the Holy Spirit interacting with the few who oversaw the building of the Tabernacle.

> Now the LORD spoke to Moses, saying, "See, I have called by name Bezalel...**I have filled him with the Spirit** of God in wisdom, in understanding, in knowledge, and in all kinds of craftsmanship."
> Exodus 31:1-3 NASB

To be "filled with the Spirit" has no similarity to filling a glass with water. The "filling" speaks of being controlled by God, not in the sense of a robot, but rather in the way God guides his people in the choices they make. It is a form of strengthening or empowerment. We could say that God empowered Bezalel with special ability to craft the Tabernacle.

He came *upon* some; he *filled* or empowered others. But he did not do this for all Israelites. It does not seem normative in any way that God indwelt his people in the Old Testament. Yes, there were exceptions to the rule, but it seems they were just that: exceptions.

All of this is very important. Step by step God was revealing himself and the meaning of his "family" presence to mankind. As we progress in the story, we will see how things have changed.

3 THE TABERNACLE

In my previous books, we looked at the seven major pieces of furniture in the Tabernacle. However, there was one article we just skimmed over. It was called the bronze basin, or in some translations, the laver.

THE BASIN

The basin was made of polished bronze mirrors, melted and recast into this article of furniture. Its exact shape and size are not stated in Scripture, but we do know its function.

> The LORD said to Moses, "You shall also make a basin of bronze, with its stand of bronze, for washing. You shall put it between the tent of meeting and the altar, and you shall put water in it." *Exodus 30:17-18 ESV*

Since the whole Tabernacle system was part of the Ceremonial Law, the basin also had a role in being…

> …our schoolmaster to bring us unto Christ. *Galatians 3:24 KJV*

We see that in the way an Israelite would approach God in the Holy of Holies. As he entered through the one gate and offered a sacrifice on the bronze altar, it pictured us entering into a relationship with God, through Jesus, the only way to eternal life and having our sins forgiven by his sacrifice on the cross.

But in order for the Israelite to move past the bronze altar, he had to be a priest. In the same way, as we move past the cross, we have become…

> …a royal priesthood…belonging to God, that [we] may declare the praises of him who called [us] out of darkness into his wonderful light. *1 Peter 2:9 NIV*

It was then that the Israelite priest came to the bronze basin. (See Tabernacle on page 67, halfway between the altar and the tent.)

> Aaron and his sons are to wash their hands and feet with water from it. Whenever they enter the Tent of Meeting, they shall wash with water so that they will not die. *Exodus 30:19-20 NIV*

The floor of the court and the sanctuary was bare ground—call it "dirt" if you will. With normal, everyday contact, the feet of the priests would become dirty. The Lord instructed the priests to wash their hands and feet regularly with water as they went about their service for him.

In the same way, when we put our trust in Jesus as Saviour, our sin-debt is forgiven. However, in our everyday living we are not sinless—we become besmirched with the grime of the world and our own wrong choices. In daily life we need to visit the basin of God's Word, to…

> …cleanse [our lives] with the washing of water by the word.
>
> Ephesians 5:26 KJV

The Bible clearly teaches that it is through the Word that we experience cleansing in our lives.

> How can a young man keep his way pure? By guarding it according to your word.　　Psalm 119:9 ESV

Jesus promised:

> Now [you] are clean through the word which I have spoken unto you.　　John 15:3 KJV

Just as the basin was made out of mirrors provided by the Israelites, so when we look into the Word of God, it functions as a mirror for our souls, showing us our need for cleansing and purity.

> But the man who looks intently into the perfect law that gives freedom, and continues to do this, not forgetting what he has heard, but doing it—he will be blessed in what he does.
>
> James 1:25 NIV

Though our eternal sin-debt was forgiven through Christ's sacrifice on the cross, we need to be "washed" daily through his Word. Only then can we serve the Lord, as did the priests in the Tabernacle.

> Now that you have purified yourselves by obeying the truth so that you have sincere love for your brothers, love one another deeply, from the heart.　　1 Peter 1:22 NIV

This is why we need to constantly read the Bible—our Map. In a sense, as you read this present book, you are doing just that. You are reading hundreds of verses. But don't neglect to read the Bible for yourself and think about what it says. Scripture promises that it will have a cleansing effect on your mind.

> Your word I have treasured in my heart, That I may not sin against You.　　Psalm 119:11 NASB

Walking daily in the light of God's Word, the Holy Spirit will be at work in our lives, and we can have confidence that…

> …the blood of Jesus His Son cleanses us from all sin.
>
> 1 John 1:7 NASB

PRIESTS

In this book we will not address the subject of priests in detail. Scripture teaches that all believers are "priests," however, this does not mean we wear special garments, offer sacrifices or recite a liturgy. Rather, it highlights our role before the world as those…

> …belonging to God, that [we] may declare the praises of him who called [us] out of darkness into his wonderful light.
>
> *1 Peter 2:9 NIV*

You will sometimes hear Christians talk about the "priesthood of believers." It is just a way of saying that we can enter directly into God's presence without an intermediary, such as a clergyman or an ordained priest.

---

4 THE CHOSEN PEOPLE

To help us clearly understand the Bible, the Ceremonial Law contains foundational instructions that are very significant to our story. While at Mount Sinai:

> The LORD said to Moses, "Speak to the Israelites and say to them: 'These are my appointed feasts, the appointed feasts of the LORD, which you are to proclaim as sacred assemblies.'"
>
> *Leviticus 23:1-2 NIV*

The Israelites were to observe certain holidays—literally "holy days" or unique days. The first holy day was called the *Sabbath* and was to be celebrated every Saturday.

> You have six days each week for your ordinary work, but the seventh day is a Sabbath day of complete rest, an official day for holy assembly.
>
> *Leviticus 23:3 NLT*

Not only would the Sabbath be a day of rest, but God said…

> …to the Israelites, "You must observe my Sabbaths. This will be a sign between me and you for the generations to come, so you may know that I am the LORD, who makes you holy."
>
> *Exodus 31:13 NIV*

A Different People

The observance of the Sabbath was a reminder to the Israelites and the nations of the world that God had set apart the Jewish people as a unique or holy nation. It would be through them that he would bring the Scriptures to the world. In light of that fact, the Israelites were to conduct themselves differently than others. God told Moses:

> *"Speak to the entire assembly of Israel and say to them: 'Be holy because I, the LORD your God, am holy.'"* Leviticus 19:2 NIV

As believers, we too are instructed to be a unique people:

> *Be holy in all your conduct, because it is written, "Be holy, for I am holy."* 1 Peter 1:15-16 NKJV

To be holy or unique does not mean that we are to be weird or eccentric. Nor does it necessarily have anything to do with observing Saturday as a rest day. It does mean, however, that we are to conduct ourselves in a way that is appropriate to those who belong to God's family. We will discuss this in more detail as we continue along.

Prophecy

To understand the next holy days, we must become familiar with two types of prophecies found in the Bible:

1. Event Prophecies: These prophecies are predictions of events, either past or yet to come. For example, 700 years before Jesus was born, the prophet Micah foretold the birthplace of the Messiah.

> *But you, Bethlehem Ephrathah, though you are small among the clans of Judah, out of you will come for me one who will be ruler over Israel, whose origins are from of old, from ancient times.* Micah 5:2 NIV

Jesus fulfilled this prophecy precisely.

Various religions and cults recognize that prophecy authenticates the Holy Bible, but only the Koran attempts to duplicate this aspect of Scripture. Koranic scholars ascribe 22 prophecies to the Koran.[3] Of those 22 prophecies, only one would meet biblical criteria as a prophecy and even that one is questionable. In contrast, the Bible contains hundreds of event prophecies.

2. Illustrative Prophecies: These complex prophecies are unique to the Bible. No other religious literature attempts to duplicate them, yet the Bible has many such prophecies. Biblical scholars call illustrative prophesies *types*, and their fulfillments are called *antitypes*—"anti"(Greek/Latin) being the corresponding *opposite* of a type. This may sound complex, but you are already familiar with many of these prophetic types and their fulfillments (antitypes).

The holidays that God asked Israel to observe were actually illustrative prophecies. We will commit the next four sections just to these feasts since they are very significant.

VISUAL AIDS

Before we end this section, we need to be reminded that the Old Testament accounts of God's dealings with Israel function as a lesson book for us. In a very real sense, Israel, as God's chosen people, was a visual aid to the whole world describing what Yahweh's character was like and his dealings with mankind. The Jewish Sabbath and their biblical feasts are part of that picture; they are placed there to teach us key lessons.

> *For whatever was written in earlier times was written for our instruction, so that through perseverance and the encouragement of the Scriptures we might have hope.*　　*Romans 15:4 NASB*

5 THE FEAST OF PASSOVER

At Mount Sinai the Lord instructed the Israelites to observe seven annual feasts. Each feast is an illustrative prophecy—a visual aid to help us understand Yahweh's agenda in history.

The first feasts were held in the spring (March or April) and were celebrated together across a handful of days. They consisted of:

1. The Feast of Passover
2. The Feast of Unleavened Bread
3. The Feast of Firstfruits

PASSOVER

In my previous books I mentioned the Passover. But let's take a quick review and look at it in a little more depth. The Scriptures say:

> *On the fourteenth day of the first month at twilight is the LORD's Passover.*　　*Leviticus 23:5 NKJV*

Remember when the children of Israel were slaves in Egypt? God delivered them from Pharaoh with great plagues, the last plague being the death of the firstborn child. God had said that if the Israelites followed his Word, they would be safe from this tragedy. Do you recall how on the fourteenth day of their first month, the Israelites were to sacrifice a lamb? Well, the Bible tells us that Jesus is our Lamb. John the Baptist said of Jesus:

"Look, the Lamb of God, who takes away the sin of the world!"

John 1:29 NET

The Passover is a good example of illustrative prophecy. The Passover lamb is the "type"; Jesus is the "antitype." But just look at the some of the details in this prophecy!

The Prophetic Significance of the Feast of Passover	
Pictured by: — Type[4] —	**Fulfilled by:** — Antitype[4] —
Death required of firstborn	Death required of all mankind
Passover lamb	Jesus Christ, the Lamb of God
Lamb without blemish	Jesus without sin
Lamb had to be a male	Jesus was a man
The lamb's blood spilled on the door frames	The blood of Jesus spilled on a wooden cross
Lamb's death in place of firstborn	Jesus' death in our place
On the first Passover, the lamb died on 14th day of the Jewish month called *Nissan*	1400+ years later, on the 14th of Nissan, Jesus died on the day the Passover was commemorated
The lamb was slaughtered at twilight, traditionally starting at 3:00 p.m. on into evening	Jesus died at 3:00 p.m., the time of the evening sacrifice in the Jewish Temple in Jerusalem
The lamb's bones not broken	The bones of Jesus not broken
Safety only found in house	Safety only found in Christ
Judgment passed over the house of all who took God at his word	Judgment passes over all who take God at his word

The Bible says that when the Lord came in judgment, wherever he saw the blood applied, he passed over that house. Why? It was because death had already come to a substitute lamb.

In the same way, God provided a way for his judgment on sin to pass over us and in so doing, all the judgment we deserved came to rest upon Jesus, our substitute Lamb.

In fulfillment of this prophecy, Scripture says:

Christ, our Passover lamb, has been sacrificed. 1 Corinthians 5:7 ESV

The Passover is a remarkable prophecy, given and fulfilled in detail. It is prophecies like these that should cause us to take the Bible seriously. Much more could be said, but we need to move on to the next prophecy, illustrated by the Feast of Unleavened Bread.

---

1. The Feast of Passover
2. **The Feast of Unleavened Bread**
3. The Feast of Firstfruits

---

6 THE FEAST OF UNLEAVENED BREAD

The Feast of Unleavened Bread was tied in so closely with the Passover that often only one was mentioned, even when both were in mind. The Bible says God instructed Moses:

> *"On the fifteenth day of that month the LORD's Feast of Unleavened Bread begins; for seven days you must eat bread made without yeast."*
> Leviticus 23:6 NIV

This feast occurred the day after Passover. In it, the Israelites were instructed to make bread without yeast. In the Bible, yeast is used as a picture of the permeating effects of sin. We see the significance of this in the Passover feast. On the night before Jesus was crucified...

> *...He took bread, gave thanks and broke it, and gave it to them, saying, "This is My body which is given for you; do this in remembrance of Me."*
> Luke 22:19 NKJV

The loaf without yeast pictured Jesus without sin. Just as the unleavened bread was broken for the disciples, so the sinless Jesus was sacrificed for us on the cross.

But the Feast of Unleavened Bread started on the day after Passover and continued for seven days. Note the seven days. What does this imply?

NEW START

To understand this Feast correctly, we must start our thinking with that first Passover. On that very day, God changed the Jewish calendar, saying:

> *"This month shall be unto you the beginning of months: it shall be the first month of the year to you."*
> Exodus 12:2 KJV

God gave the Israelites a new calendar. It was a reminder that the Passover marked a new start in life, with Egyptian slavery forever left behind.

It is the same with us. When we turned in faith to Jesus, our Passover Lamb, our sin-debt was forever blotted out. The guilt and shame of our past sins were gone.

> *This means that anyone who belongs to Christ has become a new person. The old life is gone; a new life has begun!*
> 2 Corinthians 5:17 NLT

Just like the ancient Israelites, figuratively speaking, we have a new "year," a new life before us, a new beginning. But it doesn't stop there.

We are to continue on, as exemplified in the Feast of Unleavened Bread. We are to pursue lives free of evil, although this pursuit will not be complete until we stand perfect before God in Heaven. (The number "seven" is used in Scripture to refer to *maturity, completeness* or *perfection.*) The Bible says:

> Don't you know that a little yeast works through the whole batch of dough? Get rid of the old yeast that you may be a new batch without yeast—as you really are. For Christ, our Passover lamb, has been sacrificed. Therefore let us keep the Festival, not with the old yeast, the yeast of malice and wickedness, but with bread without yeast, the bread of sincerity and truth.　　　　　　　　　　*1 Corinthians 5:6-8 NIV*

As believers, the hallmark of our lives needs to be sincerity and truth, not anger and wickedness. It is this reality that should set us apart as being holy or unique.

Perhaps at this point you're feeling a little like Simon Peter—a failure. If so, keep reading. This book is written for those who *know* they are sinners. Even though God loved you just as you were, a lost sinner, now that you are a believer, he loves you too much to leave you just as you are. He wants to guide you down the right roads in life and make sure you get to where he wants you to go. He wants you to know him, to respect, trust and love him. It has to do with your sanctification—the King's will.

The Prophetic Significance of the Feast of Unleavened Bread	
Pictured by: — Type⁴ —	**Fulfilled by:** — Antitype⁴ —
The Israelites as a group	All believers, collectively
Celebrating with new bread	Living with sincerity and truth
Being without yeast	Being without sin
Feast length was seven days; the number seven being used in the Bible for *maturity* or *perfection*	Growing to spiritual *maturity* until we pass into the presence of the Lord Jesus Christ

7 The Feast of Firstfruits

We now come to the third spring feast.

> 1. The Feast of Passover
> 2. The Feast of Unleavened Bread
> **3. The Feast of Firstfruits**

> *The LORD said to Moses, "Speak to the Israelites and say to them: 'When you enter the land I am going to give you and you reap its harvest, bring to the priest a sheaf of the first grain you harvest.'"*   *Leviticus 23:9-10 NIV*

In ancient Israel, barley was planted in the fall and harvested in the spring. During harvest, the grain was cut with a sickle and tied into bundles called *sheaves*. God instructed the people to bring the first sheaf into the Temple as an offering to the Lord. They were to bring it on the day immediately following the Sabbath which would have been Sunday.

> *He shall wave the sheaf before the LORD, to be accepted on your behalf; on the day after the Sabbath the priest shall wave it.*   *Leviticus 23:11 NKJV*

This sheaf was the first of many more to be harvested, and so it was called the firstfruit.

A Picture or Type

This Feast was a picture of resurrection from death, what the Bible sometimes politely refers to as being "asleep." No doubt, part of this picture was built around the nature of a seed. Just as a farmer places a "dead" seed in the ground only to see it spring to life, so Jesus was placed dead in the grave only to spring to life on resurrection morning.

> *But now Christ has been raised from the dead, the firstfruits of those who have fallen asleep.*   *1 Corinthians 15:20-23 NET*

And just as the farmer harvested his first sheaf of grain—the firstfruits being an indication of many more sheaves to come—so when Jesus rose from the dead, his resurrection, being the first one, was a promise of many more resurrections to come.

> *[He] has become the firstfruits of those who have fallen asleep.*
> *1 Corinthians 15:20 NKJV*

When believers die, their spirits are…

> …*away from the body and at home with the Lord [in Heaven].*
>
> 2 Corinthians 5:8 ESV

But when Jesus returns again, those who have "fallen asleep" will be resurrected with new bodies—glorified bodies—bodies just like the one Jesus had after his resurrection (see chart on p. 13).

> *For since death came through a man, the resurrection of the dead also came through a man. For just as **in Adam** all die, so also **in Christ** all will be made alive. But each in his own order: Christ, the firstfruits; then when Christ comes, those who belong to him.*   1 Corinthians 15:21-23 NET

The Prophetic Significance of the Feast of Firstfruits

Pictured by:	Fulfilled by:
— Type[4] —	— Antitype[4] —
A bundle or sheaf of grain	The Lord Jesus Christ
Celebrated on the day after the Sabbath which is Sunday	Jesus, who was resurrected on Sunday, around sunrise.
First bundle of grain taken from field at the start of harvest	Jesus, who was the first human[5] resurrected with a glorified body
The first sheaf of grain was a promise of many future sheaves to be taken from the field, as harvest moved towards completion	The resurrection of Jesus was a promise of many future resurrections to come, when all believers will be resurrected with glorified bodies

SUMMARY

Firstfruits completes the first cluster of three feasts. These three feasts form a prophetic picture, or type of the antitype—the death and resurrection of our Lord. They were inaugurated 1400 years before they were fulfilled in Jesus the Messiah. Such amazing precision in prophecy should give us confidence in the truthfulness of God's Word. Having that confidence in the Word helps us in our daily lives, as we follow the Map God has given us to guide our path.

8 The Feast of Pentecost

We now come to the fourth festival, the Feast of Pentecost, held in the late spring.

Early Spring:
1. The Feast of Passover
2. The Feast of Unleavened Bread
3. The Feast of Firstfruits

Late Spring:
4. **The Feast of Pentecost**
   (also called the Feast of Weeks)

According to Jewish tradition, the Ten Commandments along with the rest of the Law were given on the Feast of Pentecost. It was the date when God entered into his contract or covenant with Israel. Whether this is significant to the overall story we can't be certain, but the timing of the Feast is noteworthy.

> *"You shall count seven full weeks from the day after the Sabbath, from [The Feast of the Firstfruits]. You shall count fifty days to the day after the seventh Sabbath. Then you shall present a grain offering of new grain to the LORD."*
>
> Leviticus 23:15-16 ESV

The people called this feast *Pentecost*, literally, the "fiftieth" day, as the feast came exactly 50 days after the Feast of Firstfruits. On Pentecost, the Israelites were to make an offering of new grain. This would have been wheat. Although it was planted in the fall at the same time as barley, it matured later. The significant point is that it had to be *new* grain.

Pentecost

> *From the places where you live you must bring two loaves of bread for a wave offering; they must be made from two tenths of an ephah of fine wheat flour, baked with yeast, as first fruits to the LORD.*
>
> Leviticus 23:17 NET

Note the two loaves and that they were to be baked *with yeast*. Keep this in mind. Also, there was to be a sin offering of animals.

And the priest shall wave them with the bread of the firstfruits for a wave offering before the LORD, with the two lambs: they shall be holy to the LORD for the priest. Leviticus 23:20 KJV

To make sense of this, remember how I emphasized that it is helpful to first read one of the following foundational books:

- The Stranger on the Road to Emmaus
- All that the Prophets have Spoken
- By This Name

In these books you saw the fulfillment of the early spring feasts.

		Prophecy pictured by: — Type[4] —	**Fulfilled when:** — Antitype[4] —
1	**Friday** 1st month 14th day	The Feast of Passover	Jesus, our Passover Lamb, died in our place, removing the death penalty from all who trust in him
2	**Saturday** The Sabbath 1st month 15th day and onward for seven days	The Feast of Unleavened Bread	As new believers, this feast set the path forward for us, to live pure lives as we grow towards spiritual maturity
3	**Sunday** 1st month 16th day immediately after the Sabbath	The Feast of Firstfruits	Jesus became the first person resurrected from the dead,[5] proving his power to raise all believers to eternal life

In previous books, I took the biblical story up to the point of Jesus ascending into Heaven, 40 days after his resurrection. But ten days later—50 days after the resurrection—something significant happened that fulfilled the prophetic Feast of Pentecost. This event was so important on God's calendar that an entire feast was dedicated to it. It had to do with our Guide—the Holy Spirit, the third person of the Trinity. As we progress in the story, we will see how this prophetic festival was fulfilled.

To make sure no one would forget this Old Testament prophecy, the Lord closed his instructions about Pentecost with these words:

> This is to be a lasting ordinance for the generations to come, wherever you live.　　　　　　　　*Leviticus 23:21 NIV*

THE FALL FEASTS

We complete our list with the fall feasts, prophecies that illustrate the events surrounding the return of Jesus to the earth at his second coming. In this book we will not elaborate on their meaning. The three fall feasts bring the total number to seven.

Early Spring:

1. The Feast of Passover
2. The Feast of Unleavened Bread
3. The Feast of Firstfruits

Late Spring:

4. The Feast of Pentecost (sometimes called the Feast of Weeks)

Fall:

5. The Feast of Trumpets
6. The Day of Atonement
7. The Feast of Tabernacles

After Yahweh instituted these feasts, the Bible says:

> Moses announced to the Israelites the appointed feasts of the LORD.　　　　　　　　*Leviticus 23:44 NIV*

From this point on, all seven of these feasts were to be celebrated in the spring and fall of every year, on down through the centuries.

9 THE PROPHETS

Though the Israelites were Yahweh's chosen people, they were often poor representatives of their Creator. When Moses was up on the mountain receiving the 613 laws from God, the Israelites were at the foot of the mountain breaking the first commandment:

> I am the Lord your God...You shall have no other gods before Me.　　　　　　　　*Exodus 20:2-3 NASB*

The people had made an idol—a golden calf—and were worshipping it. In fact, they called the calf Yahweh!

God sent Moses down the mountain to deal with their sin.

> *Moses saw that the people were running wild and that Aaron had let them get out of control and so become a laughingstock to their enemies.* Exodus 32:25 NIV

The Israelites had become a laughingstock to the Gentiles. And of course, by association, God was also ridiculed. But should we find ourselves being hard on the Israelites, we are often just as guilty.

Many unbelievers like nothing more than to find something they can use to laugh at Christians. We need to conduct ourselves in such a way that we don't bring shame to the name of the Lord. Of course, that includes all appearance of running wild and being out of control. We are to be careful in this matter, not out of obligation, but out of love for the Lord, for we too should not want our God to be made a laughingstock in the eyes of unbelievers.

ONE OR THE OTHER

As Moses came down the mountain and entered the camp, he immediately created a distinction. Essentially he told the people that they could worship the calf or they could worship Yahweh, but they could not do both. It was one or the other. Moses said:

> *"Whoever is for the Lord, come to me." And all the Levites [the priests' assistants] rallied to him.* Exodus 32:26 NIV

As believers we should rally to the Lord and live in such a way that our lives are a statement about the goodness of God.

JOSHUA

Moving on with the story by forty years we find Moses passing from the scene. A soldier by the name of Joshua took over the leadership of the nation. He challenged the Israelites:

> *"Be strong and courageous. Do not be terrified; do not be discouraged, for the LORD your God will be with you wherever you go."* Joshua 1:9 NIV

For a time the people listened to Joshua, but then they drifted. They would return to the Lord and then drift some more. This went on for about 800 years. Over and over again, God appealed to them...

> But they rebelled and grieved His Holy Spirit.   Isaiah 63:10 NKJV

We will learn more about grieving the Holy Spirit as we progress. It is not something we want to do since the Holy Spirit is our guide.

COME AND GO

As we come to the final stories of the Old Testament, we need to take note of how the Holy Spirit related to mankind before Jesus came to earth. It was quite different back then and not altogether clear. It seems that in Old Testament times, the Holy Spirit empowered certain believers for certain tasks.[6] The person may have been a believer for some time before this happened. The Holy Spirit would come, and in some cases go, and there was no promise of him remaining with an individual throughout life. Not every believer had the empowering presence of the Holy Spirit, nor in the same way. King David, though undoubtedly a believer at a young age, only received the Holy Spirit after...

> ...Samuel took the horn of oil and anointed him in the presence of his brothers, and from that day on the Spirit of the LORD came upon David in power.   1 Samuel 16:13 NIV

Later in life after he had sinned badly, David feared that the Spirit might leave him. He prayed:

> "Create in me a clean heart, O God, And renew a steadfast spirit within me. Do not cast me away from Your presence, And do not take Your Holy Spirit from me." Psalm 51:10-11 NKJV

The Holy Spirit remained with David and at the end of his life, he was able to say:

> "The Spirit of the LORD spoke by me, And His word was on my tongue."   2 Samuel 23:2 NKJV

Although it is clear that the Holy Spirit did not leave David, the same could not be said of Saul, the king who preceded David. Saul started his rule with the Holy Spirit upon him, but after a time the Spirit left him never to return.

As one reads the Old Testament narrative, you come to the realization that man does not do well without the guiding and constant presence of the Holy Spirit. No matter how influential one may be, no matter how intelligent one is, the truth remains that without the Holy Spirit, we don't accomplish anything of lasting value. It is…

> "Not by might nor by power, but by My Spirit," Says the LORD of hosts.   *Zechariah 4:6 NKJV*

10 THE VISUAL AID

The history of Israel in the Old Testament can largely be summarized in three stages:

1. God would send a messenger to deliver a message to the people.

   Then the Spirit of God came upon Zechariah son of Jehoiada the priest. He stood before the people and said, "This is what God says: Why do you disobey the Lord's commands and keep yourselves from prospering?"   2 Chronicles 24:20 NLT

2. The people would reject both the message and the messenger. The prophets Jeremiah and Zechariah wrote:

   They refused to take correction. They have made their faces harder than rock; They have refused to repent. Jeremiah 5:3 NASB

   They made their hearts diamond-hard lest they should hear the law and the words that the LORD of hosts had sent by his Spirit through the former prophets.   Zechariah 7:12 ESV

3. As a result of this rejection, God would send judgment in the form of foreign invaders.

   You prolonged your kindness with them for many years, and you solemnly admonished them by your Spirit through your prophets. Still they paid no attention, so you delivered them into the hands of the neighboring peoples. Nehemiah 9:30 NET

This cycle happened so often that for a Jew to awaken in the morning and hear a multitude of voices speaking a foreign language, had the effect of a flashback to Babel. A foreign tongue was a byword for judgment. In this sense, the prophet Jeremiah wrote:

> "Behold, I am bringing a nation against you from afar, O house of Israel," declares the LORD.
>
> "It is an enduring nation, It is an ancient nation, A nation whose language you do not know, Nor can you understand what they say."   Jeremiah 5:15 NASB

Although the Israelites could not understand the foreign tongues of their invaders, the message of their swords was not so quickly forgotten. In time, Israel would repent and God would deliver them, but soon they would rebel again, opposed to the message of a different prophet. This happened over and over again.

Dispersion

Eventually God brought on the Israelites the ultimate judgment for a Jew. For the Israelites, to be in the land was a sign of God's blessing. To be exiled out of the land, scattered and persecuted, was a sign that they were under God's judgment.

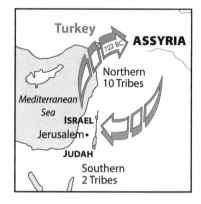

The Assyrians invaded the ten northern tribes in 722 BC and took them into captivity. The records of Sargon II of Assyria indicate that he deported 27,290 inhabitants of Israel. In keeping with the Assyrian way of doing things, Sargon then diluted those left behind, importing foreigners into the land to water down the nationalistic spirit of the Israelites.

The Samaritans

The Israelites who were left behind married these foreigners, resulting in a new race called the *Samaritans*. This mixed race settled in the middle of the country—south of the Sea of Galilee and north of Jerusalem. Those Jews with pure blood despised the Samaritans to the point that they would not even travel through the region known as Samaria. Instead, they would take the long way around.

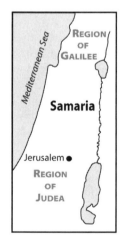

Throughout this time, the two southern tribes continued in the land until they were deported to Babylon 150 years later. Once again God was speaking to the Jews with foreign tongues. Isaiah had warned Israel:

> *For by people of strange lips and with a foreign tongue the LORD will speak to this people.* Isaiah 28:11 ESV

Again, the prophet Jeremiah wrote:

> *It shall come about when they say, "Why has the LORD our*
> *God done all these things to us?" then you shall say to them,*
> *"As you have forsaken Me and served foreign gods in your*
> *land, so you will serve strangers in a land that is not yours."*
>
> Jeremiah 5:19 NASB

SUMMARY

God is not pleased when those he created deny him or follow other gods, but he does not coerce individuals to accept him. Instead, he appeals to their hearts through his written Word. That being said, there are consequences for sin which are part of the laws of cause and effect that God has put in place — laws that govern both the spiritual and physical universe.

In Scripture we see this with the nation of Israel — God's Chosen People. They were God's visual aid to the Gentile nations. When they rebelled against Yahweh, we see God enforcing stringent judgments on them to show visually his disapproval of their conduct. The judgment could take place in two ways:

1. God would bring invaders into Israel to occupy the land, or…

2. God would remove the Israelites from their land and send them into exile.

Either way, when the Jews heard foreign tongues dominating the streets, they knew judgment was upon them.

Both of these judgments were very visual. Every other nation could see what was going on and know how Yahweh felt about the lifestyle of his Chosen People.

In looking at Israel, we as believers (whether Jew or Gentile) should not be harsh in our perception of the ancient Israelites. Instead, we should humbly recognize that often we fail just as they did and learn from them. If we are to safely navigate through the reefs of life and arrive safely at our heavenly harbour, we must take heed to both our Map and our Guide. We must listen to the counsel of the Bible and the guiding of the Holy Spirit.

Chapter Four

CHAPTER FOUR ❖ 89

1 THE SPIRIT IN THE GOSPELS

We now jump 400 years ahead in history. By this time, some of the Jews had returned from exile and settled back in their land. But now they were a colony, part of the Roman Empire.

From a biblical standpoint, we now leave the Old Testament and enter the New Testament. As we do, we see that the Holy Spirit continues to work in the same way he had in previous centuries.

JOHN THE BAPTIST

Remember the events surrounding the birth of John the Baptist? John's father, Zechariah, had been told by the angel that John would…

> …be filled with the Holy Spirit.   *Luke 1:15 NIV*

John was to be filled or guided by the Holy Spirit in such a way as to accurately pass on a very critical message. To be filled in such a manner was an uncommon occurrence in the Bible, but here you find it happening to John.

MARY

Then remember how Mary, the future mother of Jesus, asked the angel how she, a virgin, could conceive a child?

> *The angel answered and said to her, "The Holy Spirit will come upon you, and the power of the Most High will overshadow you; and for that reason the holy Child shall be called the Son of God.*   *Luke 1:35 NASB*

This was obviously very unusual, but nonetheless possible, because the Holy Spirit would make it so.

JOSEPH

Then there were the words spoken to Joseph, Mary's future husband:

> *An angel of the Lord appeared to him in a dream, saying, "Joseph, son of David, do not be afraid to take to you Mary your wife, for that which is conceived in her is of the Holy Spirit.*   *Matthew 1:20 NKJV*

Joseph badly needed that assurance. God provided it in a special dream. The conception of this baby was to be a unique event, something that would never occur again.

Elizabeth

You may also recall that while Mary was expecting Jesus, she visited Elizabeth, the wife of Zechariah. Elizabeth was quite far along in her pregnancy with John, later known as John the Baptist.

> When Elizabeth heard Mary's greeting, the baby [John] leaped in her womb, and Elizabeth was filled with the Holy Spirit. In a loud voice she exclaimed: "Blessed are you among women, and blessed is the child you will bear!" Luke 1:41-42 NIV

Elizabeth was empowered in a unique way by the Holy Spirit to affirm to Mary that the baby Mary was carrying was indeed special. It was another one-of-a-kind event, but what Mary undoubtedly needed to hear.

Zechariah

Then when John the Baptist was finally born, we find his father offering a long prayer of praise to God.

> His father Zechariah was filled with the Holy Spirit and prophesied: "Praise be to the Lord, the God of Israel, because he has come and has redeemed his people." Luke 1:67-68 NIV

The prayer continues for many verses, peppered full of prophecies about the coming Messiah. We saw earlier that the Holy Spirit enabled the Old Testament prophets to foretell the future, and now we see the same thing happening here. The words Zechariah spoke that day would be rehearsed over and over as John grew up and started his ministry. They would be remembered again in detail when Jesus came on the scene. God had his reasons for enabling Zechariah, through the Holy Spirit, to do something that in his natural ability he could not do. But that being said, this was a one-of-a-kind event.

Simeon

Scripture tells us that eight days after the birth of Jesus, his parents brought him to the Temple to dedicate him according to the instructions given in the Ceremonial Law.[1]

> Now there was a man in Jerusalem, whose name was Simeon, and this man was righteous and devout, waiting for the consolation of Israel [the Messiah], and the Holy Spirit was upon him. And it had been revealed to him by the Holy Spirit that he would not see death before he had seen the Lord's Christ. Luke 2:25-26 ESV

As Joseph and Mary listened in awe, Simeon gave some very specific prophecies concerning Jesus. No doubt, God engineered this to steady Mary and Joseph in their responsibility of raising Jesus.

For the purposes of our study, we need to understand that all of these occurrences of the Holy Spirit at work were largely one-time events, not common to every believer of that day.

As we continue to read through the four Gospels—the books of Matthew, Mark, Luke and John—we see the Holy Spirit at work in much the same way as we saw in the Old Testament. He came upon certain individuals for a specific purpose and did not always remain with them for long. This is just one significant fact that points to the real division between the Old and New Testaments, as occurring around the events of the cross rather than around the birth of the Messiah. But before we see how history has changed in the way the Holy Spirit works, we need to lay some more foundations.

2 THE BAPTISM OF JESUS

We continue our story with John the Baptist, now an adult, beginning his ministry.

> Now this is the testimony of John, when the Jews sent priests and Levites from Jerusalem to ask him, "Who are you?" He confessed, and did not deny, but confessed, "I am not the Christ."   John 1:19-20 NKJV

The Greek word *Christ* is the same as the Hebrew word *Messiah*. Both mean "the anointed one."

> Now those who were sent were from the Pharisees. And they asked him, saying, "Why then do you baptize if you are not the Christ, nor Elijah, nor the Prophet?"   John 1:24-25 NKJV

Why indeed? The Bible is clear that water baptism does not make us acceptable to God. It is only an outward picture of what has transpired inwardly. Baptism implies *identification*. A common meaning of the word *baptizo* originated in the early Greek textile industry. In the process of dyeing fabric, a piece of cloth was plunged into a vat of dye, whereby it took on the colour of the pigment. The cloth was totally identified with the dye. To be baptized by John was to say you totally identified or agreed with his message. In that sense, you became a follower or disciple of John. The Pharisees wanted to know John's motivation for doing this.

John answered them, "I baptize with water, but among you stands one you do not know, even he who comes after me, the strap of whose sandal I am not worthy to untie."

John 1:26-27 ESV

"I baptized you with water; but He will baptize you with the Holy Spirit."

Mark 1:8 NASB

Two Baptisms

We see here two different baptisms—*baptism with water* and *baptism with the Holy Spirit.* They are not the same. John was performing the first baptism in the Jordan River. Jesus would initiate the second baptism in the future and it would involve the Holy Spirit. John was making a prophetic claim about this future baptism. He said it was something yet to happen, to be performed by Jesus. It was so significant that he made it a point of prophecy.

The Trinity

*In those days **Jesus** came from Nazareth of Galilee and was baptized by John in the Jordan. And when he came up out of the water, immediately he saw the heavens being torn open and the **Spirit** descending on him like a dove. And a **voice came from heaven**, "You are my beloved Son; with you I am well pleased."*

Mark 1:9-11 ESV

The water baptism of Jesus is remarkable in that you see present the three persons of the Trinity. Together they form a tri-unity—one God whose personal name is Yahweh.

The Lamb of God

The next day John saw Jesus coming toward him and said, "Look, the Lamb of God, who takes away the sin of the world!"

John 1:29 NIV

Prophetically, John was pointing out that Jesus would die in our place, just as the Passover Lamb had died in the place of the firstborn—just as the Temple sacrifices died in the place of those bringing them. Our sin would be taken away or forgiven as we put faith in Jesus, our sacrificial substitute.

And John bore witness: "I saw the Spirit descend from heaven like a dove, and it remained on him. I myself did not know him, but he who sent me to baptize with water said to me, 'He on whom you see the Spirit descend and remain, this is he who baptizes with the Holy Spirit.'"

John 1:32-33 ESV

Yahweh had told John what to expect. He had given him a clear sign as to who this Messiah would be. Now John was letting everyone know that the Son of God, the second person of the Trinity, had arrived on earth. As we saw in an earlier chapter, he had been active on earth numerous times before as a theophany (review page 58), but this time his coming to earth was significantly different. It is rightly referred to as his first coming.

THE DISCIPLES

> *The next day John was there again with two of his disciples. When he saw Jesus passing by, he said, "Look, the Lamb of God!" When the two disciples heard him say this, they followed Jesus.* John 1:35-37 NIV

> *One of the two who heard John speak and followed Jesus was Andrew, Simon Peter's brother. He first found his own brother Simon and said to him, "We have found the Messiah" (which means Christ). He brought him to Jesus. Jesus looked at him and said, "So you are Simon the son of John. You shall be called Cephas" (which means Peter).* John 1:40-42 ESV

Both the Aramaic word *Cephas* and the Greek word *Peter* mean "rock," in the sense of a stone, not a mountain.

> *The following day Jesus wanted to go to Galilee, and He found Philip and said to him, "Follow Me." Now Philip was from Bethsaida, the city of Andrew and Peter. Philip found Nathanael and said to him, "We have found Him of whom Moses in the law, and also the prophets, wrote—Jesus of Nazareth, the son of Joseph."* John 1:43-45 NKJV

As Philip ran to tell Nathanael the good news about Jesus, he was foreshadowing a mighty army of ambassadors who would one day be raised up to tell others about Jesus.

FOLLOW ME

The call to discipleship Jesus gave was profound but simple.

> *And Jesus, walking by the Sea of Galilee, saw two brothers, Simon called Peter, and Andrew his brother, casting a net into the sea; for they were fishermen. Then He said to them, "Follow Me, and I will make you fishers of men." They immediately left their nets and followed Him.* Matthew 4:18-20 NKJV

Jesus did not choose as ambassadors those with the learning of the scholars at Qumran or with the eloquence of the Jewish

Sanhedrin. He did not seek those endued with the power of Rome. Instead, he chose humble, uneducated men to proclaim the truths that were to shake the world.

He trained these 12 men in such a way that they could train others—a process of transferability that was to be ongoing—each one reaching one, each one teaching one. But success in their efforts did not lie in the world of academic knowledge. It lay in something provided by the Holy Spirit.

3 The Honest Seeker

In my previous books I told the story about...

> ...a man of the Pharisees named Nicodemus, a ruler of the Jews. This man came to Jesus by night and said to Him, "Rabbi, we know that You are a teacher come from God; for no one can do these signs that You do unless God is with him."
>
> Jesus answered and said to him, "Most assuredly, I say to you, unless one is born again, he cannot see the kingdom of God."
>
> John 3:1-3 NKJV

The Scriptures tell us that the Holy Spirit brings life. The theological term is *regeneration*. To be regenerated is to be born again—to have gone from being spiritually dead (in Adam) to spiritually alive (in Christ). Nicodemus struggled with this whole idea. Jesus said:

> "Do not be amazed that I said to you, 'You must be born again.'"
>
> "The wind blows where it wishes and you hear the sound of it, but do not know where it comes from and where it is going; so is everyone who is born of the Spirit." John 3:7-8 NASB

Comparison

As we saw before, wind is often associated with the presence of the Holy Spirit. Jesus made a comparison between the two. Wind speaks of air that is moving, like a fresh breeze, not stale and stagnant. Fresh air invigorates and gives life and so does the Holy Spirit when he give life to those who are "born again."

Wind may be a soft puff or a mighty hurricane. Likewise, the presence of the Holy Spirit may be so subtle that you don't even notice he is near. At other times, his fearsome roar cannot be missed.

Wind is beyond our control—it cannot be stopped. In the same way, the work of the Holy Spirit is beyond human control—God cannot be stopped.

Wind is an unseen force. Though we cannot see its source or destination we know it is present by its effects. In the same way, the Holy Spirit is invisible. Though we cannot see him, his presence is displayed in the way he changes lives and provides for his own.

NEW LIFE

Nicodemus wondered just how it was possible to be born of the Spirit—to be regenerated—to be given new life. It is a question we should all know how to answer. Jesus said:

> "For God so loved the world, that he gave his only Son, that whoever believes in him should not perish but have eternal life."
>
> John 3:16 ESV

As the Lord's ambassadors, this is a good verse to memorize. To be "born from above," all we need to do is believe—to rest our confidence in Jesus as our Saviour. Jesus continued:

> "For God did not send his Son into the world to condemn the world, but that the world should be saved through him. The one who believes in him is not condemned. The one who does not believe has been condemned already, because he has not believed in the name of the one and only Son of God."
>
> John 3:17-18 NET

Jesus pictured mankind standing in God's courtroom, facing judgment.

> "Now this is the basis for judging: that the light has come into the world and people loved the darkness rather than the light, because their deeds were evil. For everyone who does evil deeds hates the light and does not come to the light, so that their deeds will not be exposed."　　John 3:19-20 NET

Whether unbeliever or believer, we do not like it when our sin is exposed. It hurts our pride and we feel shame. But…

> "…whoever lives by the truth comes into the light, so that it may be seen plainly that what he has done has been done through God."　　John 3:21NIV

As believers, we have chosen the truth. As we live in humble transparency before God, people in the world will see a difference in our lives. They will see God at work through the regenerating power of the Holy Spirit, giving us new life.

As we move on, getting to know him, respecting, trusting and loving him, we will become more and more like him. Our friends will know something has changed. And that is good.

4 The Samaritan Woman

Now when Jesus knew that the Pharisees had heard that he was winning and baptizing more disciples than John (although Jesus himself was not baptizing, but his disciples were), he left Judea and set out once more for Galilee.

But he had to pass through Samaria.

John 4:1-4 NET

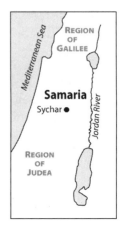

It is interesting to note that Jesus said he "had to" pass through Samaria. The region of Samaria was avoided by the Jews. Normally to travel from Judea to Galilee, the Jews took the long way around, either by the coast or along the Jordan River valley. One thing they did not do was intentionally travel through Samaria.

Now he came to a Samaritan town called Sychar, near the plot of land that Jacob had given to his son Joseph. Jacob's well was there, so Jesus, since he was tired from the journey, sat right down beside the well. It was about noon. John 4:5-6 NET

When a Samaritan woman came to draw water, Jesus said to her, "Will you give me a drink?" (His disciples had gone into the town to buy food.) John 4:7-8 NIV

According to the customs of the day, water was drawn in the early hours during the cool of the day. It was a little strange that a woman should be coming at noon, in the stifling heat of the day. The place was deserted, except for Jesus. Jesus asked for a drink.

The Samaritan woman said to him, "You are a Jew and I am a Samaritan woman. How can you ask me for a drink?" (For Jews do not associate with Samaritans.)

Jesus answered her, "If you knew the gift of God and who it is that asks you for a drink, you would have asked him and he would have given you living water." John 4:9-10 NIV

This must have been perplexing to her. Jesus had asked for a drink and yet he was saying he had some sort of "living water."

The woman said to Him, "Sir, You have nothing to draw with, and the well is deep.² Where then do You get that living water? Are You greater than our father Jacob, who gave us the well, and drank from it himself, as well as his sons and his livestock?"

> *Jesus answered and said to her, "Whoever drinks of this water will thirst again, but whoever drinks of the water that I shall give him will never thirst. But the water that I shall give him will become in him a fountain of water springing up into everlasting life."*   John 4:11-14 NKJV

Jesus was offering her water that would quench her thirst forever. This had her attention! At least once a day she made the journey to the well. It was heavy, hard work.

> *The woman said to him, "Sir, give me this water, so that I will not be thirsty or have to come here to draw water." He said to her, "Go call your husband and come back here." The woman replied, "I have no husband." Jesus said to her, "Right you are when you said, 'I have no husband,' for you have had five husbands, and the man you are living with now is not your husband. This you said truthfully!"* John 4:15-18 NET

Now it made sense why she drew from the well at noon. No one would be there—no one to gossip and sneer. This was a woman with history—she had a bad reputation.

ANOTHER SUBJECT

The fact that an obvious stranger knew her "history" touched a raw nerve. She changed the subject.

> *The woman said to him, "Sir, I see that you are a prophet. Our fathers worshiped on this mountain, and you people say that the place where people must worship is in Jerusalem."*
> John 4:19-20 NET

This is so common to humanity. When one brings up spiritual matters, especially the Bible, people are quick to change the subject. Jesus gently brought her back on track.

> *Jesus said to her, "Believe me, woman, a time is coming when you will worship the Father neither on this mountain nor in Jerusalem. You people worship what you do not know. We worship what we know, because salvation is from the Jews."*
> John 4:21-22 NET

Jesus carefully pointed out that the Samaritans had confused God's plan to reveal himself. They had a lot of truth, but it was also mixed with error. Jesus said salvation would come to the world through a Jew.

> *The woman said to Him, "I know that Messiah is coming" (who is called Christ). "When He comes, He will tell us all things."*
>
> *Jesus said to her, "I who speak to you am He."* John 4:25-26 NKJV

Jesus made it as clear as one could make it. *He* was the Messiah.

And at this point His disciples came, and they marveled that He talked with a woman; yet no one said, "What do You seek?" or, "Why are You talking with her?"

The woman then left her waterpot, went her way into the city, and said to the men, "Come, see a Man who told me all things that I ever did. Could this be the Christ?"

John 4:27-29 NKJV

AN AMBASSADOR

Without even realizing it, this woman had become an ambassador for Jesus, quickly telling others about him. She was quite effective.

They came out of the town and made their way toward him.

John 4:30 NIV

As the people made their way out to the well, Jesus used it as a teaching point with his disciples.

"Do you not say, 'Four months more and then the harvest'? I tell you, open your eyes and look at the fields! They are ripe for harvest."

John 4:35 NIV

Jesus compared the people of the world to a huge field of ripe grain. He told his disciples that they needed to open their eyes to the opportunities that were around them—opportunities to declare the good news that the Messiah had arrived.

Now many Samaritans from that town believed in him because of the report of the woman who testified, "He told me everything I ever did." So when the Samaritans came to him, they began asking him to stay with them. He stayed there two days, and because of his word many more believed. They said to the woman, "No longer do we believe because of your words, for we have heard for ourselves."

John 4:39-42 NET

People rarely respond to the Bible just because we say it is true. I have found that it is best to give people the time and tools to think through the Bible on their own. That is why I wrote the previous books for the various worldviews, so that readers could understand for themselves.

This woman's testimony motivated the others to investigate Jesus' claim so they too could say...

"...we know that this one really is the Savior of the world."

John 4:42 NET

5 THE ROYAL OFFICIAL

The previous story happened in the region of Samaria. Immediately following this, Jesus…

> … *came again to Cana in Galilee… And at Capernaum there was an official whose son was ill.*
>
> John 4:46 ESV

Herod Antipas, the ruler of Galilee, probably employed this man. Some translations call him a "royal official." For this reason many Bible scholars identify him as a Gentile. His place of duties was in the town of Capernaum.

> *When this man heard that Jesus had come from Judea to Galilee, he went to him and asked him to come down and heal his son, for he was at the point of death.* John 4:47 ESV

Capernaum is about 32 km (20 miles) from Cana, an uphill walk all the way. If he pushed hard, he could make the trip in a day.

You can imagine the worried father seeing his son suffering to the point of death. Rather than sit by waiting for the inevitable, he leaves, going for the only help he could imagine, to the one he has heard is performing the impossible — supernatural miracles!

Not knowing if his son is still alive, he arrives in Cana, worn by the journey. Knowing the imposition of asking Jesus to make the trip, he nonetheless begs Jesus to return with him to Capernaum.

> *The royal official said, "Sir, come down before my child dies."*
> *Jesus replied, "You may go. Your son will live."*
> *The man took Jesus at his word and departed.* John 4:49-50 NIV

When reading the Bible, it is best to let Scripture define its own words. This story gives a clear definition of the word *faith*. It means to "take God at his word." Over the centuries the concept of faith has accumulated all sorts of theological baggage. We end up with various adjectives to describe faith — real faith, genuine faith, saving faith, intellectual faith and so forth. It becomes very confusing. But really, faith (a noun) is just belief (the verb) — belief in God's Word as being true. The Bible says the royal official simply…

> …*took Jesus at his word and departed.* John 4:50 NIV

It is not hard to imagine the father's thoughts as he travelled the long hours home. Was it really true that his son would live? Faith does not imply "no doubts." Remember, it is not the *faith* that is important, but the *object* of the faith. The object was Jesus, and his word would not change. But as he walked the many hours towards home, this very human man must have wondered if it could really be true that his son would live.

Meanwhile at home, his servants had watched with increasing alarm at the son's imminent death. And then, all of sudden, the downward spiral reversed, the fever broke, and the son rapidly began to recover. Overwhelmed, and not wanting the father to be anxious any longer, at least two of the servants set out in haste to find dad and give him the good news.

> As [the father] was going down, his servants met him and told him that his son was recovering. John 4:51 ESV

We don't know, but it is possible that when the father first saw the servants at a distance, his heart sank, for such messengers could only be bearing bad tidings. But then, no, the father was told that the son was well on the road to good health! Then came a dawning. The father…

> … asked [his servants] the hour when [the son] began to get better, and they said to him, "Yesterday at the seventh hour the fever left him." John 4:52 ESV

The seventh hour is 1:00 p.m. by modern reckoning. Immediately the father did the math.

> The father knew that was the hour when Jesus had said to him, "Your son will live."

> And he himself believed, and all his household. John 4:53 ESV

It seems that now we see the father's faith taking on greater depth, even affecting his whole household. He had believed when Jesus said his son would be healed, but now he believed even more. This man was in the process of getting to know Jesus better and as he did, his respect, trust and love grew stronger too.

It is the nature of faith to grow in strength as we walk with God through each day's struggles and opportunities. It is important to not focus on the *faith*, for it may be small and it may waver, but rather focus on the *object* of our faith, God himself. Each one of us needs to daily "take God at his word."

ANCIENT PREJUDICES

In these last three stories, we have seen Jesus interacting first with the Jewish Nicodemus, then with the Samaritan woman and now with the Gentile royal official. These stories appear sequentially in the gospel of John. It seems hardly a coincidence that between these three groups—Jew, Samaritan and Gentile—vast barriers of prejudice existed. Jesus gently but persistently broke down these barriers, one at a time. Take note of them and the sequence we see recorded in the book by the apostle John, as this will happen again later in our story.

6 THE MIRACLES OF JESUS

Early in his ministry Jesus headquartered in the town of Capernaum, on the north shore of the Sea of Galilee, sometimes known as the Lake of Gennesaret. This was Simon Peter's hometown.

> *While the sun was setting, all those who had any who were sick with various diseases brought them to Him; and laying His hands on each one of them, He was healing them.*
>
> *Demons also were coming out of many, shouting, "You are the Son of God!" But rebuking them, He would not allow them to speak, because they knew Him to be the Christ.*
>
> *Luke 4:40-41 NASB*

Jesus did not want demonic spirits as his ambassadors.

> *Now it happened that while the crowd was pressing around Him and listening to the word of God, He was standing by the lake of Gennesaret; and He saw two boats lying at the edge of the lake; but the fishermen had gotten out of them and were washing their nets.*
>
> *And He got into one of the boats, which was Simon's, and asked him to put out a little way from the land. And He sat down and began teaching the people from the boat.*
>
> *When He had finished speaking, He said to Simon, "Put out into the deep water and let down your nets for a catch."*
>
> *Simon answered and said, "Master, we worked hard all night and caught nothing, but I will do as You say and let down the nets."*
>
> *When they had done this, they enclosed a great quantity of fish, and their nets began to break; so they signaled to their partners in the other boat for them to come and help them. And they came and filled both of the boats, so that they began to sink.*
>
> *Luke 5:1-7 NASB*

This was obviously a supernatural event, witnessed by many experienced fishermen.

> *When Simon Peter saw that, he fell down at Jesus' feet, saying, "Go away from me Lord, for I am a sinful man!"*
>
> *For amazement had seized him and all his companions because of the catch of fish which they had taken.*   Luke 5:8-10 NASB

SUPERNATURAL

Whether healing the diseased or enabling an unusual catch of fish, these were obvious miracles. By definition, a miracle is not a natural phenomenon — it is supernatural.

Depending on the culture you come from, miracles can be given much more importance than some might realize. With that in mind and for the purpose of clarity, I am going to classify miracles as Class-A and Class-B.[3] We will start with Class-A and then later in the book, we will look at Class-B miracles.

Most of the miracles Jesus performed would be Class-A. They have a number of defining characteristics:

Class-A miracles are not debatable in the court of public or legal opinion. They are a clear act of the supernatural. They cannot be explained as luck or chance. Only a fool would debate Class-A miracles.

With Class-A miracles, the one performing the miracle is clearly identifiable. You know who is responsible for the event. Jesus clearly performed his miracles. He did not allow them to be ascribed to magicians, sorcerers or demons.

Class-A miracles have clear primary purposes with obvious secondary purposes.[4] In the case of Jesus, the primary purpose was to authenticate a message and the messenger.[5] John, the disciple of Jesus (not John the Baptist), recorded eight miracles in his book, the gospel of John. He closed the book with these words:

> *Now Jesus performed many other miraculous signs in the presence of the disciples, which are not recorded in this book. But these are recorded so that you may believe that Jesus is the Christ, the Son of God, and that by believing you may have life in his name.*   John 20:30-31 NET

Class-A miracles had credible witnesses, often many. For example, when Jesus fed 5000 with a boy's lunch, he had 5000 witnesses — and that was just the men!

Studying the storyline of Scripture leaves you with the sense that God used Class-A miracles with economy—he didn't perform them haphazardly. There are vast chunks of Scripture that make no mention of a supernatural event. In the Bible, miracles are grouped together in three main blocks of time:

1. During the lives of Moses and Joshua
2. During the time of the prophets Elijah and Elisha
3. During the time of Jesus and the apostles

Between these periods of time you do find some miracles, but not with the same concentration.

Coming back to the story, Class-A miracles should leave us feeling like Peter. There he stood, in one of two boats swamped with a huge catch of fish, and…

> …when Simon Peter saw that, he fell down at Jesus' feet, saying, "Go away from me Lord, for I am a sinful man!"
> *Luke 5:8 NASB*

Peter knew that only God was capable of such a miracle. He immediately sensed his sinfulness…

> For he and all who were with him were astonished at the catch of fish which they had taken.
> *Luke 5:9 NKJV*

We too need to remain in awe of Yahweh and his mighty power. In so doing, we can leave the timing and need for miracles in his hands. He has given us the same job he gave to Peter on that day.

> Jesus said to Simon, "Do not be afraid; from now on you will be catching men." And when they had brought their boats to land, they left everything and followed him. *Luke 5:10-11 ESV*

7 THE WALK ON THE WATER

Peter witnessed numerable Class-A miracles that left a deep impression on him. Peter knew many of those who benefitted from them.

> And there came a man named Jairus, who was a ruler of the synagogue [in Capernaum]. And falling at Jesus' feet, he implored him to come to his house, for he had an only daughter, about twelve years of age, and she was dying. *Luke 8:41-42 ESV*

Jesus immediately left with Jarius to go to his house. Along the way he healed a woman who had suffered for many years. He took the time to talk to her, to encourage her.

While he was still speaking, someone from the ruler's house came and said, "Your daughter is dead; do not trouble the Teacher any more." But Jesus on hearing this answered him, "Do not fear; only believe, and she will be well." And when he came to the house, he allowed no one to enter with him, except Peter and John and James, and the father and mother of the child. And all were weeping and mourning for her, but he said, "Do not weep, for she is not dead but sleeping."

Luke 8:49-52 ESV

And they began making fun of him, because they knew that she was dead. But Jesus gently took her by the hand and said, "Child, get up." Her spirit returned, and she got up immediately. Then he told them to give her something to eat. Her parents were astonished, but he ordered them to tell no one what had happened.

Luke 8:53-56 NET

Peter had seen it for himself! Class-A miracles were unforgettable. They left an impression.

WIND AND WAVES

Some days later, a large crowd gathered on the hillside, next to the Sea of Galilee. The people had nothing to eat and Jesus performed another miracle, this time feeding 5000 men plus women and children with a small boy's lunch. Peter was there too.

Immediately [Jesus] made the disciples get into the boat and go before him to the other side, while he dismissed the crowds. And after he had dismissed the crowds, he went up on the mountain by himself to pray. When evening came, he was there alone, but the boat by this time was a long way from the land, beaten by the waves, for the wind was against them. And in the fourth watch of the night he came to them, walking on the sea.

Matthew 14:22-25 ESV

It is stated so matter-of-factly that you almost miss what is happening. Jesus was walking on top of the water! This occurred during the fourth watch—between 3:00 and 6:00 a.m. The wind would have been raging and the waves at the apex of their fury. But here comes Jesus as if out for a late night stroll.

When the disciples saw Him walking on the sea, they were terrified, and said, "It is a ghost!" And they cried out in fear.

But immediately Jesus spoke to them, saying, "Take courage, it is I; do not be afraid."

Matthew 14:26-27 NASB

Obviously, the disciples were exhausted. Could it be that they were collectively hallucinating? That was unlikely. Perhaps it was Peter's impetuous nature that caused him to call out:

"Lord, if it is You, command me to come to You on the water."

And He said, "Come!"

And Peter got out of the boat, and walked on the water and came toward Jesus. Matthew 14:28-29 NASB

Peter actually walked on the water—just like Jesus!

But when he saw the strong wind he became afraid. And starting to sink, he cried out, "Lord, save me!" Matthew 14:30 NET

Peter knew where to look for help. He didn't call for the disciples to bring the boat closer. He didn't try to swim, though he could have. He didn't confidently state self-affirmations, "I can do it! I can do it!" No. Instead he called out to the Lord.

Immediately Jesus reached out his hand and caught him, saying to him, "You of little faith, why did you doubt?" When they went up into the boat, the wind ceased. Then those who were in the boat worshiped him, saying, "Truly you are the Son of God." Matthew 14:31-33 NET

Not only did this Class-A miracle save the disciples lives, it also authenticated the deity of Jesus. He was God in human flesh. Of course, as a prime participant, Peter did not miss a thing.

There are those who try to downplay the fact that Jesus was fully God and who try to make him a lesser god of some sort. This is an error of the highest magnitude. Yet people believe what they wish, including a lie, even after much evidence to the contrary. Others seemingly "follow" God, but only as long as it is beneficial to them.

TWO RESULTS

This was true with Jesus. When the miracles and benefits ceased ...

...many of his disciples turned back and no longer followed him.

"You do not want to leave too, do you?" Jesus asked the Twelve.

Simon Peter answered him, "Lord, to whom shall we go? You have the words of eternal life. We believe and know that you are the Holy One of God." John 6:66-69 NIV

Many left, but Peter stayed. Peter may have been impetuous, but here he spoke well. He believed.

CHAPTER FIVE

1 THE SEED

Why do some Christians grow spiritually and others do not? Jesus gave an answer to this question.

> While a large crowd was gathering and people were coming to Jesus from town after town, he told this parable: "A farmer went out to sow his seed.
>
> • As he was scattering the seed, some fell along the path; it was trampled on, and the birds of the air ate it up.
>
> • Some fell on rock, and when it came up, the plants withered because they had no moisture.
>
> • Other seed fell among thorns, which grew up with it and choked the plants.
>
> • Still other seed fell on good soil. It came up and yielded a crop, a hundred times more than was sown."
>
> When he said this, he called out, "He who has ears to hear, let him hear." *Luke 8:4-8 NIV*

THE WORD

Jesus was challenging his listeners to be teachable. He continued:

> "This is the meaning of the parable: The seed is the word of God." *Luke 8:11 NIV*

This is an important connection. The seed is the Bible. Previously we have identified it as our Map for life. This parable concerns the way we respond to that Map.

SAVED?

To understand the parable, we need some background as to how Scripture uses the word *saved*.

• Salvation: The word *saved* is used in the sense of being delivered from the eternal penalty of sin. This is why Christians speak of being "saved."

• Sanctification: The word *saved* also commonly applies to being saved from the daily power of sin.

• Physical: Scripture speaks of being *saved* from problems such as sickness, a natural catastrophe, or even the present consequence of sin (a judgment on sin that happens right here on earth).

At minimum, it would seem the "four soils" parable applies to both *salvation* and *sanctification*. In a sense, these verses show people's generic responses to God's Word. In this section I will focus my comments on our daily walk with the Lord—our sanctification.

The Hard Soil

The first response is illustrated when Jesus speaks of the Word that is sown on hard ground.

> Those along the path are the ones who have heard [the Scriptures]; then the devil comes and takes away the word from their hearts, so that they may not believe and be saved.
> *Luke 8:12 NET*

Like the hard soil of the path, people can harden their hearts to what God is trying to teach them. In such cases, Satan snatches away the Word from their minds so they will not be "saved" from either the future or present consequences of sin. It really isn't a wise way to live. One should be like the Bereans when exposed to God's Word. Remember they were the ones who...

> ...received the word with great eagerness, examining the Scriptures daily to see whether these things were so.
> *Acts 17:10-11 NASB*

The Rocky Soil

Jesus continued:

> The seed on the rocky soil represents those who hear the message and immediately receive it with joy. But since they don't have deep roots, they don't last long. They fall away as soon as they have problems or are persecuted for believing God's word.
> *Mark 4:16-17 NLT*

People will mock and question your faith. Without deep spiritual "roots" it can be overwhelming. To gain roots you must dig into the Bible and read it for yourself. The purpose of this present book is to start you on that journey. You cannot neglect your "road map" without getting off track. Remember Peter? He denied the Lord three times! We are no different. Without roots we will all fail at some time in some way.

The Weed-Infested Soil

> The seed that fell among the thorns represents others who hear God's word, but all too quickly the message is crowded out by the worries of this life, the lure of wealth, and the desire for other things, so no fruit is produced. *Mark 4:18-19 NLT*

Notice how the thorny weeds take a person off-course:

- By being overwhelmed by the worries of life.
- By believing that happiness in life can be found in a little more wealth.
- By craving other things: status, a different job—any ambition for "greener grass that grows on the other side of the fence."

When believers focus on distractions such as these, Scripture is clear. Spiritually…

> …they never grow into maturity. *Luke 8:14 NLT*

In contrast, maturity is the result of taking your eyes off yourself and your life situation and focusing them on Jesus.

> Let us throw off everything that hinders and the sin that so easily entangles, and let us run with perseverance the race marked out for us. Let us fix our eyes [or focus] on Jesus.
> *Hebrews 12:1-2 NIV*

THE GOOD SOIL

Jesus concluded:

> And the seeds that fell on the good soil represent honest, good-hearted people who hear God's word, cling to it, and patiently produce a huge harvest. *Luke 8:15 NLT*

These are believers with teachable hearts. Much later, Peter encouraged people to have the same attitude:

> Like newborn babies, crave pure spiritual milk, so that by it you may grow up in your salvation, now that you have tasted that the Lord is good. *1 Peter 2:2-3 NIV*

Scripture is our spiritual milk. We neglect it to our harm. If we leave our Map in the "back seat," we will take a wrong turn. We need to make it a goal to become thoroughly acquainted with the Bible so our Guide, the Holy Spirit, can lead us.

Though Jesus spoke of four soils, there were only two results. There were those who gained no lasting effect from their exposure to the Bible, and those who grew and matured, producing a "crop," as the Bible says.

We saw this before. When Jesus taught, many left him. But then there were those like Peter. Peter stayed. We need to ask ourselves a question. "What sort of soil are we—hard, rocky, thorny or good? What will be our response to the Word?"

2 The Traditions

It is in the heart of man to add to or take away from God's Word. We have a tendency to muddy the Map. One area of concern relates to religious traditions.

Clean and Unclean

As a result of the first books I wrote, I have had new believers contact me from many places on the globe. I know that some who are reading these words right now come from religious backgrounds that place a heavy emphasis on traditions: baptisms, washings, attendance at religious services or visits to the temple, prayers, fasting, the giving of money, offering sacrifices, burning candles, the veneration of gods, idols or saints, the services of priests, confessions of sin—the list goes on. Religions that put a heavy emphasis on outward form have existed since Babel and it was no different in the time of Jesus.

> *Then some Pharisees and teachers of the law came to Jesus from Jerusalem and asked, "Why do your disciples break the tradition of the elders? They don't wash their hands before they eat!"*
> Matthew 15:1-2 NIV

This was not a matter of sanitation. The washing of hands had a spiritual connotation. The Pharisees pointed out that the disciples were not following the religious traditions.

> *After Jesus called the crowd to Him, He said to them, "Hear and understand.*
>
> *"It is not what enters into the mouth that defiles the man, but what proceeds out of the mouth, this defiles the man."*
> Matthew 15:10-11 NASB

This was a simple parable.

> *Then the disciples came and said to Him, "Do You know that the Pharisees were offended when they heard this statement?"*
> Matthew 15:12 NASB

Apparently, they got the point. Truth often does offend. That being said, when we talk about the Bible, we must be careful that we are not offensive in our manner. Let the truth offend, but let us be humble. Although the Pharisees understood the parable, the disciples were not so sure.

> *Peter said to him, "Explain the parable to us."*

And [Jesus] said, "Are you also still without understanding? Do you not see that whatever goes into the mouth passes into the stomach and is expelled? But what comes out of the mouth proceeds from the heart, and this defiles a person. For out of the heart come evil thoughts, murder, adultery, sexual immorality, theft, false witness, slander. These are what defile a person. But to eat with unwashed hands does not defile anyone."   Matthew 15:15-20 ESV

Jesus made the point that sin is an inward issue. Ignoring tradition, an outward matter, is not sin.

When dealing with religions that have no basis in the Bible, it is somewhat easier to sort through the right and wrong of traditions. But when it comes to those groups that claim a biblical connection, it can become quite confusing. It is important to distinguish between "religious Christianity" and "true Christianity." Religious Christianity is orientated around observing outward form—traditions, rites and rituals. True Christianity is centred on the heart.

Some traditions may be relatively harmless, but others have been destructive. We must remember that the Bible, and only the Bible, is our final authority for life. It is our road map. Any rite or ritual added to it can confuse the journey. Repeatedly, the Bible makes the point that…

You shall not add to the word that I command you, nor take from it.   Deuteronomy 4:2 ESV

Many religions want their book or collection of books to have equal authority with the Bible. Others place tradition on the same level as Scripture. Both are dangerous and both are wrong. Jesus had strong words for those who did such things.

He replied, "Isaiah was right when he prophesied about you hypocrites; as it is written: 'These people honor me with their lips, but their hearts are far from me. They worship me in vain; their teachings are but rules taught by men.'

"You have let go of the commands of God and are holding on to the traditions of men."   Mark 7:6-8 NIV

As believers we must seek to live solely by God's Word, not by the traditions of any religious system. Only then can the Holy Spirit guide us. Only then will we be growing spiritually, just as the seed that fell upon the good soil.

THE DEMAND FOR A SIGN

It was not only their sacred traditions that caused Jesus to confront the powerful religious establishment.

> Then the Pharisees and Sadducees came, and testing Him
> asked that He would show them a sign from heaven.
>
> Matthew 16:1 NKJV

This happened often. The religious leaders wanted a sign from Jesus to verify his identity. It really didn't make sense. The abundance of Class-A miracles that Jesus performed should have been sufficient evidence for any "sign seeker," but his signs were not fitting the religious ideal they had in mind. The apostle Paul would later write:

> Jews demand miraculous signs and Greeks [or Gentiles] look
> for wisdom, but we preach Christ crucified.
>
> 1 Corinthians 1:22-23 NIV

People still want proof of the Messiah. They want a sign. We need to be cautious of sign-seekers, not only because their desire is misplaced, but because we can begin to feel that we must prove the reality of Christ. We need not give in to that pressure—it can lead us into error. If God wants to provide a sign, he is fully capable of doing that. As for us, we need to simply explain the reason for "Christ crucified." We need to stick to the Word.

3 THE ROCK

The miracles and teaching of Jesus certainly set the communities of Israel alive with opinions about his identity. The Sadducees seemed to think he was a lunatic. The Pharisees said that he was a Samaritan and indwelt by a demon. The scribes said he was uneducated. So...

> ...when Jesus came into the district of Caesarea Philippi, he
> asked his disciples, "Who do people say that the Son of Man
> is?" And they said, "Some say John the Baptist, others say
> Elijah, and others Jeremiah or one of the prophets."
>
> Matthew 16:13-14 ESV

Although these were worthy men to be identified with and certainly much better than the scribes and Pharisees and their opinions, they still were not good enough. To be identified as John, Elijah or Jeremiah still left Jesus as a man—yes, a good man—but not the God-man. Today many religions recognize Jesus as a prophet or even as a god (small "g"), but they would vehemently deny he is the Creator—Yahweh himself.

WHAT ABOUT YOU?

Jesus asked his disciples:

> *"But who do you say that I am?"*
>
> *Simon Peter answered and said, "You are the Christ, the Son of the living God."* Matthew 16:15-16 NKJV

Peter declared Jesus to be:

- The Christ: In other words, the Messiah, the Anointed One, the Promised Deliverer. Peter also said Jesus was...

- The Son of God: That is, having all the attributes of Deity. The Bible says, the Son...

> *...is the radiance of His [God's] glory and the exact representation of His nature.* Hebrews 1:3 NASB
>
> *For in Christ all the fullness of the Deity lives in bodily form.* Colossians 2:9 NIV
>
> *...Christ Jesus: Who, being in very nature God, did not consider equality with God something to be grasped, but made himself nothing, taking the very nature of a servant, being made in human likeness.* Philippians 2:5-7 NIV

As believers, we need to be clear in our minds about the Deity of Christ. The gospel of John in the New Testament is a good book to read that deals specifically with this subject.

THE REPLY

Jesus' answer to Peter's above declaration has caused a lot of controversy over the centuries. He said:

> *"Blessed are you, Simon son of Jonah, for this was not revealed to you by man, but by my Father in heaven. And I tell you that you are Peter, and on this rock I will build my church, and the gates of Hades will not overcome it."* Matthew 16:17-18 NIV

Often when we think of a church we have a physical building in mind. However, the Bible never uses the word that way. Rather, the word *church* is used to refer to all believers collectively. We will look at the church in greater detail in the coming chapters. For now let me explain the controversy around this verse.

CONFUSION

For almost three centuries after the time of Christ, believers were unmercifully persecuted. Then the Roman emperor, Constantine, proclaimed religious tolerance, which in turn led to the development of a "Christianized" worldview that retained many pre-Christian concepts. Over time this form of Christianity became the national religion. The preceding verse was erroneously used to establish Peter as the founding leadership with power over both church and state.

PRIEST NOT KING

Although "Christianity" was not the only religion that combined power with faith, it was the one that should have known better. Such a concept actually violates the model we see in Scripture. According to Jewish Law and God's promises, the offices of priest and king were not to be combined. Kings were to be chosen from the tribe of Judah.[1] The high priest could only be selected from the tribe of Levi. It would seem that this was God's way of preventing abuse of power and faith.

To extend Peter's authority beyond his lifespan, to create an ongoing power with both religious and political authority, evoked much disagreement and controversy.[2] The reason being, there is scant Scripture to support such an interpretation.

Is there any lesson we can learn from this confusion? I think there is. As a rule of thumb, good Bible interpretation avoids building major points of teaching around highly debated verses. The Bible is abundantly clear on all major points of truth. This is not one of them. Personally, I think we need to just keep it simple. As we read our Map, we must be careful not to journey along roads that don't exist.

FAMILY

If you come from a church background involving a lot of "Christian" tradition, be careful how you approach that tradition with your family. If they do not clearly understand the gospel, you will be asking them to give up faith in their religion without them knowing that they can solely trust in Jesus. It's better to gently bring them to an understanding of the gospel first, before you tear down a tradition they hold dear. Jesus gave this advice to his disciples:

> I am sending you out as sheep in the midst of wolves, so be wise as serpents and innocent as doves.   Matthew 10:16 ESV

The gospel that you believe in your heart is what is important (not outward traditions), and with wisdom, you may be able to bring your family and friends to that understanding as well.

4 THE MOUNT

As you study the life of Jesus, you see him slowly revealing to the disciples his plan and purpose in coming to earth. But there came a day when his message took on a different tone, and...

> From that time Jesus began to show his disciples that He must go to Jerusalem, and suffer many things from the elders and chief priests and scribes, and be killed, and be raised up [to life] on the third day. Matthew 16:21 NASB

Jesus did something that is humanly impossible. He foretold how and where he would die. He also described events leading up to that death.

It is interesting that from this point on Jesus performed only a few miracles. The focus shifted from establishing his identity to fulfilling his work on the cross. Peter, upon hearing Jesus foretell his death...

> ...took him aside and began to rebuke him. "Never, Lord!" he said. "This shall never happen to you!" Matthew 16:22 NIV

Peter was looking at life from the human viewpoint—a viewpoint espoused by Satan. In contrast, Jesus had the divine viewpoint and he could see who was influencing Peter's thinking.

> Jesus turned to Peter and said, "Get away from me, Satan! You are a dangerous trap to me. You are seeing things merely from a human point of view, not from God's." Matthew 16:23 NLT

As earthly beings, it is natural for us to look at life from the human viewpoint, but the Holy Spirit wants to guide us into the divine viewpoint. That can only happen as we read our Map, the Word of God.

> Then Jesus said to his disciples, "If anyone would come after me, he must deny himself and take up his cross and follow me. For whoever wants to save his life will lose it, but whoever loses his life for me will find it. What good will it be for a man if he gains the whole world, yet forfeits his soul? Or what can a man give in exchange for his soul? For the Son of Man is going to come in his Father's glory with his angels, and then he will reward each person according to what he has done.
> Matthew 16:24-27 NIV

Jesus spoke of rewards for those who live according to the divine viewpoint. We will look at this more in a coming chapter.

The Transfiguration

One week after Jesus spoke of his death, he took Peter, James and John up a mountain to give them a glimpse of his true identity.

> And he was transfigured before them, and his face shone like the sun, and his clothes became white as light. Matthew 17:2 ESV

Jesus' outward form was transformed into the same dazzling light that had filled the Holy of Holies in the Tabernacle. The radiance of his majesty had been there all along, but the people could not see it.

> Two men were talking with [Jesus], Moses and Elijah, who appeared in glory and spoke of his departure, which he was about to accomplish at Jerusalem. Luke 9:30-31 ESV

Peter was astounded by it all. It seems he blurted out whatever idea came to his mind.

> Peter exclaimed, "Rabbi, it's wonderful for us to be here! Let's make three shelters as memorials—one for you, one for Moses, and one for Elijah." He said this because he didn't really know what else to say, for they were all terrified.
> Mark 9:5-6 NLT

> He was still speaking when…a bright cloud overshadowed them, and a voice from the cloud said, "This is my beloved Son, with whom I am well pleased; listen to him."
> Matthew 17:5 ESV

God the Father had spoken from Heaven.

> When the disciples heard this, they fell on their faces and were terrified. But Jesus came and touched them, saying, "Rise, and have no fear." And when they lifted up their eyes, they saw no one but Jesus…as they were coming down the mountain, Jesus commanded them, "Tell no one the vision, until the Son of Man is raised from the dead." Matthew 17:6-9 ESV

At that time, the disciples didn't know what to make of it all, but years later Peter would write:

> We did not follow cleverly invented stories when we told you about the power and coming of our Lord Jesus Christ, but we were eyewitnesses of his majesty. 2 Peter 1:16 NIV

They had been given a glimpse of his glory on the mountain.

For he received honor and glory from God the Father when the voice came to him from the Majestic Glory, saying, "This is my Son, whom I love; with him I am well pleased." We ourselves heard this voice that came from heaven when we were with him on the sacred mountain! 2 Peter 1:17-18 NIV

Peter, whom Jesus had named as espousing Satan's viewpoint, would one day be a strong spokesman for the divine viewpoint—he knew what he was talking about. As he said, they were not "cleverly invented stories."

5 THE SAMARITAN

The leaders of Jesus' day had immense power, both political and religious. They constantly tried to catch Jesus in some technical point of Bible interpretation in order to discredit him.

And a lawyer stood up and put Him to the test, saying, "Teacher, what shall I do to inherit eternal life?" Luke 10:25 NASB

This was not a sincere question. Knowing that, Jesus asked him:

"What is written in the Law? How do you read it?" And he answered, "You shall love the Lord your God with all your heart and with all your soul and with all your strength and with all your mind, and your neighbor as yourself." Luke 10:26-27 ESV

The lawyer gave a brief overview of the Ten Commandments. To "love the Lord" summarized the first four commands, and to "love your neighbour" summarized the last six.

And [Jesus] said to him, "You have answered correctly; do this, and you will live." Luke 10:28 ESV

Of course, there was a problem. The lawyer was unable to keep these rules perfectly.

The purpose of the Law was to show us our sin, not to provide a way to Heaven. When Jesus agreed with the lawyer, the responsibility for doing what he had just stated began to descend on his shoulders. He realized he could not measure up to the demands of the Law and so he began to look for an excuse to get out of his dilemma.

He should have asked Jesus, "How can I do this? I am a sinner. I need help."

But he, wanting to justify himself, said to Jesus, "And who is my neighbor?" Luke 10:29 NKJV

THREE MEN

To answer his question, Jesus related a parable having to do with a barren road that descends sharply from Jerusalem to Jericho.

> *Jesus replied and said, "A man was going down from Jerusalem to Jericho, and fell among robbers, and they stripped him and beat him, and went away leaving him half dead.*
>
> *"And by chance a priest was going down on that road, and when he saw him, he passed by on the other side.*
>
> *"Likewise a Levite also, when he came to the place and saw him, passed by on the other side."* Luke 10:30-32 NASB

Both the priest and the Levite were religious leaders. They would have been expected to show care for this half-dead man, but they did not.

> *"But a certain Samaritan, as he journeyed, came where he was: and when he saw him, he had compassion on him."*
> Luke 10:33 KJV

Jesus knew the mindset of the Jews toward Samaritans. They neither wanted nor expected help from them. But this Samaritan...

> *"...went to him and bound up his wounds, pouring on oil and wine. Then he set him on his own animal and brought him to an inn and took care of him. And the next day he took out two denarii and gave them to the innkeeper, saying, 'Take care of him, and whatever more you spend, I will repay you when I come back.'"* Luke 10:34-35 ESV

Jesus now focused on the lawyer's question.

> *"Which of these three do you think proved to be a neighbor to the man who fell into the robbers' hands?"*
>
> *[The lawyer] said, "The one who showed mercy toward him."*
> *Then Jesus said to him, "Go and do the same."*
> Luke 10:36-37 NASB

Jesus did not tell the lawyer how to be born again. (He was insincere with his question on eternal life.) But Jesus did give him the requirement of the Law. The Law makes us aware of our sin. The lawyer needed time for that to sink in. Later, his heart may have been prepared for a sincere question, "How can a man be born again?"

It is a point well worth remembering. When we share the story of Jesus, we need to help people first see that they are lost before we can explain how they can be saved.

TEN HEALED

In his teaching and actions, Jesus hammered away at the wall that existed between Jew and Samaritan.

> *As Jesus continued on toward Jerusalem, he reached the border between Galilee and Samaria. As he entered a village there, ten lepers stood at a distance, crying out, "Jesus, Master, have mercy on us!"*
>
> *He looked at them and said, "Go show yourselves to the priests." And as they went, they were cleansed of their leprosy.*
>
> *Luke 17:11-14 NLT*

As required by the Ceremonial Law, Jesus sent them to see the priests, to be certified as "healed." The priests were enemies of Jesus. If they wanted a sign from God, here it was!

For this to be established as true, the Civil Law required three witnesses.[3] But now, here we have nine witnesses—we will see what happened to the tenth in a moment. The religious leaders might be able to explain away one leper being healed, but not nine—and all at the same time. This was a Class-A miracle—undeniable! It forced the priests to come to terms with the identity of Jesus. It was an identity they did not like and would not accept. As we have seen before, it is in man's nature to suppress the knowledge of God.[4]

> *And one of them, when he saw that he was healed, returned, and with a loud voice glorified God, and fell down on his face at His feet, giving Him thanks. And he was a Samaritan.*
>
> *Luke 17:15-16 NKJV*

Don't miss those last words. It was a Samaritan thanking a Jew.

> *Then Jesus answered, "Were not ten cleansed? Where are the nine? Was no one found to return and give praise to God except this foreigner?" And he said to him, "Rise and go your way; your faith has made you well."* *Luke 17:17-19 ESV*

It is likely he returned to Samaria. He along with the woman Jesus met at the well may have laid the foundation for a significant event that would happen later in Samaria. We will read about it in the pages to come.

6 The Classroom

For three and a half years, the greatest Teacher the world has ever known instructed the disciples. He taught them beside the sea, walking along the path or on the mountainside. Day by day they heard his words of cheer to the weary and heavy-laden, and his rebukes to the proud and hypocritical. Wherever he found open minds, he took the time to explain how man might be made right with his Maker. He did not order his disciples around, but said, "Follow Me." As a result, they shared his hunger and weariness. On the streets, by the lakeside, in the Temple, they were with him, learning from him. In every way and every day, they saw him live out all aspects of life.

Left All

Then Peter began to say to Him, "See, we have left all and followed You."

So Jesus answered and said, "Assuredly, I say to you, there is no one who has left house or brothers or sisters or father or mother or wife or children or lands, for My sake and the gospel's, who shall not receive a hundredfold now in this time—houses and brothers and sisters and mothers and children and lands, with persecutions—and in the age to come, eternal life."   Mark 10:28-30 NKJV

To live for Jesus brings a multitude of blessings, right here on earth, maybe not in wealth or material goods, but in joy and fulfillment. Jesus also said to expect at least some persecution. For a number of you reading this book, you already know the reality of those words. It is also encouraging to note that Jesus mentioned something we can count on—eternal life in the age to come.

Predicts His Death

Jesus took the Twelve aside and told them, "We are going up to Jerusalem, and everything that is written by the prophets about the Son of Man will be fulfilled. He will be handed over to the Gentiles. They will mock him, insult him, spit on him, flog him and kill him. On the third day he will rise again."
                   Luke 18:31-33 NIV

To be able to foretell such specific details about your own personal death is beyond human capability.

But the disciples understood none of these things, and the meaning of this statement was hidden from them, and they did not comprehend the things that were said. Luke 18:34 NASB

THE END OF THE AGE

Near the end of his life on this earth, Jesus made his official entrance to Jerusalem on the back of a donkey while the crowds roared their approval.

Over the next four days he was in and around the Temple precincts.

Some of his disciples were remarking about how the temple was adorned with beautiful stones and with gifts dedicated to God. But Jesus said, "As for what you see here, the time will come when not one stone will be left on another; every one of them will be thrown down." Luke 21:5-6 NIV

What Jesus was prophesying was the final act in the age-old cycle of Israel's history of rebellion, slavery, repentance and deliverance.

1. Remember how we saw that God would send a messenger to deliver a message to the people. In this case, it had come in the form of John the Baptist and then the Messiah himself. Both had challenged the people and their leaders concerning the direction of their lives.

2. The cycle would continue when the people rejected both the message and the messenger. Herod Antipas had beheaded John the Baptist and in just a few days Jesus would be mocked, insulted, spit upon, flogged and nailed to a cross. How much more fully could a messenger be rejected?

3. As a result of this, God would send judgment in the form of foreign invaders. For centuries God had warned the people that when they heard foreign tongues in the street, they should beware of impending judgment. When the disciples commented about the beauty of the Temple, Jesus foretold its destruction.

Jesus knew that in a few decades (AD 70), the Romans would invade Israel to crush a rebellion. Titus, who would later become Caesar of the Roman Empire, would overwhelm the forces defending Jerusalem. Josephus, the secular historian, would later write:

Caesar gave orders that they should now demolish the entire city and temple, …the wall, it was so thoroughly laid even with the ground by those that dug it up to the foundation, that there was left nothing to make those that came thither believe it had ever been inhabited.[5]

Knowing this future event, Jesus told the disciples:

"Not one stone will be left on another; every one of them will be thrown down."
Luke 21:6 NIV

The nation of Israel would be scattered to the four corners of the earth, fulfilling an even older prophecy:

You will be uprooted from the land…The Lord will scatter you among all nations, from one end of the earth to the other.
Deuteronomy 28:63-64 NET

Warning

I have found that when new believers become aware of how much prophecy in the Bible has been accurately fulfilled, they immediately become curious. Like the disciples, they have questions:

"Teacher, when therefore will these things happen? And what will be the sign when these things are about to take place?"
Luke 21:7 NASB

To ask questions of this nature is a good thing. But we also need to be cautious.

He replied: "Watch out that you are not deceived. For many will come in my name, claiming, 'I am he,' and, 'The time is near.' Do not follow them. When you hear of wars and revolutions, do not be frightened. These things must happen first, but the end will not come right away." Luke 21:8-9 NIV

We must be careful about those who make hard and fast predictions about the future. We may be able to muse about the political, religious and social events in the world, and wonder if they are the precursors of things that will lead up to the return of Jesus, but it must remain musing only. Our focus needs to remain on knowing the Lord and seeking to serve him, not speculating on his arrival.

CHAPTER SIX

1 The Dirty Feet

Four days after Jesus made his official entrance into Jerusalem, the three spring feasts began, each following on the heels of the other.

1. The Feast of Passover
2. The Feast of Unleavened Bread
3. The Feast of Firstfruits

The Bible says:

> *Just before the Passover feast, Jesus knew that his time had come to depart from this world to the Father. Having loved his own who were in the world, he now loved them to the very end. The evening meal was in progress, and the devil had already put into the heart of Judas Iscariot, Simon's son, that he should betray Jesus.*
>
> *Because Jesus knew that the Father had handed all things over to him, and that he had come from God and was going back to God, he got up from the meal, removed his outer clothes, took a towel and tied it around himself. He poured water into the washbasin and began to wash the disciples' feet and to dry them with the towel he had wrapped around himself.* John 13:1-5 NET

Since everyone wore sandals in that day and age, feet would become dusty with travel. Upon arriving at a destination, it was normal to be met by a servant who then washed the traveller's feet. In washing the disciples' feet, Jesus was performing the task of a servant.

> *Then he came to Simon Peter. Peter said to him, "Lord, are you going to wash my feet?"* John 13:6 NET

Peter was taken aback that it was the Messiah who was taking on this lowly job. It was not a task fit for a King.

> *Jesus replied, "You do not realize now what I am doing, but later you will understand."*
>
> *"No," said Peter, "you shall never wash my feet."* John 13:7-8 NIV

Peter's pride got the best of him. He was embarrassed that the Lord should put himself in this role. Peter would wash his own feet if it came to that!

> *Jesus replied, "If I do not wash you, you have no share with me."*
> John 13:8 NET

Jesus made the point that Peter could not share in the Lord's work if he refused this lesson in servanthood.

> Simon Peter said to him, "Lord, wash not only my feet, but also my hands and my head!"   John 13:9 NET

Peter asked for a complete bath!

> Jesus answered, "A person who has had a bath needs only to wash his feet; his whole body is clean."   John 13:10 NIV

RELATIONSHIP

It would seem here that Jesus was drawing a parallel to the big picture of the Christian life. When we put our trust in Jesus, God clothes us in His righteousness—equivalent to a full bath. From God's perspective we are pure and clean—equipped for Heaven. It is at this point that the relationship broken by sin is restored. As new believers we now belong to the family of God.

> Once you were alienated from God and were enemies... but now he has reconciled you by Christ's physical body through death.   Colossians 1:21-22 NIV

FELLOWSHIP

But there is a reality we all face. Though our sin-debt has been forgiven and the relationship restored, as long as we are here on earth, we still sin. When that happens, there is a rift in the family fellowship. Fellowship is different than relationship.

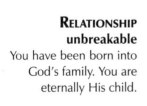

RELATIONSHIP
unbreakable
You have been born into God's family. You are eternally His child.

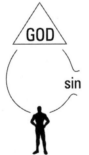

FELLOWSHIP
breakable
Your sin breaks the pleasant harmony you have with your heavenly Father.

That difference can be seen in a healthy family where the father is a reasonable and honourable man.

If the son does not obey his father, is he any less a son?

- Of course not. The relationship is the same; the disobedient son is still a son.

Is the father pleased with the disobedient son?

- No, not at all. The father-son fellowship is definitely affected. The son has disappointed his father.

If a son obeys his father, does it make him more of a son?

- No. The relationship never changed. But the father-son fellowship is definitely different. The father will delight in his son and the son will find joy in his father.

THE HARD REALITY

The hard reality is that as we tread the grimy streets of life, we as believers need daily cleansing—we need to have our "feet washed." When we sin, we need to acknowledge that fact to God and if we have wronged our fellow man, then we must seek to be reconciled to him as well. God has promised that...

> If we confess our sins, he is faithful and just and will forgive us our sins and purify us from all unrighteousness.
>
> 1 John 1:9 NIV

Although confession may take the form of a prayer, it is really more of an attitude than one specific act or prayer. Confession has the idea of agreeing with God or saying the same thing as God says about something—simply put, just acknowledging or being honest with God about the struggles in our lives. It should be an everyday habit that is part of our lives as Christ-ones. We can have confidence that our fellowship with our heavenly Father will be immediately restored when we acknowledge our sin.

DAILY CLEANSING

Cleansing always comes as a result of the Holy Spirit using the Word of God in our lives. As we read and ponder Scripture regularly, the Holy Spirit cleanses us.

> Now [you] are clean through the word which I have spoken unto you.
>
> John 15:3 KJV

Remember the priests in the Tabernacle? They washed their hands and feet as part of their daily service to the Lord. In the same way, Peter didn't need a "bath" since he was already a believer, but he did need his spiritual "feet" washed if he was to serve the Lord. And so do we.

CONFESSION

Some of you may have been exposed to a concept of confession whereby you must visit a clergyman to state your sin. Usually this is done anonymously. Upon stating your sin in a confessional booth, you are assigned certain acts of penance to perform.

This whole system is difficult to support from Scripture. Rather than entering into a confessional booth, the Bible says that, through Jesus, we can enter into God's presence and acknowledge our sin directly to him.

> *For there is one God, and one mediator also between God and men, the man Christ Jesus.*   1 Timothy 2:5 NASB

---

2 THE SERVANT'S ATTITUDE

After Jesus had finished washing the disciples' feet, he returned to his place at the table.

> *"Do you understand what I have done for you? You call me 'Teacher' and 'Lord,' and do so correctly, for that is what I am. If I then, your Lord and Teacher, have washed your feet, you too ought to wash one another's feet. For I have given you an example – you should do just as I have done for you."*
> John 13:12-15 NET

Some have taken this to mean that we should literally wash the feet of others. Personally, I think Jesus was using this as a metaphor for servanthood—that as believers, we need to have a humble, servant-like attitude. The words *arrogant* and *believer* do not belong together. Jesus continued:

> *I tell you the truth, no servant is greater than his master, nor is a messenger greater than the one who sent him. Now that you know these things, you will be blessed if you do them.*
> John 13:16-17 NIV

The definition of the word *blessed* is a little slippery. The story of Jesus washing his disciples' feet nails it down. We find joy and contentment when we are taken up with serving others.

MID MEAL

Now remember that the washing of feet occurred as the disciples and Jesus prepared to commemorate the Passover together. It was in the middle of the meal that Judas Iscariot left for his rendezvous with the chief priests in order to betray Jesus. They would pay him 30 pieces of silver for his treachery, which in that day was the price of a slave. Judas valued his pocketbook over his friendships. Perhaps with that in mind, Jesus said:

> *"A new commandment I give to you, that you love one another, even as I have loved you, that you also love one another.*
>
> *"By this all men will know that you are My disciples, if you have love for one another."* John 13:34-35 NASB

As believers we are to help each other out. There are many times when we as Christians fail in demonstrating love, but I can also say that many more times I have experienced care and concern even from complete strangers simply because they were believers.

Knowing the stress his little band of disciples would encounter in the coming hours, Jesus encouraged his disciples with a promised home in Heaven.

> *"Do not let your hearts be troubled. Trust in God; trust also in me. In my Father's house are many rooms; if it were not so, I would have told you. I am going there to prepare a place for you. And if I go and prepare a place for you, I will come back and take you to be with me that you also may be where I am."* John 14:1-3 NIV

Ever since that night, believers have encouraged themselves with these words.

EAGER

Scripture tells us Jesus was determined to go to the cross. You get a sense of that during this meal.

> *And He said to them, "I have earnestly desired to eat this Passover with you before I suffer; for I say to you, I shall never again eat it until it is fulfilled in the kingdom of God."* Luke 22:15-16 NASB

You may wonder what the disciples were thinking as Jesus plainly spoke of his coming suffering. The Bible tells us the crucifixion took them by complete surprise. It was only after Jesus had resurrected that they remembered how he had foretold the exact way he would die. As they ate, Jesus...

> ...took bread, gave thanks and broke it, and gave it to them, saying, "This is My body which is given for you; do this in remembrance of Me."
>
> Luke 22:19 NKJV

We must not read into the story here. They weren't eating Jesus' flesh. Scripture uses bread as a metaphor for Jesus.

> "Truly...I say to you, he who believes has eternal life. I am the bread of life."
>
> John 6:47-48 NASB

Bread to the Jews was like rice to Asians. It was a basic essential of physical life. In the same way, Jesus as the Bread of Life was the only one through whom we could have spiritual life. Just as the Passover bread was broken, so it was the physical body of Jesus that would soon be broken by the scourging and the cross. Remember this, since later in the book we will talk more about the bread as a reminder of Jesus.

> And when He had taken a cup and given thanks, He gave it to them, saying, "Drink from it, all of you; for this is My blood of the covenant, which is poured out for many for forgiveness of sins."
>
> Matthew 26:27-28 NASB

Again the symbolism is similar. This was not actual blood but rather wine or juice picturing the fact that Jesus' blood would be poured out in his suffering. The Bible tells us that...

> ...without [death through the] shedding of blood there is no forgiveness [of the sin-debt].
>
> Hebrews 9:22 NASB

> But now in Christ Jesus you who used to be far away have been brought near by the blood of Christ.
>
> Ephesians 2:13 NET

With the meal over, and after...

> ...they had sung a hymn, they went out to the Mount of Olives.
>
> Matthew 26:30 NKJV

FORGOTTEN

As the disciples walked along…

> …they began to argue among themselves about who would
> be the greatest among them.   *Luke 22:24 NLT*

Wasn't it just a few hours earlier that Jesus had taught and shown
the disciples the nature of true humility? They had already forgotten
the lesson given in the washing of feet. Self-aggrandizement and
servanthood are strangers to each other.

> Jesus told them, "In this world the kings and great men
> lord it over their people, yet they are called 'friends of the
> people.' But among you it will be different. Those who are
> the greatest among you should take the lowest rank, and the
> leader should be like a servant.
>
> "Who is more important, the one who sits at the table or the
> one who serves? The one who sits at the table, of course. But
> not here! For I am among you as one who serves."
>   *Luke 22:25-27 NLT*

As believers we are not to move through life in an arrogant,
demanding sort of way. Over and over again, we are told to
be servants.

3 THE PROMISED SPIRIT

As the disciples argued over who would be the greatest, Jesus
gave them a quick peek behind the scenes. He wanted them to
know that there was one influencing their minds who was far
more powerful than they were—one who is exceedingly evil.
Jesus said:

> "Simon, Simon, Satan has asked to sift you as wheat. But
> I have prayed for you, Simon, that your faith may not fail.
> And when you have turned back, strengthen your brothers."
>   *Luke 22:31-32 NIV*

It was Satan who was behind their seeking for self-glory. But Peter
did not see things that way. In his self-confidence and pride…

> Peter said to him, "Lord, I am ready to go with you both to
> prison and to death."   *Luke 22:33 ESV*

We now return to where our story began. It was at this point that
Peter vowed to follow the Lord through thick and thin. Jesus didn't
question Peter's sincerity, but he did question Peter's strength.

Did Peter have it within himself to follow through on what he believed? The answer was no. Peter was up against a deceiver far more evil than he could imagine, one much stronger than any determination he could muster in himself.

Just as wheat is sifted by shaking the kernels, so Satan shook Peter to the core of his being. After it was all over, Peter knew that he had denied Jesus, not because he did not know what was the right thing to do, but because his courage had faltered. It left Peter a spiritual wreck, humiliated beyond words.

To resist Satan, Peter needed help from outside himself, from someone who would place the right thoughts in his mind. He needed someone who would guide him in what to say when confronted by young servant girls asking awkward questions.

It was in this context that Jesus promised to send a Helper, one who would give the disciples the counsel they needed.

> "And I will ask the Father, and he will give you another Counselor to be with you forever—the Spirit of truth." John 14:16-17 NIV

In Koine Greek, the word *another* means "another of the same kind." When the Holy Spirit arrived, the disciples would find in him the same attributes as those found in the Father and the Son. Jesus said:

> "But the Counselor, the Holy Spirit, whom the Father will send in my name, will teach you all things and will remind you of everything I have said to you." John 14:26 NIV

In the Old Testament the Holy Spirit came upon certain individuals to help them perform special tasks. But now Jesus was making a promise that had broader implications. He would send the Holy Spirit to work in a way that he had never done before.

> "But I tell you the truth, it is to your advantage that I go away; for if I do not go away, the Helper will not come to you; but if I go, I will send Him to you." John 16:7 NASB

When He Comes

> "When he comes, he will convict the world of guilt in regard to sin and righteousness and judgment." John 16:8 NIV

In Greek the word *convict* is a legal term which means "to bring to light, to expose the facts, to convince of truth." The Spirit would convict the world of guilt in three areas:

> "…in regard to sin, because men do not believe in me."
> John 16:9 NIV

The Spirit would expose man's greatest sin—the sin of unbelief in Jesus as Saviour.

> *"...in regard to righteousness, because I am going to the Father, where you can see me no longer."*   John 16:10 NIV

After Jesus left the world, the Holy Spirit would work to convince mankind that Jesus' death as a payment for our sin was the most "right" or righteous action ever accomplished.

> *"...and in regard to judgment, because the prince of this world now stands condemned."*   John 16:11 NIV

Although still active in this present world, Satan is a defeated foe. Like a condemned criminal, his final judgment is sure—an eternity in the Lake of Fire.

Jesus told his disciples that the Holy Spirit would be like a prosecuting attorney, convincing the unbelieving world that they were indeed guilty sinners in need of a perfect Saviour to rescue them from the same judgment.

GUIDE

Jesus continued:

> *"I still have many things to say to you, but you cannot bear them now. When the Spirit of truth comes, he will guide you into all the truth, for he will not speak on his own authority, but whatever he hears he will speak, and he will declare to you the things that are to come."*   John 16:12-13 ESV

As stated at the beginning, we all need a Map and a Guide in life. Jesus told the disciples that after he left, he would send the Holy Spirit to guide them down the right road. The Spirit would bring glory, not to himself, but to Jesus.

> *"He will glorify Me, for He will take of what is Mine and declare it to you."*   John 16:14 NKJV

FINAL HOURS

In those final hours before his death, Jesus continually encouraged his disciples.

> *"I came from the Father and entered the world; now I am leaving the world and going back to the Father.*
>
> *"I have told you these things, so that in me you may have peace. In this world you will have trouble. But take heart! I have overcome the world."*   John 16: 28,33 NIV

4 The Empty Cross

The day Jesus was crucified must have been the lowest day of Peter's life. In the wee hours of that morning he had publically denied Jesus—three times, with curses—and that was after he had adamantly stated in front of the other disciples that he would follow Jesus to his death. What would they be thinking? Peter the coward! Don't ask Peter to cover your back in a crisis!

But it wasn't the other disciples who were on Peter's mind. Upon his third denial…

> …*immediately, while he was still speaking, the rooster crowed. And the Lord turned and looked at Peter.*   Luke 22:60-61 ESV

It was that look—it was Jesus of whom Peter was thinking. He had denied his Lord when it counted the most. The shame of it all! What had he been thinking?

> *And Peter remembered the saying of the Lord, how he had said to him, "Before the rooster crows today, you will deny me three times."*   Luke 22:61ESV

Peter had failed miserably.

> *And he went out and wept bitterly.*   Luke 22:62 ESV

No Escape

The Bible does not say where Peter went. It is doubtful he could have gone far. Being outside of the courtyard did not bring solace. As the night gave way to early morning, Jesus was paraded through the streets to the Temple. The clamour attracted gawkers and scoffers like flies to the dead. By the time Jesus was before Pontius Pilate, the Roman governor, the crowd was substantial. There would have been loud taunts and jeers from the mob. No doubt, Peter could hear the commotion, although at a distance.

I remember being in London when two renowned football teams were playing. We could plainly hear the roar of the spectators even though we were a full kilometre away. Granted, the crowd was much larger at the football stadium, but Jerusalem in that day was a small place, not even a kilometre across at its widest. Peter could hardly have escaped the roar of the crowd shouting:

> *"Crucify him! Crucify him!"*   Luke 23:21 NIV

Perhaps he heard the crack of the lash, the jeers as Jesus was led through the streets, maybe even the ring of the hammer on the nails being pounded through flesh. It is possible that Peter heard it all. But it wasn't just the noise—it was also the quiet.

In our modern world we are conditioned to a certain level of background noise, the result of electricity and vehicles. But I have visited places in the world that lack both. You soon notice how sound travels and how quiet it can be. On the day Jesus was crucified, it is quite probable that the streets were empty, eerily so. And as the hours passed, even the jeers would have faded to a deathly silence. It was as though the whole world paused to contemplate the One on the cross.

And then there was the midday darkness, three hours of pitch black. And an earthquake. This was supernatural and Peter knew it. He knew it was all about Jesus, the Son of God.

For Peter, it was the worst day of his life—a day of despair.

A DAY OF SHAME

As for humanity, it was the most shameful day of all time. The Lord of the universe…

> …was despised and rejected by men; a man of sorrows, and acquainted with grief; and as one from whom men hide their faces he was despised, and we esteemed him not. Isaiah 53:3 ESV

On that day, mankind nailed the Creator to a cross. Over the centuries this has been blamed on the Jews, but we must remember it was a Gentile court that had the power to enact the death penalty, and it was Gentiles who drove the nails through his hands and feet. Yes, the Jews were there, but no less guilty were the Gentiles—all mankind was at fault. It was our sin that put him there. It was a day of shame.

A DAY OF HOPE

But it was also a day of hope. For Jesus…

> …was pierced for our transgressions, he was crushed for our iniquities; the punishment that brought us peace was upon him, and by his wounds we are healed.
>
> We all, like sheep, have gone astray, each of us has turned to his own way; and the LORD has laid on him the iniquity of us all. Isaiah 53:5-6 NIV

It was on this day that the words *mercy* and *grace* took on their full breadth of meaning.

It has been said that *mercy* is "not getting what we deserve." We deserve to face the same judgment as Satan and yet, because of Jesus' death on the cross, we can now escape that entirely. Jesus was punished in our place.

And *grace* has been defined as "getting what we do not deserve." We do not deserve it, but now we can have fellowship with God. We have eternal life forever in Heaven, given freely—as a gift.

Though the mountains be shaken and the hills be removed, yet my unfailing love for you will not be shaken. Isaiah 54:10 NIV

We, who in our sins had no hope, now have been shown mercy and grace. The day of Christ's death could not have been better for mankind—it was truly a day to be thankful.

The day Jesus died is central to all of history, to all of eternity. Long after this earth has passed away, we will remember his sacrifice on the cross. We may forget this life, but we will never, never forget the cross.

For Christ, our Passover lamb, has been sacrificed.
1 Corinthians 5:7 ESV

5 The Empty Tomb

Sunday was the day after the Sabbath. It was the Feast of Firstfruits. The eastern sky was just showing a rim of light when the ladies left for the tomb. They left early, long before they would have to face sneering faces on the street.

For Peter the day was grim. Sleep had been out of reach. If beating one's fists on walls and floors were helpful, Peter should have been feeling better. But he wasn't. Shame and guilt were overwhelming at times. Sure, the other disciples had not said a word, but it went without saying that he had been absent from the cross, noticeably so.

It was all over now. If only Jesus had spoken a few words to him, anything, just…anything. Jesus had spoken to Judas Iscariot, a certifiable traitor—a premeditated one. Well, Peter had denied Jesus, but at least he had not planned it. Rumour had it that Judas had committed suicide. Perhaps Peter wondered if he should too.

The Jewish culture is an Eastern culture where shame is a significant burden. Whether Peter contemplated following the example of Judas or not, we don't know, but we do know Peter was human and no doubt his feelings ran the gamut.

> When the Sabbath was over, Mary Magdalene, Mary the mother of James, and Salome bought aromatic spices so that they might go and anoint him. And very early on the first day of the week, at sunrise, they went to the tomb. They had been asking each other, "Who will roll away the stone for us from the entrance to the tomb?" But when they looked up, they saw that the stone, which was very large, had been rolled back. Then as they went into the tomb, they saw a young man dressed in a white robe sitting on the right side; and they were alarmed.
> Mark 16:1-5 NET

A resurrection was not something they had contemplated—it wasn't even a thought in the corner of their minds. So when they saw the angel they were afraid. He said:

> "Do not be alarmed. You seek Jesus of Nazareth, who was crucified. He has risen; he is not here. See the place where they laid him. But go, tell his disciples and Peter that he is going before you to Galilee. There you will see him, just as he told you."
> Mark 16:6-7 ESV

AND PETER

They were given specific instructions to tell the disciples—and Peter.

> Trembling and bewildered, the women went out and fled from the tomb.
> Mark 16:8 NIV

> ...and returning from the tomb they told all these things to the eleven and to all the rest. Now it was Mary Magdalene and Joanna and Mary the mother of James and the other women with them who told these things to the apostles.
> Luke 24:9-10 ESV

The women were met with a skeptical audience. In the culture of the day, women were not considered reliable witnesses in any situation.

> And their words seemed to them like idle tales, and they did not believe them.
> Luke 24:11 NKJV

But Peter was different.

> Peter got up and ran to the tomb.
> Luke 24:12 NASB

He could hardly believe what he was hearing! He had hope—yes, just a tiny spark, but nonetheless, hope. The women had relayed the angel's exact words. With elevated voice you can see Peter asking, "Are you sure the young man, the one in the white robe, said, 'Tell the disciples and Peter?' He did say, 'and Peter,' did he? Specifically?" The women had affirmed it was so. Now Peter was on the way to the tomb—running. He was joined by another disciple, John.

> Both were running, but the other disciple outran Peter and reached the tomb first. He bent over and looked in at the strips of linen lying there but did not go in. Then Simon Peter, who was behind him, arrived and went into the tomb. He saw the strips of linen lying there, as well as the burial cloth that had been around Jesus' head. The cloth was folded up by itself, separate from the linen. *John 20:4-7 NIV*

It was amazing. It looked as if someone had tidied up before leaving. The body of Jesus was definitely absent, but so was the young man in a white robe. Maybe the other disciples were right; the women were not to be trusted as witnesses. Peter, pushing out of the tomb and past John...

> ...went away, wondering to himself what had happened. *Luke 24:12 NIV*

> Then the other disciple, who came to the tomb first, went in also; and he saw and believed. For as yet they did not know the Scripture, that He must rise again from the dead. *John 20:8-9 NKJV*

Sunday Evening

It was now evening—the day of the resurrection. Some Bible scholars think that by this time Jesus had engaged in a private conversation with Peter. And it seems it may be so, for when two disciples returned from meeting Jesus on the road to Emmaus, they were told by the others:

> "The Lord has risen indeed, and has appeared to Simon!" *Luke 24:34 ESV*

What went on in the conversation remains confidential to Peter and the Lord, but you can be sure mercy and grace were evident. As to his relationship with God, Peter was undoubtedly a believer; however, when he denied knowing Christ, his fellowship with the Lord had been seriously hindered. Scripture says Peter wept bitterly when he realized Jesus knew of his denial and, no doubt, Jesus ached inside at being disowned just as any of us would. That is the nature of a break in fellowship — grief, hurt, disappointment.

Peter was in desperate need of having his "feet washed" — of having his fellowship restored. Jesus made room for Peter on that day. We need to remember that. More often than we may like to admit, all of us play the part of Peter in the journey of life — we deny our Lord. We too need to make time to be with the Lord for the same private conversation.

We also need to learn, as Peter did, to…

> …not to think of himself more highly than he ought to think, but to think with sober judgment. Romans 12:3 ESV

We need to be humble and recognize our constant need for a Map and a Guide in this life. As believers, going it alone is not a safe option.

DOORS LOCKED

Peter was present when…

> On the evening of that day, the first day of the week, the doors being locked where the disciples were for fear of the Jews, Jesus came and stood among them and said to them, "Peace be with you." When he had said this, he showed them his hands and his side. John 20:19-20 ESV

Jesus authenticated his physical presence by showing the fearful disciples the scars in his hands and his side.

> The disciples were overjoyed when they saw the Lord. John 20:20 NIV

But one disciple missed this meeting. His name was Thomas.

CHAPTER SEVEN

1 THE RESURRECTION

There is no other miracle in the Bible that draws more skepticism than the resurrection of Jesus. The apostles knew this and wrote:

> *And if Christ has not been raised, then all our preaching is useless, and your faith is useless. And we apostles would all be lying about God…*

> *And if Christ has not been raised, then your faith is useless and you are still guilty of your sins. In that case, all who have died believing in Christ are lost! And if our hope in Christ is only for this life, we are more to be pitied than anyone in the world.* 1 Corinthians 15:14-15,17-19 NLT

THEORIES

Skeptics have floated a number of theories to disavow the resurrection. These theories were discarded as invalid long ago, but they still make their rounds in some circles.

The Swoon Theory: This is the belief that Jesus didn't really die on the cross, but merely passed out. When he was laid in the cool tomb he resuscitated.

This theory assumes that a Roman squad botched the execution. It assumes that the centurion who thrust his spear into Jesus' heart did not know what he was doing. It assumes that a man, wrapped as a cadaver, could escape from the yards of cloth wound around his body. It assumes that a man in a weakened state could pry open the huge rock blocking the tomb from inside, without alerting the guards, slip away and then present himself as a healthy individual to his disciples the same day. This theory assumes far too much. It is not credible.

The Conspiracy Theory: This argument suggests that Jewish and Roman authorities removed the body from the tomb for safekeeping.

But if they had the body of Jesus, why did they not produce it later when the apostles were publicly proclaiming the resurrection? They could have stopped Christianity dead in its tracks. This theory also offers no explanation for all those who said they had spoken with Jesus after his resurrection.

The Wrong Tomb Theory: Proponents of this idea state the women visited the wrong grave. Since it was early in the morning, still dark, and the women were grieving deeply, they merely visited the wrong tomb—an empty one.

If this were true, the disciples who did not believe the women in the first place, would soon have corrected their mistake. And if the body were still in the tomb, then when the resurrection was publicly declared, the chief priests would have been quick to produce the body to quash any rumours.

The Hallucination Theory: This theory holds to the idea that the resurrection occurred only in the minds of the disciples.

This is not tenable because so many people with different personalities and backgrounds would have needed to hallucinate all at the same time. The theory has no supporting evidence.

FACT

The truth of the matter is, none of the apostles expected Jesus to resurrect. They had to be won over from their skepticism.

> *Now Thomas (called Didymus), one of the twelve, was not with them when Jesus came. The other disciples told him, "We have seen the Lord!"*
>
> *But he replied, "Unless I see the wounds from the nails in his hands, and put my finger into the wounds from the nails, and put my hand into his side, I will never believe it!"*
>
> John 20:24-25 NET

Thomas had not seen Jesus and he was not prone to believing in a resurrection, no matter how hard his friends tried to persuade him otherwise. So much for resurrection theories.

> *Eight days later the disciples were again together in the house, and Thomas was with them. Although the doors were locked, Jesus came and stood among them and said, "Peace be with you!"* John 20:26 NET

After the resurrection Jesus was fitted with a body that could do amazing things. It was still a physical body, but it could pass through walls, moving instantly from one location to another. It is referred to as a *glorified body.*

Personally, if I had been Jesus, I would have made a visit to see Pilate. I would have just shown up in his bedroom to perch on the end of his bed and ask a few questions. But one of the characteristics of a glorified body is that it is not subject to sin or sinful thoughts, so obviously such a visit would not have happened. But here, a week after the resurrection, we have Jesus appearing in a room, having passed through locked doors.

> Then [Jesus] said to Thomas, "Put your finger here, and examine my hands. Extend your hand and put it into my side. Do not continue in your unbelief, but believe."
> Thomas replied to him, "My Lord and my God!"
>
> John 20:27-28 NET

Thomas immediately recognized the implications of a resurrected Messiah. Jesus was just who he said he was. He was the Creator God himself—Yahweh! We see here the roots of the oldest confession of faith:

> That if you confess with your mouth, "Jesus is Lord [Yahweh]," and believe in your heart that God raised him from the dead, you will be saved. Romans 10:9 NIV

Because the resurrection authenticates Jesus as God himself, Satan has tried hard to discredit it over the centuries.

FAITH

Jesus said to Thomas:

> "Because you have seen me, you have believed; blessed are those who have not seen and yet have believed." John 20:29 NIV

Faith is built on understood facts—it is not something you can muster up in yourself out of thin air. If you do, you may find yourself trusting in notions that are false.

The better you know someone—his identity and reputation—the greater the possiblity you will have faith in that person; the more likely you will take him at his word.

Some need more information than others, but all must have at least some facts in order to have genuine biblical faith.

This is why Scripture was written. It is a goldmine of facts upon which to build our faith.

2 THE DOUBTER

Thomas is the most famous of doubters, but he is not alone. It is human to doubt. Over the years I have talked to many Christians who have struggled with doubts about their faith. Many have wondered if they were really "saved" or not. They are not sure if they are on the road to Heaven. Usually "doubters" fall into four categories.

NO FACTS

There are those who struggle with doubts simply because they do not have enough information on which to hang their faith. I have found that young teens are especially prone to doubts of this nature. They are old enough to question what they may have learned from Christian parents or church leaders, but they are not old enough to have learned the Scriptures well enough to dispel doubts. There is only one solution for these doubts: they need a solid dose of Bible basics.

Faith cometh by hearing…the word of God. Romans 10:17 KJV

Faith is not some sort of mystical feeling—it only exists if there are known facts upon which faith can rest.

WRONG FOCUS

Then there are those who struggle with doubts because of the method used to bring them to salvation. Many church leaders have them say a "sinner's prayer" to get saved. Or they have them "go forward" or "sign a card" as a result of an invitation. There is nothing inherently wrong with these methods, but for many new believers, it causes them to wonder if they really *meant it* when they prayed the sinner's prayer, or whether they said the right words. They question their own sincerity.

If you find yourself in this group, then let me say that none of these things, including the prayer, are required to become a believer. Indeed, if you are trusting in this "ritual," then you have put your trust in the wrong place. You are looking at something you did—maybe a prayer—rather than at Jesus and what he has done for you. You have the wrong focus.

Your faith must rest solely in the fact that Jesus—God himself—died in your place. He took your sin and offers you his righteousness. You accept that offer by faith. To be counted as a believer, all you need to do is rest in these facts as being true—just take Jesus at his word. That is the essence of faith.

NEED ASSURANCE

I find another group that has yet to come to grips with the reality of eternal life. They struggle because it seems too easy—the gospel is too good to be true. And yet one of the apostles wrote:

> I write these things to you who believe in the name of the Son of God that you may know [at this present time] that you have [as a present possession] eternal life. *1 John 5:13 ESV*

Right now, not after we die, we can have the assurance of eternal life. If it were possible for eternal life to be gone tomorrow, it would not be eternal life today. No, God wants us to be confident of our place in his family. When we stumble, we need not fear that we will be thrown out of his family. Jesus has promised:

> "Truly, truly, I say to you, whoever hears my word and believes him who sent me has eternal life. He does not come into judgment, but has passed from death to life." *John 5:24 ESV*

Don't doubt the promises of God. They are solid and sure. Eternal life is eternal. It doesn't go away just because you doubt or struggle.

CONFUSED

There are also those who feel they are not good Christians. They struggle with sin and when it comes to good works, they come up short. They have the perpetual feeling of needing to do more to please God. It is a heavy weight they carry. They are confused. Here are some thought-provoking questions:

- On what basis can I keep myself saved?
- How good of a life must I live to keep myself saved?
- How much faith must I have to keep myself saved?

If you try to come up with a list of good things to do that would add up to great faith, then you have things backwards in your mind. Read the following chart carefully and it will show how our good living—our good works—fit into the picture. We will then touch on this subject again later in the book.

If you struggle with doubts about your faith, keep reading. We will talk more on this issue. And yes, remember you are not alone. Even after all the time he spent with Jesus, it was one of the disciples who gave us the phrase "doubting Thomas."

The Place of Good Works

We are not saved **by** the good things we do. *For it is by grace you have been saved, through faith—and this not from yourselves, it is the gift of God—not by works, so that no one can boast.* *Ephesians 2:8-9 NIV*	We are saved **to do** good deeds or good works. *For we are God's workmanship, created in Christ Jesus to do good works.* *Ephesians 2:10 NIV*
Good works are not the path to eternal life. *He saved us, not because of righteous things we had done, but because of his mercy.* *Titus 3:5 NIV*	Good works are the **result** or the **fruit** of having eternal life. *I want you to stress these things, so that those who have trusted in God may be careful to devote themselves to doing what is good.* *Titus 3:8 NIV*
If good works could save us, we would boast about how good we are. *If, in fact, Abraham was justified by works, he had something to boast about.* *Romans 4:2 NIV*	Since we are saved by simply "taking God at his word," we boast about God's goodness. *May you always be filled with the fruit of your salvation—the righteous character produced in your life by Jesus Christ.* *Philippians 1:11 NLT*
Message to those investigating the path to God: *Jesus told them, "This is the only work God wants from you: Believe in the one he has sent."* *John 6:29 NLT*	Message to the believer: *For the grace of God... teaches us to say "No" to ungodliness and worldly passions, and to live self-controlled, upright and godly lives in this present age... eager to do what is good.* *Titus 2:11-12, 14 NIV*

3 THE JUDGMENTS

Jesus was resurrected on the Sunday after Passover, the day the Israelites celebrated the Feast of Firstfruits. In God's overall historical plan, the Lord had placed this prophetic feast in history so no one would miss what had happened.

THE FEAST OF FIRSTFRUITS

Let me refresh your mind to what we learned in an earlier chapter. Just as a farmer places a "dead" seed in the ground only to see it spring to "life," so in Scripture, the Feast of Firstfruits was a picture of resurrection.

And just as the farmer harvested his first sheaf of grain—the firstfruits being an indication of many more sheaves to come—so when Jesus rose from the dead, his resurrection, being the first one, was a promise of many more resurrections to come.

> *But now Christ has been raised from the dead, the firstfruits of those who have fallen asleep [having died].*
>
> *For since death came through a man, the resurrection of the dead also came through a man. For just as **in Adam** all die, so also **in Christ** all will be made alive. But each in his own order: Christ, the firstfruits; then when Christ comes, those who belong to him.* 1 Corinthians 15:20-23 NET

When Jesus returns to earth, those "in Christ" who have "fallen asleep" will be resurrected and they, along with the believers living at that time, will be given new bodies—glorified ones—the same kind of body Jesus had after his resurrection.

> *Now we do not want you to be uninformed, brothers and sisters, about those who are asleep, so that you will not grieve like the rest who have no hope. For if we believe that Jesus died and rose again, so also we believe that God will bring with him those who have fallen asleep as Christians.*
>
> *For we tell you this by the word of the Lord, that we who are alive, who are left until the coming of the Lord, will surely not go ahead of those who have fallen asleep.*
>
> *For the Lord himself will come down from heaven with a shout of command, with the voice of the archangel, and with the trumpet of God, and the dead **in Christ** will rise first. Then we who are alive, who are left, will be suddenly caught up*

*together with them in the clouds to meet the Lord in the air.
And so we will always be with the Lord. Therefore encourage
one another with these words.* 1 Thessalonians 4:13-18 NET

It is the resurrection that is the linchpin of the Christian faith.

The Bema Seat Judgment

Many scholars would understand the Bible to teach that some
time soon after our collective arrival in Heaven…

*We must all appear before the judgment seat of Christ, so
that each one may be paid back according to what he has
done while in the body, whether good or evil.*
2 Corinthians 5:10 NET

The words *judgment seat* come from one Greek word *bema*. The
bema was a raised platform upon which a ruler would sit. The
Romans often used it in a forum to make legal decisions. However,
the Bible also seems to use it in a way consistent with the Greek
games. In this case, a judge would sit on the bema to watch the
contestants, making sure they were playing by the rules. The
Bible often draws this parallel to the life of a believer.

*Do you not know that all the runners in a stadium compete,
but only one receives the prize? So run to win.*
1 Corinthians 9:24 NET

The winner would be taken before the bema seat to receive a
laurel wreath upon his head, equivalent to being presented the
gold medal on the Olympic podium. The Bible says that the
wreath was perishable, but as believers we run to receive an
imperishable award.

*Each competitor must exercise self-control in everything. They
do it to receive a perishable crown, but we an imperishable one.*
1 Corinthians 9:25 NET

The Judgment Seat of Christ is not to determine whether we belong
in Heaven or not. That was settled when we put our trust in Christ.
The Bema Seat Judgment, or what the Bible sometimes calls *the
Day*, determines rewards for faithful service—for doing good
works. The question concerns what sort of reward we will receive.

When you put your trust in Christ, a foundation was laid for
serving the Lord. But…

*…each one must be careful how he builds. … If anyone builds
on the foundation with gold, silver, precious stones, wood,*

hay, or straw, each builder's work will be plainly seen, for
the Day will make it clear, because it will be revealed by fire.
1 Corinthians 3:10-13 NET

This is not hellfire. It is a "fire" that tests the quality of a work.
Works done for Christ are compared to gold, silver and precious
stones. Self-serving effort is seen as wood, hay and straw.

And the fire will test what kind of work each has done. If
what someone has built survives, he will receive a reward. If
someone's work is burned up, he will suffer loss.
1 Corinthians 3:13-15 NET

At the Bema Seat we will either receive a reward or have nothing.
Losers are not humiliated or beaten up. That being said, I cannot
help but believe that if we walk away from that podium with
nothing to show for our lives, we will feel deeply disappointed.
Perhaps that is why the Bible says that God in Heaven…

…will wipe away every tear from their eyes.
Revelation 21:4 NET

I cannot emphasize strongly enough that the Bema Seat is not
about judgment on sin; it is about rewards for faithful service.
When we put our trust in Christ, the gavel was gone. No longer
do we face a courtroom judge. And though we may run the race
poorly, Scripture says:

If someone's work is burned up, he will suffer loss. He himself
will be saved, but only as through fire.   *1 Corinthians 3:15 NET*

Oh the love—the grace—that God has extended to us sinful
men, that he should make it this way. We serve him, not because
we are driven out of fear, but because we love him.

THE GREAT WHITE THRONE JUDGMENT[1]

There is another judgment that you need to be aware of, a courtroom
where only unbelievers will be present. It is a judgment that will
occur at the end of this age.

Then I saw a great white throne and him who was seated on it. From his presence earth and sky fled away, and no place was found for them. And I saw the dead, great and small, standing before the throne, and books were opened. Then another book was opened, which is the book of life. And the dead were judged by what was written in the books, according to what they had done.

And the sea gave up the dead who were in it, Death and Hades gave up the dead who were in them, and they were judged, each one of them, according to what they had done.

Revelation 20:11-13 ESV

It seems that those who have done good deeds will receive a lighter sentence than those whose lives were marked by evil deeds. That being said, all unbelievers face the second death.

Then death and the grave were thrown into the lake of fire. This lake of fire is the second death. And anyone whose name was not found recorded in the Book of Life was thrown into the lake of fire.

Revelation 20:14-15 NLT

SUMMARY

There are significant differences between the Bema and the Great White Throne judgments—one concerns only believers, the other only unbelievers.[1] As Christians, we can be thankful that we do not face the latter. That being said, we need to live in such a way that we honour the one who saved us from such a future.

The Bema Seat	The Great White Throne
Focuses on gain or loss of rewards pertaining to the kind of works or service of the believer	Focuses on loss of salvation pertaining to those whose names are not written in the Book of Life
Comparable to a judge in a sporting or arts event	Comparable to a judge in a courtroom
Lake of Fire is not in the picture	Lake of Fire is in the picture

Now back to the story—to the events immediately following the resurrection of Jesus.

4 THE FISHING TRIP

Afterward Jesus appeared again to his disciples, by the Sea of Tiberias. It happened this way: Simon Peter, Thomas (called Didymus), Nathanael from Cana in Galilee, the sons of Zebedee, and two other disciples were together. "I'm going out to fish," Simon Peter told them, and they said, "We'll go with you." So they went out and got into the boat, but that night they caught nothing.

Early in the morning, Jesus stood on the shore, but the disciples did not realize that it was Jesus.

He called out to them, "Friends, haven't you any fish?"

"No," they answered.

He said, "Throw your net on the right side of the boat and you will find some." When they did, they were unable to haul the net in because of the large number of fish. John 21:1-6 NIV

Then the disciple whom Jesus loved said to Peter, "It is the Lord!" So Simon Peter, when he heard that it was the Lord, tucked in his outer garment (for he had nothing on underneath it), and plunged into the sea.

Meanwhile the other disciples came with the boat, dragging the net full of fish, for they were not far from land, only about a hundred yards.

When they got out on the beach, they saw a charcoal fire ready with a fish placed on it, and bread. Jesus said, "Bring some of the fish you have just now caught."

So Simon Peter went aboard and pulled the net to shore. It was full of large fish, one hundred fifty-three, but although there were so many, the net was not torn. "Come, have breakfast," Jesus said. John 21:7-12 NET

This must have been quite a meal. Imagine having Jesus as your chef.

But none of the disciples dared to ask him, "Who are you?" because they knew it was the Lord. Jesus came and took the bread and gave it to them, and did the same with the fish. This was now the third time Jesus was revealed to the disciples after he was raised from the dead. John 21:12-14 NET

SIMON PETER

When they had finished eating, Jesus said to Simon Peter, "Simon son of John, do you truly love me more than these?"
John 21:15 NIV

We are not told what "these" referred to. Perhaps Jesus was nodding to the other disciples, his friends. Personally, I think he was indicating the boats and the nets. Maybe it was both. Whatever the case, the question drilled down to priorities in life. Peter, what is more important to you?

- What your friends think?
- These possessions that you own?
- Or me?

[Peter] replied, "Yes, Lord, you know I love you."

Jesus told him, "Feed my lambs." John 21:15 NET

In the Old Testament God often referred to himself as a shepherd with his people being the flock. This carries over to the New Testament where Scripture speaks of…

…our Lord Jesus, that great Shepherd of the sheep.
Hebrews 13:20 KJV

Jesus told Peter to…

"Feed my lambs." John 21:15 NET

Jesus asked Peter to be an undershepherd, to teach young believers.

Jesus said a second time, "Simon, son of John, do you love me?" He replied, "Yes, Lord, you know I love you." Jesus told him, "Shepherd my sheep." John 21:16 NET

Jesus told Peter to teach older believers.

Jesus said a third time, "Simon, son of John, do you love me?"
John 21:17 NET

Scripture specifically says that Jesus asked essentially the same question three times. As the other disciples sat listening quietly, they could not have missed the obvious parallel. Peter had denied

Jesus publically, three times; Jesus was reinstating Peter publically, three times.

> Peter was distressed that Jesus asked him a third time, "Do you love me?" and said, "Lord, you know everything. You know that I love you."
>
> Jesus replied, "Feed my sheep.
>
> ...After he said this, Jesus told Peter, "Follow me."
>
> John 21:17,19 NET

Peter was back.

Only in Jesus do you find such a level of undeserved love. No other belief system or religion offers such forgiveness. It is all because God is a God of grace.

GRACE

Jesus welcomed Peter back solely on the basis of grace. At minimum he deserved a severe scolding, but instead Peter was shown underserved love — that special type of love called *grace*.

If Peter felt he deserved to be forgiven by Jesus, then Jesus could not have shown him grace — he could only have given him a reward.

If Peter felt he could buy or earn forgiveness, then Jesus could not have shown him grace — it would have been a simple business transaction.

But neither was possible. Grace is always underserved — it is always a gift, and to add any of our "goodness" to the equation destroys grace. The Bible says:

> If it is by grace, it is no longer on the basis of works; otherwise grace would no longer be grace. Romans 11:6 ESV

Grace is a slippery subject for us humans. We always feel we can do something that will make God love us more than he already does. We add into the equation our good works — or at least our good intentions. But grace ceases to be grace if any good work is added.

During times of war, soldiers often hide in trenches or holes in the ground to seek protection from snipers and exploding artillery shells. These holes are called foxholes. During the world wars it became common to hear of "foxhole conversions." As the shells began to explode around the foxhole, a soldier would begin to call out to God to save him. For some, this was their experience:

- (BOOM!) God, save me. I will stop smoking!

- (CRASH!) I will stop drinking alcohol!
- (KA-BOOM!) I will stop carousing! Cussing! Just save me.

The soldier might promise a whole list of things he would stop doing. As the exploding shells came closer, he would shift to things he would be willing to do.

- (CRACK-BANG!) God, save me. I will go to church!
- (BANG!) I will pray every day! I will read the Bible!! You can have all my money!
- (KA-BOOM!) I will become a missionary, a priest...I will serve you! You can be master of my life!
- (BOOMMMMM!) I will make you my Lord! My King! Just save me.

Now, all of these things might be good and right, but God does not accept promises and good intentions as a basis for salvation. They are works. And works cannot be mingled with grace or it destroys grace. Even as believers, we daily walk with God only by his grace. Peter had neither...

- things he could deny himself, nor
- things he could promise to do...

...to win favour with Jesus. He was at the mercy of Jesus showing him grace. And Jesus did show Peter underserved love when he welcomed him back.

Coming back to the foxhole illustration, what a soldier needed to say was this:

- (BOOM!) God, I know I am a sinner and cannot save myself. I deserve death—I deserve hell. (CRASH!) But you said that you died in my place for my sin. You said if I put my faith in you, then you would save me; you would forgive my sin. (KA-BOOM!) I want you to know that I am taking you at your word, right here, right now. I believe you are telling me the truth! I am trusting you!

This is the kind of prayer that clings to God's grace. God has committed himself to honouring such a cry from the heart.

Grace is a gift, and a gift is always free. Not only do we need God's grace to be saved from the Lake of Fire, but as believers, we need God's grace to live daily as Christians. Peter was undoubtedly a believer, but he needed grace when he miserably failed.

So let us come boldly to the throne of our gracious God. There we will receive his mercy, and we will find grace to help us when we need it most.   Hebrews 4:16 NLT

Grace is a daily necessity for the believer, but clinging to grace is not easy for us even as believers. We need to be constantly reminded that God's grace is given freely. That's what makes it *grace*.

5 THE COMMAND

The Bible makes it abundantly clear that Yahweh is a God worthy of all of our love, all of our praise, all of our service. We must be careful to not treat him as a high-five, backslapping, feel-good, gushy-mushy, buddy-buddy kind of God. Nor are we to view him as being somewhat of a cranky, putting-off, leave-me-alone grouch—a grumpy God.

Yahweh, in all his majesty, is a God of perfect love and justice. We see love in his underserved grace; justice in his holy anger. In embracing his love for us, we should never treat lightly God's wrath towards sin. Yahweh is to be lifted up in our eyes, not brought down to our level.

This is very important as we discuss this subject of grace. Grace can be warped one way or the other. So how do we keep balanced?

In simple terms, we need to watch out for thoughts in our minds that would confuse or minimize, even belittle, God's love. Wrong thoughts on grace tend to gather around these ideas:

An Addition: We think in our minds, "God I am willing to trust you for salvation, but to be truly saved and to stay saved I know I need to be baptized, become a member of a church, give my money, pray often, et cetera."

Our respect and love for the Lord should motivate us to do good deeds, but we must never confuse faith and works as being one and the same. We are to serve the Lord because He alone is worthy, not because we can add to that worthiness. When we try to obtain God's favour through good living, we bring the grandeur of God's grace down to a human level.

For by grace you have been saved through faith, and that not of yourselves; it is the gift of God, not of works, lest anyone should boast.   Ephesians 2:8-9 NKJV

An Exchange. In the backroom of our minds we think, "God I will do 'this' for you if you do 'that' for me. What we are really saying is, "God, you save me and I will serve you."

Such thinking shows we either:

- don't understand the concept of grace, or...
- we are not resting in his grace.

Instead, we are treating Yahweh on a human level, as if our right living or good intentions are acceptable elements in negotiating God's good favour. We are being gripped by that "foxhole conversion" mentality we looked at in the last section. It is a view often built around a grumpy God that we feel we must appease. And if we don't succeed, we get "blown up!"

In contrast, the Bible tells us the sort of thinking that motivates genuine service:

> I beseech you therefore, brethren, by the mercies of God, that you present your bodies a living sacrifice, holy, acceptable to God, which is your reasonable service. And do not be conformed to this world, but be transformed by the renewing of your mind, that you may prove what is that good and acceptable and perfect will of God.　　Romans 12:1-2 NKJV

To truly honour God is not an exchange of services or a negotiated deal. Rather, it is reasonable service because he is worthy. It is because we trust, love and respect him that we serve him.

A Wrong Focus: This flawed understanding of grace can present itself in two different ways. We think:

1. God you are worthy, but I have this addiction, this loss, this problem (something viewed as too big for even God to resolve); or...

2. God you are worthy, but I am too. (This idea has gained prominence with the emphasis on self-esteem brought on by the fathers of modern psychology.)

But neither is right. Instead, we need to keep our interests, our eyes focused on Jesus every moment of every day. A.W. Tozer (1897-1963) was a pastor who wrote many years ago:

"The victorious Christian neither exalts nor downgrades himself. His interests have shifted from self to Christ. What he is or is not no longer concerns him. He believes that he has been crucified with Christ and is not willing either to praise or depreciate such a man."[2]

Read that quote again, slowly. It summarizes life for the believer so well that my wife and I put it on the wall for us to read and be reminded. It gives everything a proper perspective.

DOUBTS

Keeping our eyes off ourselves and on Jesus is a good life principle to remember when doubts enter our thinking. The Bible says that not long after the resurrection…

> …the eleven disciples went away into Galilee, into a mountain where Jesus had appointed them.
>
> And when they saw him, they worshipped him: but some doubted.
> Matthew 28:16-17 KJV

Now think about this for a moment. For three years the disciples had travelled with Jesus. They had shared life with him; they knew every word Jesus spoke, every action he took. It should not surprise us that they worshipped him, for he was worthy.

But then take note. Even after all the miracles, the resurrection, *everything*, some of the disciples still doubted. They doubted who Jesus was! They doubted what he had just done for them on the cross and in the tomb. They doubted him!

Doubt is just so human. Personally, when I hear Christians say they have never had doubts, it makes me wonder.

When we doubt, it is good to remember the young man who said to Jesus:

> "I do believe; help me overcome my unbelief!" Mark 9:24 NIV

This is a good prayer to pray when we go through times of doubt. It is also good to remember that doubt does not mean that all faith has fled. It just means we need to get into the Word of God faithfully, regularly, drinking heavily of God's grace, getting our eyes off ourselves and back on him. Only then will we know him. Only then will we trust, respect and love him.

THE GREAT COMMISSION

Even though the disciples still struggled with unbelief, Jesus focused their minds on the future. He gave them a command that has come to be known as the Great Commission.

> Then Jesus came up and said to them, "All authority in heaven and on earth has been given to me. Therefore go and make disciples of all nations, baptizing them in the name of the

Father and the Son and the Holy Spirit, teaching them to obey everything I have commanded you." Matthew 28:18-20 NET

The disciples, indeed all believers, were commissioned by Jesus to "go into all the world" and be part of seeing others become disciples. (We will be taking a deeper look at baptism shortly.) This commission to tell others was not to be a passing fad, but rather a lifelong lifestyle. Jesus completed his command with these words:

"And remember, I am with you always, to the end of the age."
Matthew 28:18-20 NET

How could this be? Jesus would soon be leaving the earth. The answer lay within the promise Jesus had given—the promise to send the Holy Spirit.

6 The Ascension

Beginning with that milestone in history, the Sunday when Jesus was resurrected…

He appeared to them over a period of forty days and spoke about the kingdom of God. Acts 1:3 NIV

For forty days Jesus remained on the earth.

He appeared to [Peter], then to the twelve. Then he appeared to more than five hundred of the brothers and sisters at one time, most of whom are still alive, though some have fallen asleep. Then he appeared to James, then to all the apostles.
1 Corinthians 15:5-7 NET

After his suffering, he showed himself to these men and gave many convincing proofs that he was alive. Acts 1:3 NIV

Distinction

Gathering them together, He commanded them not to leave Jerusalem, but to wait for what the Father had promised, "Which," He said, "you heard of from Me; for John baptized with water, but you will be baptized with the Holy Spirit not many days from now." Acts 1:4-5 NASB

Once again we see different types of baptisms; in this case, baptism with water and baptism with the Holy Spirit. They are not the same. Jesus was foretelling the soon arrival of the Holy Spirit on earth who would come in a special way.

So when they had come together, they asked him, "Lord, will you at this time restore the kingdom to Israel?" Acts 1:6 ESV

The disciples, being good Israelites, were wondering if Jesus was about to restore the monarchy that had existed in the time of King David, 1000 years earlier.

> *He said to them: "It is not for you to know the times or dates the Father has set by his own authority. But you will receive power when the Holy Spirit comes on you; and you will be my witnesses in Jerusalem, and in all Judea and Samaria, and to the ends of the earth."* Acts 1:7-8 NIV

I will briefly comment on three aspects in this verse:

1. **Power:** Once again Jesus was saying that when the Holy Spirit arrived, he would give them an inner strength they had never had before. Peter must have taken notice. He knew he needed it.

2. **Witnesses**: The disciples—indeed all believers—were to go everywhere telling others about this good news. It was something that was to be a hallmark of their lives—a lifelong lifestyle.

3. **Extent**: The message surrounding the empty cross and the empty tomb would travel from city to region, from region to country, and from country to the ends of the earth. For 2000 years the gospel has been doing just that.

BEFORE THEIR EYES

> *After he had said this, while they were watching, he was lifted up and a cloud hid him from their sight.* Acts 1:9 NET

Jesus ascended into Heaven. This was not an unseen, middle of the night spiritual experience. Jesus returned to Heaven in his glorified body—in full view of the disciples who were witnesses to that fact.

> *And while they were gazing into heaven as he went, behold, two men stood by them in white robes, and said, "Men of Galilee, why do you stand looking into heaven? This Jesus, who was taken up from you into heaven, will come in the same way as you saw him go into heaven."* Acts 1:10-11 ESV

The angels said Jesus would return again in a physical way, in the same way he had ascended. When that day comes...

> *The Lord himself will come down from heaven with a shout of command, with the voice of the archangel, and with the trumpet of God, and the dead in Christ will rise first. Then we who are alive, who are left, will be suddenly caught up together with them in the clouds to meet the Lord in the air. And so we will always be with the Lord. Therefore encourage one another with these words.* 1 Thessalonians 4:16-18 NET

The Bible calls the return of Jesus our "blessed hope." While we wait for that time, we have been given a job to do: being messengers of that hope.

> *For the grace of God that brings salvation has appeared to all men. It teaches us to say "No" to ungodliness and worldly passions, and to live self-controlled, upright and godly lives in this present age, while we wait for the **blessed hope**—the glorious appearing of our great God and Savior, Jesus Christ, who gave himself for us to redeem us from all wickedness and to purify for himself a people that are his very own, eager to do what is good.* Titus 2:11-14 NIV

Upper Room

After the ascension of Jesus from earth to Heaven, the disciples...

> *...returned to Jerusalem from the mountain called the Mount of Olives (which is near Jerusalem, a Sabbath day's journey away). When they had entered Jerusalem, they went to the upstairs room where they were staying. Peter and John, and James, and Andrew, Philip and Thomas, Bartholomew and Matthew, James son of Alphaeus and*

Simon the Zealot, and Judas son of James were there. All these continued together in prayer with one mind, together with the women, along with Mary the mother of Jesus, and his brothers.
Acts 1:12-14 NET

As instructed by Jesus, the disciples waited for the arrival of the Holy Spirit. The wait must have seemed long at times, but once again they had to trust the Lord to keep his word. In all there was…

…a gathering of about one hundred and twenty persons.
Acts 1:15 NASB

They would wait for ten days until Pentecost (the Feast of Weeks), the next big event on God's prophetic calendar.

WITNESSES, NOT LAWYERS

It is encouraging to see friends come to the same understanding of the Bible as we have. As we talk with them, we need to be patient in our approach and sensitive in what we say. We need not cram it down their throats. The Bible tells us to be witnesses, not lawyers. A witness testifies to what he knows to be true; a lawyer argues and tries to convince. See pages 286 and 287 for tools to help explain the Bible to people with non-biblical worldviews.

CHAPTER EIGHT

1 THE FEAST OF PENTECOST

After his resurrection Jesus remained on earth for 40 days. It was during this time that Jesus said to his disciples:

> "Do not leave Jerusalem, but wait there for what my Father promised, which you heard about from me. For John baptized with water, but you will be baptized with the Holy Spirit not many days from now."   Acts 1:4-5 NET

After Jesus ascended to Heaven, the disciples waited just as instructed. The "not many days" passed—ten exactly—and the Feast of Pentecost was upon them. As we saw before, this feast was called Pentecost, as the feast came exactly 50 days after the Feast of Firstfruits—the day that Jesus had resurrected.

Early Spring:
1. The Feast of Passover
2. The Feast of Unleavened Bread
3. The Feast of Firstfruits

Late Spring:
4. **The Feast of Pentecost**
   (also called the Feast of Weeks)

> Now when the day of Pentecost had come, they were all together in one place. Suddenly a sound like a violent wind blowing came from heaven and filled the entire house where they were sitting. And tongues spreading out like a fire appeared to them and came to rest on each one of them. Acts 2:1-3 NET

It is important to note that the disciples were not blown about with an actual wind or threatened with literal fire. Rather, a noise filled the house and it sounded like a great wind. The key word is *like*. In the same sense, the fire wasn't real, but only what appeared to be *like* fire rested on every one of them.

We saw before that wind and fire were powerful visual aids of God's presence. The sound of wind pointed directly to the Holy Spirit. Without doubt, the disciples were gripped with amazement.

> All of them were filled with the Holy Spirit and began to speak in other tongues as the Spirit enabled them. Acts 2:4 NIV

BABEL REVERSED

The disciples had not prayed or pleaded for the Holy Spirit to come. Rather, the Spirit had arrived simply because of God's plan and promise. The speaking in "tongues" happened quite unexpectedly as the Holy Spirit "enabled" them.

The tongues they spoke were actual languages, but languages they had never learned or studied. Another translation puts it this way:

> All of them were filled with the Holy Spirit, and they began to speak in other languages as the Spirit enabled them. Acts 2:4 NET

It was a temporary reversal of God's judgment at the Tower of Babel. This was a profound miracle—a supernatural event.

> Now there were staying in Jerusalem God-fearing Jews from every nation under heaven. Acts 2:5 NIV

These Jews had travelled from abroad to gather in Jerusalem for Pentecost—the Feast of Weeks. In the middle of their festivities, they had been shaken by an unbelievable sound—like a wind. Curiosity drove them to the source of the noise.

> And when this sound occurred, the crowd came together, and were bewildered because each one of them was hearing them speak in his own language. Acts 2:6 NASB

As they gathered, they heard amazing lessons taught in the native tongues of the regions from which they had travelled. Sixteen separate languages are mentioned.

> Completely baffled, they said, "Aren't all these who are speaking Galileans? And how is it that each one of us hears them in our own native language? Parthians, Medes, Elamites, and residents of Mesopotamia, Judea and Cappadocia, Pontus and the province of Asia, Phrygia and Pamphylia, Egypt and the parts of Libya near Cyrene, and visitors from Rome, both Jews and proselytes,[1] Cretans and Arabs—we hear them speaking in our own languages about the great deeds God has done!" Acts 2:7-11 NET

WONDERS OF GOD

The miraculous message they spoke declared the "great deeds God has done." It is likely the lesson included the details surrounding the death and resurrection of Christ, since later, after the language miracle was over, Peter explained the gospel using one of the local trade languages—either Greek or Aramaic.

A UNIQUE COMING

The Bible says that the gathered crowd were all...

> ...astounded and greatly confused, saying to one another, "What does this mean?" But others jeered at the speakers, saying, "They are drunk on new wine!"
>
> But Peter stood up with the eleven, raised his voice, and addressed them: "You men of Judea and all you who live in Jerusalem, know this and listen carefully to what I say. In spite of what you think, these men are not drunk, for it is only nine o'clock in the morning. But this is what was spoken about through the prophet Joel: 'And in the last days it will be,' God says, 'that I will pour out my Spirit on all people.'"
>
> *Acts 2:12-17 NET*

On a number of occasions Jesus had told the disciples that they would receive the Holy Spirit. It is doubtful they knew exactly what he meant. But now the Holy Spirit had arrived. This was such a singular event in God's calendar that he had set aside a whole feast to prophetically drive home its significance. The prophecy was now being fulfilled both visually and audibly. No one could have missed the arrival of the Holy Spirit.

What we see here parallels the coming of the second person of the Trinity—Jesus. We saw that Jesus, as a theophany, visited the earth numerous times in the Old Testament. However, none of those visits compared to his arrival in Bethlehem. When Jesus was placed in a manger, his arrival was accompanied by unique signs and was rightly understood as his first coming. You could not have missed it.

The same could now be said of the third person of the Trinity—the Holy Spirit. We saw that the Holy Spirit was active on earth in the Old Testament. However, none of this previous activity could be compared to his arrival at Pentecost. Nothing like this had ever happened before. We can rightly understand it as the Holy Spirit's official arrival on earth. And you couldn't have missed it.

2 THE BODY OF CHRIST

The day of Pentecost was the origin of something that had never existed before—the beginning of *the body of Christ.*

We need to gain an understanding of what this is all about, as it is a phrase used in Scripture and is common vocabulary among believers. Some of this may seem a little technical, but when you understand it, it will keep you from falling into common misinterpretations of the Bible. It is also a little awe-inspiring to get a glimpse of the inner workings of the Trinity. The phrase *body of Christ* is both rich in symbolism and practical in meaning.

SYMBOLISM

When we talk about the body of Christ, we are not referring to the physical body of Jesus. Rather, we are speaking of a group of people.

> *Now you are the body of Christ, and members individually.*
> 1 Corinthians 12:27 NKJV

The leader or head of this "body" is the Lord Jesus.

> *And God placed all things under his feet and appointed him to be head over...his body.* Ephesians 1:22-23 NIV

When the day of Pentecost dawned, the body of Christ consisted of 120 followers of Jesus gathered together, waiting in an upper room.

ONE-TIME EVENT

At Pentecost, the Lord Jesus baptized or placed the Holy Spirit into the body of Christ—the group of 120 believers. This was not water baptism. Rather, it was an event that John the Baptist had prophesied and Jesus had referred to often. Just ten days before, Jesus had told the disciples:

> *"John baptized with water, but you will be baptized with the Holy Spirit not many days from now."* Acts 1:5 ESV

This was a first-time, one-time event, and God, in the overall scheme of things, had seen fit to mark the official arrival of the Holy Spirit with a prophetic feast—the day of Pentecost.

The Baptism that Happened on Pentecost to 120 Jews

2000 years ago, on the day of Pentecost, Jesus sent the Holy Spirit from Heaven to earth, placing him into the believers gathered in the city of Jerusalem.

The Holy Spirit

The Body of Christ

Ongoing Events

Although Pentecost was a one-time, historical "baptism" event, the Bible speaks of another form of baptism that has continued down through the centuries. You must not confuse the two.

This other form of baptism occurs when individuals put their trust in Jesus as Saviour. At that point they become identified with Christ—as Christ-ones—and become members of that body which began on the day of Pentecost. It is unlikely they are aware of it, but that is what has happened—they have been placed into a huge family with other believers.

We will see in the next section that by the end of Pentecost, 3000 new believers had been added to this body. It has been growing ever since.

Specifically, it is the role of the Holy Spirit to add the new believer into the Body—the individual is placed or baptized into the body of Christ.

For by one Spirit are we all baptized into one body.
1 Corinthians 12:13 KJV

There is no water in this verse. It is something that happens at a spiritual level to every new believer, regardless of age or background. Think of it this way. As we saw in an earlier chapter, there are just two families you can be identified with.

The Baptism that has Happened Since Pentecost

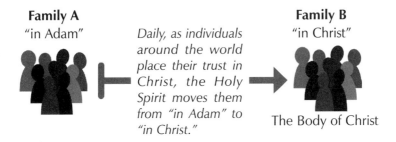

Family A
"in Adam"

Daily, as individuals around the world place their trust in Christ, the Holy Spirit moves them from "in Adam" to "in Christ."

Family B
"in Christ"

The Body of Christ

Once you were part of Family A, whatever that identity may have included—professor, plumber, priest or prostitute. But when you put your trust in Jesus, you were transferred from Family A to Family B—made up of those who belong to God's family, the body of Christ. The Holy Spirit did this transfer on your behalf the moment you believed.

As we saw before, you now have a new identity. In biblical terms you are now considered part of an "in" crowd—literally, you are viewed as being "in Christ."

This new identity does not come with biblical adjectives. Never does the Bible describe a Christian as radical, gay, straight, capitalist, socialized, right-wing, left-wing, liberal, conservative, struggling, triumphant, true—or any other adjective—Christian. What it does say is that a believer has a completely new identity, as one who is "in Christ." We belong to those who are "forgiven"—declared as righteous.

> *Do you not know that the unrighteous will not inherit the kingdom of God? Do not be deceived! The sexually immoral, idolaters, adulterers, passive homosexual partners, practicing homosexuals, thieves, the greedy, drunkards, the verbally abusive, and swindlers will not inherit the kingdom of God.* **Some of you once lived this way.** *But you were washed, you were sanctified, you were justified in the name of the Lord Jesus Christ and by the Spirit of our God.*   1 Corinthians 6:9-11 NET

This sample list of sins states what our past identity may have been. But it also declares clearly that it was something in the past. We now have a new identity as those who have been washed, sanctified, justified—all true of those who are now "in Christ."

Family A **Family B**
"in Adam" "in Christ"

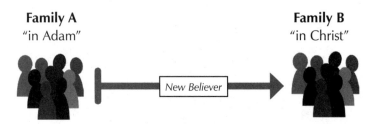

New Believer

The Body of Christ

This transfer from "in Adam" to "in Christ" can be difficult for friends to understand. They often don't understand. They cannot see anything outwardly simply because this move from Family A to Family B has all occurred on a spiritual level. To help make this clear, God introduced a visual aid to explain to our friends what has occurred to us. That visual aid is called *water baptism.*

Water baptism illustrates how the new believer is moved from the "in Adam" crowd to the "in Christ" family — the body of Christ. It provides a wonderful opportunity to explain to friends and family what happened when you trusted in Christ. It is a good time to explain the gospel itself, as well as the meaning of baptism. I will explain more on this in just a moment, but let me close this section with one final comment on Pentecost.

UP TILL NOW

Pentecost is a significant milestone in the Bible. Centuries before, Yahweh had Moses institute the Feast of Pentecost as a yearly celebration on the Jewish calendar. This was done to point to a future notable day in history when the Holy Spirit would expand his role in the world. At this stage in the story, we can say that day had finally arrived and the ancient prophecy had been fulfilled.

3 THE BAPTISM BY WATER

There is much confusion surrounding water baptism, so it deserves a more in-depth look. As I mentioned in the previous section, water baptism is significant since it illustrates something that cannot be seen with the eyes. It explains our new identity "in Christ."

As new believers, we simply took Jesus at his word, believing that he died in our place and was raised for our justification. When we trusted Christ, something happened on the spiritual plane that most new believers know nothing about.

> Do you not know that all of us who have been baptized into Christ Jesus were baptized into his death? We were buried therefore with him by baptism into death, in order that, just as Christ was raised from the dead by the glory of the Father, we too might walk in newness of life.
>
> For if we have been united with him in a death like his, we shall certainly be united with him in a resurrection like his.
>
> Romans 6:3-5 ESV

When we trusted in Christ, we identified with Jesus in his death and resurrection. At that moment, God the Holy Spirit moved us from "in Adam" to "in Christ," thus making us part of the body of Christ. The wonder of it all is that our "past" is past and our "now" is now — we have a new life in Christ. It is well said that water baptism is an outward act that illustrates an inner reality.

ADULT BAPTISM

Water baptism usually has several modes and whatever mode is used depends greatly on the church.

Sprinkling: Though this is the most common mode of baptizing an infant, sprinkling is also used with adults. The person performing the baptism dips their fingers in a basin of water and sprinkles the water on the head of the one being baptized.

Pouring: In this form of baptism, the head of the one being baptized is held over a basin. Water is then poured out of a pitcher onto the head.

Immersion: This form of baptism usually occurs in a river, lake or a specially designed water tank at the front of a church building. The one being baptized enters the water and stands waist deep with the one performing the baptism. The individual is then laid back or forward into the water, fully immersed (picturing death to the old life), and then lifted back up out of the water (picturing resurrection to a new life).[2] Immersion pictures how…

> We were buried…with him by baptism into death, in order that, just as Christ was raised from the dead by the glory of the Father, we too might walk in newness of life. Romans 6:4 ESV

Because immersion illustrates Jesus' death and resurrection so clearly, I am partial to this mode. I believe there is strong historical and biblical evidence for this being the form of baptism found in the Bible. As important as it is, I don't think the *mode* of baptism is nearly as significant as explaining the *reason* for baptism. Onlookers

need to understand that baptism is a visual aid explaining what Christ has done for a new believer by placing him or her into a new spiritual family. To me it is critical that the gospel be well-presented[3] and that the "why" of baptism be clearly explained. It is too easy for an unbeliever to confuse baptism with a weird rite used to join a religious "club."

If a young child understands the gospel, then he or she is old enough to be baptized, assuming parents are agreeable. This is different than infant baptism.

INFANT BAPTISM

Although infant baptism is quite common in some churches, one is hard-pressed to find it in the Bible. It does not illustrate the verses we have just read, thus parents do it solely based on the traditions of the church. Whatever meaning the organized church or clergy may want to give it, infant baptism would best be understood as a dedication by the parents to raise their child in a church setting.[4]

Probably one of the biggest difficulties with infant baptism is that a baby cannot understand the gospel message. And we know that it is only with understanding that a person can be saved from the consequences of sin.

Those who have been baptized as infants need to be careful how they explain to family their wish to be baptized as adults. Words such as these may help:

"Dad and Mom, I am honoured that you were concerned for my spiritual welfare as a child. My baptism as an infant showed you wanted me to grow up knowing about God. But now that I am an adult, it is important to me to let all my family and friends know that this is my desire as well. Would you do me the honour of attending my adult baptism?"

Remember, water baptism is a picture explaining an inner work of God. If family and friends are unnecessarily angry with you, it becomes counterproductive to the purpose of water baptism.

SUMMARY

Before a baptism, invite your friends and family to attend. At the baptism, the one leading the meeting should explain the gospel and then teach on what baptism "is" and "is not." The one being baptized should then be given an opportunity to say how he or she became a believer, assisted in this by answering certain questions that prompt a reply. Then the one performing the baptism will announce something along this line: "Upon the confession of your faith, I now baptize you in the name of the Father, the Son and the Holy Spirit." This is out of obedience to Jesus who said:

> *"Therefore go and make disciples of all nations, baptizing them in the name of the Father and of the Son and of the Holy Spirit, and teaching them to obey everything I have commanded you. And surely I am with you always, to the very end of the age."*   Matthew 28:19-20 NIV

Just remember: water baptism does not save a person from the eternal consequences of sin. It is only an illustration to help both you and the onlookers understand an inner reality.

4 THE LORD AND MESSIAH

On the day of Pentecost, a great crowd was gathered, drawn by the sound of the mighty wind and the miracle of unlearned languages. Peter stood up and addressed the crowd:

> *"Men of Israel, listen to this: Jesus of Nazareth was a man accredited by God to you by miracles, wonders and signs, which God did among you through him, as you yourselves know."*
> Acts 2:22 NIV

Peter made the point that he was not talking about unknown, obscure events done in a corner. The fact that Jesus had performed incredible miracles was not a secret. Those who had been healed or eaten multiplied fish were present and talking.

This seems to have been recognized by the secular historian, Josephus. Born at the time of Christ, he wrote late in the first century:

> *"Now, there was about this time Jesus, a wise man, if it be lawful to call him a man, for he was a doer of wonderful works —a teacher of such men as receive the truth with pleasure. He drew over to him both many of the Jews, and many of the Gentiles. He was Christ; and when Pilate, at the suggestion of the principal men amongst us, had condemned him to the cross, those that loved him at the first did not forsake him, for he appeared to them alive again the third day, as the divine prophets had foretold these and ten thousand other wonderful things concerning him; and the tribe of Christians, so named from him, are not extinct at this day."*[5]

ACCREDITED

Peter connected with this "knowing" audience. He continued:

> "This man was handed over to you by God's set purpose and foreknowledge; and you, with the help of wicked men, put him to death by nailing him to the cross. But God raised him from the dead, freeing him from the agony of death, because it was impossible for death to keep its hold on him."
>
> Acts 2:23-24 NIV

It had been only seven weeks since Jesus had been crucified and the news of a resurrection had kept the gossip mills alive. As Peter continued his message, he knew his audience was familiar with all these events.

> "This Jesus God raised up, and we are all witnesses of it. So then, exalted to the right hand of God, and having received the promise of the Holy Spirit from the Father, he has poured out what you both see and hear." Acts 2:32-33 NET

Peter, in a nutshell, explained what the wind, flames and tongues were all about. The Holy Spirit had arrived. But Peter was interested in more than an explanation. He applied his message—he pointed the finger. Read carefully, for within these few words you see that Peter, the common coward, had become a man of unusual courage.

> "Therefore let all the house of Israel know beyond a doubt that God has made this Jesus whom you crucified both Lord and Christ." Acts 2:36 NET

Peter did not pull any punches. He made it clear that it was his audience[6] that had nailed Jesus to the cross.

GOD HIMSELF

However, Peter's message went even further by stating that Jesus was not only the *Christ* but also the *Lord,* which in the context of that day could have been understood as none other than Yahweh himself.[7] To say this would have taken immense courage, as the Jews were hypersensitive about any man, such as Jesus, being called God. They could have killed Peter, but…

> …when they heard this they were cut to the heart, and said to Peter and the rest of the apostles, "Brothers, what shall we do?" Acts 2:37 ESV

The Holy Spirit was convicting them of their sin and the truthfulness of what they had heard. They were now convinced that Jesus was both Lord and Christ—that he was both Yahweh and Messiah—but they were uncertain as to what that meant for them.

> *"Brothers, what shall we do?"* Acts 2:37 ESV

Peter pointed out that they needed a change of mind—they needed to repent. Previously they had rejected Jesus and crucified him. Now they needed to recognize him for who he was—the Messiah and God. They needed a Saviour. We know they changed their minds by the way they embraced Peter's message. The response was dramatic.

> *Those who believed what Peter said were baptized and added to the church that day—about 3,000 in all.* Acts 2:41 NLT

Three thousand new believers joined the body of Christ. The reality of that spiritual event was expressed in an outward act—water baptism.

THE ASSEMBLY

These believers were collectively referred to as an *assembly* or a *church*. The word *church* comes from Koine Greek, meaning "called-out ones" or "belonging to the Lord." Scripture says that these people...

> *...were continually devoting themselves to the apostles' teaching and to fellowship, to the breaking of bread and to prayer.*
>
> Acts 2:42 NASB

Often when we use the word *church* we are referring to a physical building, however the Bible never uses the word that way. Rather, it is used to refer to believers collectively—as a body. It can be used two ways:

1. The Local Church: This is an assembly of believers who meet together on a regular basis in one area. The Bible speaks of...

> *...the church at Antioch.* Acts 13:1 ESV
>
> *...the church at Jerusalem.* Acts 11:22 NASB

In urban centres there may be many local churches.

2. The Universal Church: This church consists of all believers throughout every century, regardless of their place on the globe. Only those who have put their trust in Christ can claim to belong to this church. The only time this group will be assembled together in one place is when Jesus returns again.

THE HEAD

The Lord Jesus is in charge of this assembly.

> *And God placed all things under his feet and appointed him*
> *to be head over everything for the church, which is his body.*
> *Ephesians 1:22-23 NIV*

> *And he is the head of the body, the church; he is the beginning*
> *and the firstborn [first resurrected] from among the dead, so*
> *that in everything he might have the supremacy. Colossians 1:18 NIV*

Note that the "church" is the "body of Christ." The terms are synonymous—they refer to the same group. The church or body is also referred to as the *Bride of Christ.*

As the sun set on the day of Pentecost, the body of Christ consisted of over 3000 Jews and converts to Judaism. This was the beginning.

5 THE UNIVERSAL CHURCH

Before we move on in the story, we need to take a short look at the way we use the words *Christian* and *church*. Without this background, it may be very confusing.

CHRISTIAN

From a biblical perspective, the word *Christian* means "Christ-one" or "belonging to the household of Christ." It is synonymous with the words *saved* and *believer*. It refers to those who, recognizing their sinfulness, have come to the point of trusting solely in Jesus…

> *The Lamb of God, who takes away the sin of the world!*
> *John 1:29 NKJV*

Originally, it was a word rich in meaning to be used of all genuine believers, synonymous with the body of Christ.

> *And the disciples were called Christians first in Antioch.*
> *Acts 11:26 KJV*

But that has all changed. The word *Christian* has been hijacked and abused to the point where it has lost almost all of its original meaning. Over the centuries it has been used of kings, local rulers, crusaders, national governments, nations and various religious empires—groups that have perpetuated terrible crimes in the name of Christ. Frankly, when I hear people call themselves "Christians," my initial reaction is to be very cautious until I can verify that they are using it in the sense of its original biblical meaning. Sadly, the world has far more false or cultural Christians than genuine ones.

Church

The same could be said of the word *church*. Few understand it to be synonymous with the body of Christ. Most think of it merely as a building or as a religious denomination.

The so-called "Christian" or "church community" breaks itself down into three major camps: Roman Catholic, Protestant and Orthodox. Alhough you will find genuine believers in all three communities, this does not mean that the majority who attend these churches are true, born-from-above believers. Far from it. These three religious communities are rife with those who are deeply confused or who deny the core essentials of the true biblical church. (More on those essentials in the next section.) It is important to understand that, although the world has many genuine local churches, there are far more that are deep in error, often having no connection to the true body of Christ at all.

The Universal Church

To add to the confusion, there is an obscure cult with the name *The Universal Church*. I am not referring to them. Rather, I want to take a brief look at the true universal Church, from the biblical perspective. Simon Peter wrote:

> As you come to [Jesus], the living Stone—rejected by men but chosen by God and precious to him.   1 Peter 2:4 NIV

Peter, drawing from rich Old Testament illustrations, stated that Jesus was like a living stone—a solid rock. Referring to all believers, he continued:

> You also, like living stones, are being built into a spiritual house.
> 1 Peter 2:5 NIV

He was using an analogy. Peter was comparing the universal church to a physical building with all genuine believers down through the ages being part of that spiritual building. Jesus was the keystone who holds this spiritual building—the universal church—all together. With that in mind, Peter says:

> But you are...a people belonging to God, that you may declare the praises of him who called you out of darkness into his wonderful light.   1 Peter 2:9 NIV

God has given us a privileged position, as members of the true church, to share the good news about Jesus Christ with those who do not yet know him as Saviour.

> *Therefore, we are ambassadors for Christ, God making his appeal through us. We implore you on behalf of Christ, be reconciled to God.*　　　2 Corinthians 5:20 ESV

In the church, this is called *evangelism*. The word finds its roots in Koine Greek and was associated with proclaiming a message. Unfortunately, the word *evangelism* has been badly twisted from its original meaning. Whatever its modern meaning, we still need to be ambassadors in the original sense of the word—bearers of good news. Just like Peter on the day of Pentecost, we share the good news because...

> *Once you were not a people, but now you are God's people; once you had not received mercy, but now you have received mercy.*　　　1 Peter 2:10 ESV

It is only right to share the gospel, which is literally, "the good news." It is selfish to keep it to ourselves. With all this in mind, Simon Peter wrote:

> *Dear friends, I urge you, as aliens and strangers in the world, to abstain from sinful desires, which war against your soul. Live such good lives among the pagans that, though they accuse you of doing wrong, they may see your good deeds and glorify God on the day he visits us.*　　　1 Peter 2:11-12 NIV

Sharing the gospel is the church's primary task, but with it we are to care about and meet the physical needs of people around us. Historically, believers as part of the universal church have been at the forefront of many social agendas: starting schools, founding hospitals and reaching out to the homeless. It was believers like William Wilberforce and John Newton who fought slavery, based on the principle that all mankind was created in the image of God. To their shame, the majority of believers did not support them, basing their view of slavery on the popular culture of the time. Involvement in alleviating social ills around the world is still an active part of church life. Drilling wells, sponsoring orphanages, resisting the sex trade, setting up clinics, are just a few roles found in active church life. Jesus said:

> *"Let your light so shine before men, that they may see your good works and glorify your Father in heaven."* Matthew 5:16 NKJV

We do good works, not to be praised by men, but so that God will be exalted. He is the one who gives us strength to help others.

> And God is able to make all grace abound to you, so that having all sufficiency in all things at all times, you may abound in every good work. *2 Corinthians 9:8 ESV*

As members of the universal church, we follow in the footsteps of an immense crowd who have gone on before. To all of us the apostles left this prayer.

> And we pray this in order that you may live a life worthy of the Lord and may please him in every way: bearing fruit in every good work, growing in the knowledge of God, being strengthened with all power according to his glorious might. *Colossians 1:10-11 NIV*

6 THE LOCAL CHURCH

All believers belong to the body of Christ, the universal church. But when any part of this body gathers together, they must meet somewhere as a local church.[8] The early believers met in whatever places were available—homes, synagogues and the Jewish Temple. The Bible states no specific building is necessary: a group of believers can meet beside a river, under a tree and you don't even need the river or the tree! In countries where Christians are persecuted, they may resort to secrecy when they meet, often in homes or in barns. From a biblical perspective, where you gather is not important.

What is important is that you meet. The Bible says:

> Let us not give up meeting together, as some are in the habit of doing, but let us encourage one another—and all the more as you see the Day [of Jesus' return] approaching. *Hebrews 10:25 NIV*

The Bible is clear that we need other believers in our lives to encourage us as we travel on our spiritual journey. We need what the early church called *fellowship*.

THE STYLE

New believers attending various churches can be bewildered by the variety of meeting styles. On a basic level, meetings—or what are called *services*—include prayer, singing and teaching, but the way each group conducts those events can differ greatly. Services can range from those heavy with ceremony to those that have very little structure.

The Bible gives liberty for both; neither is right or wrong. That being said, Scripture does warn us against both empty ritualism and mystical confusion. When assembled, we are told that…

>...all things should be done decently and in order.
>
> 1 Corinthians 14:40 ESV

We are to pray with meaning, not just mumbled memorized words. We need to believe the songs we sing, not just mouth empty words. We are to respect the Lord for who he is and not let spontaneity run wild. Pandemonium must not reign. Such confusion distracts from a genuine focus on the Lord. Many churches find a culturally appropriate balance between structure and spontaneity. If you don't feel comfortable in a church because of its style of service, then try to find another one to attend. It is not helpful to you spiritually to sit there and be distracted or critical.

THE LEADERSHIP

There is a confusing array of terms used of church leadership: from bishop to vicar, reverend to priest. If you want to talk to someone in authority, just ask to speak to a church leader who will refer you to the right person.

From a biblical point of view, the Bible only mentions two leadership roles in the local church: elder and deacon. Elders and deacons are leaders by example. They are Bible teachers, peacemakers, prayer leaders and visitors of the sick. They are decision-makers. Their role is not to be taken lightly and should be respected. The term *pastor* (literally, *shepherd*) is commonly used of an elder who employs his time, usually full time, in caring for the church flock.

THE TEACHING

Another issue that bewilders new believers is the broad spectrum of different types of churches. The defining line between most church groups is something called *doctrine*—what they teach. It defines what a particular group believes as true, what the early church called…

>...the apostles' teaching. Acts 2:42 NASB

Many churches have differences of opinions over non-critical doctrines, but would strongly agree on the Core Essentials listed on page 181.

When you first attend a church, ask for their *Statement of Faith* or *Doctrinal Statement*. If the Core Essentials are missing or disagree with their Statement of Faith, then ask why. Be fully prepared to go and find another church. Be cautious of any church that downplays doctrine. Doctrine does divide, for good reason, but it also unites in a marvellous way. It is critical to your spiritual journey that you find a good church.

Summary

1. The local church is a place to learn more about the Bible, becoming grounded in the Word.

2. The local church is a place to gather together and remember what Christ has done for us on the cross, commemorated in two ordinances: water baptism and the Lord's Supper, which we will be looking at in the next section.

3. The local church is a place to be encouraged and held accountable by other believers as everyone seeks to live a godly life.

4. The local church is a place to team up with other believers as part of the universal church, to reach out in evangelism and social endeavours.

Many local churches of various backgrounds strongly agree on the Core Essentials. Upon these, we should never compromise — not even for one of them.

However, local churches can differ on non-essentials, sometimes so strongly that they form separate groups. These groups are called denominations. At times it seems needful, but even then, believers can disagree without being disagreeable.

The Universal Church	The Local Church
A spiritual body, comprising all believers, now living in Heaven or still on earth (Ephesians 3:15)	A physical group, comprising a limited number of believers, now living on earth (Philippians 1:1)
The only time all will be assembled in one place will be in Heaven (Hebrews 12:22-23)	Assemble regularly, probably weekly, in a local meeting place (1 Corinthians 14:23)
Led by the Great Shepherd, the Lord Jesus Christ (John 10:14-16)	Led by undershepherds: elders (pastors), deacons (1 Peter 5:2)

THE CORE ESSENTIALS

1. **The Holy Scriptures**: We believe the 66 books found in the Old and New Testaments to be the inspired, infallible Word of God, inerrant in the original writings.

2. **The Godhead**: We believe in one God, existing eternally in three persons—Father, Son and Holy Spirit—identical in nature, power and glory.

3. **The Person and Work of Christ**: We believe that Jesus, the eternal Son, became man without ceasing to be God, born of the Virgin Mary, died a substitutionary death on the cross, providing forgiveness of sin and justification for all who trust in him. His resurrection and ascension were both literal and physical. He now lives in Heaven, as Intercessor and Advocate for all who believe.

4. **The Person and Work of the Holy Spirit**: We believe the Holy Spirit convicts the world of sin, regenerates, baptizes all believers into the body of Christ, indwells, seals and guides them unto the day of Christ's return.

5. **The Personality of Satan**: We believe Satan is an angelic being, created perfect, but now evil, opposed to God and his people. He shall be eternally punished in the Lake of Fire.

6. **The Nature of Man**: We believe that man was created in the image of God, but having fallen in sin, is now alienated from God, unable to remedy his lost condition.

7. **The Nature of Salvation**: We believe that salvation is a gift, received apart from any merit of our own, and is ours only by personal faith in the person and work of the Lord Jesus.

8. **The Church**: We believe the Church is comprised of believing Jews and Gentiles, with Christ as the one and only head.

9. **The Eternal State**: We believe in the resurrection of all mankind; the saved to eternal life, the unsaved to everlasting punishment.

10. **The Future**: We believe in the bodily return of Jesus Christ at His second coming.

7 THE LORD'S SUPPER

As we have seen, the Lord left minimal directives as to how and where his church should gather. However, he did give two orders or ordinances:

1. The first one is water baptism.

2. The second one is commonly called *Communion*, the *Lord's Supper*, the *Breaking of Bread* or *Eucharist*. The word *Eucharist* comes from Greek (eukharistia), which means "thanksgiving and gratitude."[9]

This second ordinance is a memorial instituted by Jesus, built around his prophetic fulfillment of the Old Testament Passover.

> *For I received from the Lord that which I also delivered to you: that the Lord Jesus on the same night in which He was betrayed took bread; and when He had given thanks, He broke it and said, "Take, eat; this is My body which is broken for you; do this in remembrance of Me." In the same manner He also took the cup after supper, saying, "This cup is the new covenant in My blood. This do, as often as you drink it, in remembrance of Me."*

> *For as often as you eat this bread and drink this cup, you proclaim the Lord's death till He comes. 1 Corinthians 11:23-26 NKJV*

This commemorative "meal" consists of two physical elements: a small bit of bread and a sip of wine or juice. The nature of the two elements is not important. I have been in parts of the world where sweet potato and water were used—it was all they had. It is what those elements represent that is significant.

The bread is a reminder that the body of the sinless Jesus was "broken" for us on the cross. The wine is a reminder that his blood was spilled in death—that he died in our place as our substitute.

The bread and the wine are nothing more than that—bread and wine. They do not change into the physical body and blood of the Lord Jesus. They are only visual aids to help us remember what Jesus did for us on the cross.

A decade after Pentecost, Peter wrote:

> For you know that it was not with perishable things such as silver or gold that you were redeemed from the empty way of life handed down to you from your forefathers, but with the precious blood of Christ, a lamb without blemish or defect.
>
> 1 Peter 1:18-19 NIV

PRACTICAL ASPECTS

Remembering the Lord's Supper is an ordinance that believers are to take part in until the Lord returns. Some churches or assemblies do this every Sunday, others once a month

How this "meal" is commemorated within a given local church does differ. The Bible gives no specific instructions, so there is plenty of room for variety. There are a couple of different ways the bread is served:

- **Individual Pieces**: With this method, a plate with small, precut pieces of bread, crackers or wafers are passed out.

- **Common Loaf**: The "common loaf" is the size you would feed a family. When the loaf is offered to you, you break off a small piece for yourself.

The wine[10] is also dispensed to an assembly in a couple of ways:

- **Individual Cup**: With this method, a special platter is passed up and down the rows of believers. This platter has many small cups in it, each filled with juice or wine. As the platter comes by, you select one cup.

- **Common Cup**: This method is used less, but with the "common cup" approach, all believers take a little sip out of the same large cup. If you find yourself in a church where only the leader drinks the wine, then seek another church. This is an ordinance in which every believer should participate.

With both of the above methods, you either eat the bread and drink the wine immediately after being served, or wait until all have been served and then partake together when instructed.

Observing the Lord's Supper in an unfamiliar church can be a little intimidating the first time. Just remember what it is all about—it is a time to remember the Lord. Watch what others are doing and you will learn how that particular group observes this commemorative "meal." Usually when I am given one of the elements, I take a moment, close my eyes to cut out distractions, and then pray, thanking the Lord for his sacrifice. It is a time just between God and myself.

The breaking of the bread service may be interspersed with singing, Scripture reading, prayer and others sharing what they have been learning from the Bible about the wonderful person and redemptive work of Christ. When people share like this, it is called a *testimony*. It can be a real precious time, as one is drawn back to the core of our spiritual lives—the wonder of the Creator paying our sin-debt on a cross. It is a profound reminder of the Lord's special love for us.

THE LAST DAYS

On the day of Pentecost…

> …Peter stood up with the Eleven, raised his voice and addressed the crowd: "…In the last days, God says, I will pour out my Spirit on all people."   Acts 2:14,17 NIV

What did Peter mean by "last days"? The Scriptures make it very clear that the last days began with the first coming of Jesus.

> Long ago, at many times and in many ways, God spoke to our fathers by the prophets, but in these last days he has spoken to us by his Son.   Hebrews 1:1-2 ESV

It is apparent from this passage that "these last days" began when Jesus appeared at his first coming. The "last days" has continued to this day, 2000 years later.

There may be such a thing as the last days of "the last days"—the period of time right before the Lord's return.

> But mark this: There will be terrible times in the last days. People will be lovers of themselves, lovers of money, boastful, proud, abusive, disobedient to their parents, ungrateful, unholy, without love, unforgiving, slanderous, without self-control, brutal, not lovers of the good, treacherous, rash, conceited, lovers of pleasure rather than lovers of God—having a form of godliness but denying its power.   2 Timothy 3:1-5 NIV

Although this may be the prevailing spirit in the last days of the last days, it is hard to make a dogmatic case since such wickedness has gone on for 2000 years. I tend to believe we are in the last days of the last days, but we must be careful to not set dates or "squeeze" Bible verses to make that point. It is wise to plan as if we will live until death, but also live our lives today as if it were the "last days." In each generation we should view life as Simon Peter wrote 2000 years ago:

> The end of all things is near. Therefore be clear minded and self-controlled so that you can pray.   1 Peter 4:7 NIV

CHAPTER NINE

1 THE BEGGAR

It was not long after Pentecost when…

…Peter and John were going up to the temple at the time for prayer, at three o'clock in the afternoon. And a man lame from birth was being carried up, who was placed at the temple gate called "the Beautiful Gate" every day so he could beg for money from those going into the temple courts. When he saw Peter and John about to go into the temple courts, he asked them for money. Peter looked directly at him (as did John) and said, "Look at us!" So the lame man paid attention to them, expecting to receive something from them. But Peter said, "I have no silver or gold, but what I do have I give you. In the name of Jesus Christ the Nazarene, stand up and walk!" Then Peter took hold of him by the right hand and raised him up, and at once the man's feet and ankles were made strong.

Acts 3:1-7 NET

This was a Class-A miracle. This man had an obvious and well-known handicap. It wasn't an ailment hidden from view, such as a headache or a stomach condition. Peter didn't pray for the man and then send him to the local physician. Rather, right then and there, the man was healed instantly. The beggar…

…jumped up, stood and began walking around, and he entered the temple courts with them, walking and leaping and praising God.

Acts 3:8 NET

We see here the true purpose behind a miracle—it should cause people to praise God, not the miracle worker.

All the people saw him walking and praising God, and they recognized him as the man who used to sit and ask for donations at the Beautiful Gate of the temple, and they were filled with astonishment and amazement at what had happened to him.

While the man was hanging on to Peter and John, all the people, completely astounded, ran together to them in the covered walkway called Solomon's Portico.

Acts 3:9-11 NET

Typical to humanity, anything out of the ordinary draws a crowd.

When Peter saw this, he said to them: "Men of Israel, why does this surprise you? Why do you stare at us as if by our own power or godliness we had made this man walk? The

> *God of Abraham, Isaac and Jacob, the God of our fathers,*
> *has glorified his servant Jesus."*   Acts 3:12-13 NIV

Remember, this was happening in the Jewish Temple—it was a Jewish crowd. Knowing that, Peter drew on their rich understanding of the Old Testament to explain to them what was happening. He then pointed out that they were the same ones who had taken Jesus, and…

> *"…handed him over to be killed, and you disowned him before*
> *Pilate, though he had decided to let him go. You disowned*
> *the Holy and Righteous One and asked that a murderer be*
> *released to you."*   Acts 3:13-14 NIV

Pilate had offered to release Jesus as a Passover goodwill gesture, but instead the people demanded the release of Barabbas, a convicted murderer. Guilty Barabbas went free while innocent Jesus died. Peter told the audience:

> *"You killed the Originator of life, whom God raised from the*
> *dead. To this fact we are witnesses!"*   Acts 3:15 NET

THE RESURRECTION

This could not be easily denied. If Jesus were dead in the tomb, then a brief walk to the gravesite would remove all debate. The Pharisees would have been happy to conduct a tour. But they couldn't. The tomb was definitely empty.

No doubt, Peter's audience had heard the story being perpetuated by the Jewish leaders. It had only been a couple of months since the terrified guards reported that the tomb was empty. The Jewish leaders had told the guards:

> *"You are to say, 'His disciples came by night and stole Him*
> *away while we were asleep.' And if this should come to*
> *the governor's ears, we will win him over and keep you*
> *out of trouble."*   Matthew 28:13-14 NASB

The guards were offered a lot of money.

> *And they took the money and did as they had been instructed;*
> *and this story was widely spread among the Jews, and is to*
> *this day.*   Matthew 28:15 NASB

But any thinking person had a lot of questions.

How could anyone slip past vigilant Roman guards, men who faced certain execution if they failed in their duties? And if the disciples had robbed the grave, then why weren't they being arrested? Besides, it was a known fact that the disciples were in no frame of mind to steal the body. They were terrified and hiding after the crucifixion, one even denying that he knew Jesus.

As to the guards sleeping, was it really credible that all the guards would snooze at the same time? And if they did, how was it that not even one of them was awakened by the grinding removal of the massive stone that sealed the tomb? Would grave robbers really go to such lengths to unwrap grave clothes and then neatly place them back in the tomb? And if the guards were all asleep, then how did they know that it was the disciples who stole the body? The whole story was riddled with holes.

It was also obvious that the authorities had not removed the body or they would have produced it as evidence the moment Peter began his discourse. No, what Peter was saying had the ring of truth to it. Jerusalem was full of witnesses who said Jesus had come back to life. No one could deny it.

EVIDENCE

Peter continued his message, pointing to the beggar.

> "Through faith in the name of Jesus, this man was healed—and you know how crippled he was before. Faith in Jesus' name has healed him before your very eyes.
>
> "Friends, I realize that what you and your leaders did to Jesus was done in ignorance. But God was fulfilling what all the prophets had foretold about the Messiah—that he must suffer these things." Acts 3:16-18 NLT

Yes, it was true that they had crucified Jesus, but now knowing the facts, they needed to have a change of mind about who Jesus was and what he was all about. Peter told them:

> "Repent therefore, and turn again, that your sins may be blotted out." Acts 3:19 ESV

Using the Old Testament Scriptures, Peter reinforced his message by quoting the ancient prophets. He wrapped it up by stating:

> "And you are heirs of the prophets and of the covenant God made with your fathers. He said to Abraham, 'Through your offspring all peoples on earth will be blessed.'" Acts 3:25 NIV

Peter referred to the promises Yahweh had given Abraham long ago. Now they were being fulfilled, for through Jesus all nations of the earth would be blessed.

INTERRUPTED

> *While Peter and John were speaking to the people, they were confronted by the priests, the captain of the Temple guard, and some of the Sadducees. These leaders were very disturbed that Peter and John were teaching the people that through Jesus there is a resurrection of the dead. They arrested them and, since it was already evening, put them in jail until morning.*
> *Acts 4:1-3 NLT*

Peter and John may have landed in jail...

> *...but many of those who had listened to the message believed, and the number of the men came to about five thousand.*
> *Acts 4:4 NET*

Well over 8000 Jews now belonged to the body of Christ. The church was growing by leaps and bounds.

2 THE THREATS

The healing of the beggar at the Temple gate had unleashed a whole chain of events that ended with Peter and John in prison.

> *On the next day, their rulers, elders, and experts in the law came together in Jerusalem. Annas the high priest was there, and Caiaphas, John, Alexander, and others who were members of the high priest's family. After making Peter and John stand in their midst, they began to inquire, "By what power or by what name did you do this?"*
> *Acts 4:5-7 NET*

The high priest and his family did not believe that Jesus was anything more than a fraud. It didn't enter their minds that he might be the key to what had just occurred. What they could not deny was a Class-A miracle.

> *Then Peter, filled with the Holy Spirit, replied, "Rulers of the people and elders, if we are being examined today for a good deed done to a sick man – by what means this man was healed – let it be known to all of you and to all the people of Israel that by the name of Jesus Christ the Nazarene whom you crucified, whom God raised from the dead, this man stands before you healthy. This Jesus is the stone that was rejected by you, the builders, that has become the cornerstone."*
> *Acts 4:8-11 NET*

Peter was referring to a portion of Jewish Scripture the priests would have known well. He was saying that Jesus was the cornerstone—the stone that anchored all the other stones. Peter drove home the point by reminding them that they were the very men who had rejected him. Peter went on:

> "And there is salvation in no one else, for there is no other name under heaven given among people by which we must be saved."
>
> Acts 4:12 NET

The Bible is very clear on this. Jesus taught:

> "I am the way, and the truth, and the life. No one comes to the Father except through me."
>
> John 14:6 ESV

It is only Yahweh—the LORD—who can provide salvation from the consequences of sin. That name, which is above every name, is fundamentally linked to the name Jesus by the will of God himself.

> Jesus: Who, being in very nature God, did not consider equality with God something to be grasped, but made himself nothing, taking the very nature of a servant, being made in human likeness. And being found in appearance as a man, he humbled himself and became obedient to death—even death on a cross! Therefore God exalted him to the highest place and gave him the name that is above every name, that at the name of Jesus every knee should bow, in heaven and on earth and under the earth, and every tongue confess that Jesus Christ is Lord, to the glory of God the Father.
>
> Philippians 2:5-11 NIV

COURAGE

> When they saw the boldness of Peter and John, and discovered that they were uneducated and ordinary men, they were amazed and recognized these men had been with Jesus.
>
> Acts 4:13 NET

It had only been weeks since Peter, who with a clumsy oath, had denied Jesus to a household servant. Now here he was, standing before some of the most powerful men in the land, eloquently defending his Lord. Peter had gone from a common coward to a man of immense courage. What made the difference?

The answer is found in the story. On the night before He was crucified, Jesus promised the coming of the Holy Spirit, calling him the Helper. He said:

> "When the Helper comes, whom I will send to you from the Father, that is the Spirit of truth who proceeds from the Father,

He will testify about Me, and you will testify also, because you have been with Me from the beginning." John 15:26-27 NASB

And now, here was...

...Peter, filled with the Holy Spirit. Acts 4:8 NKJV

And he was testifying with great courage.

The change happened on the day of Pentecost. Although Peter, by nature, was a coward before the cross, after Pentecost his display of courage was the direct result of the Holy Spirit being present in his life. The courage he exhibited was from the Lord, not Peter. The Holy Spirit was strengthening him as an ever-present Helper and Guide.

This change in Peter was not only true for him, but it has been true of all believers ever since. We who have been born again now have the sacred presence of the Holy Spirit.

The Spirit of God dwells in you. But if anyone does not have the Spirit of Christ, he does not belong to Him.
Romans 8:9 NASB

The same inner Guide who directed Peter on that day long ago, lives with us and is available to all who belong to Christ.

Undeniable

Peter's courage was so remarkable that the Bible says those interrogating him were astonished...

...since they could see the man who had been healed standing there with them, there was nothing they could say. So they ordered them to withdraw from the Sanhedrin and then conferred together. "What are we going to do with these men?" they asked. "Everybody living in Jerusalem knows they have done an outstanding miracle, and we cannot deny it. But to stop this thing from spreading any further among the people, we must warn these men to speak no longer to anyone in this name." Acts 4:14-17 NIV

It is notable that they did not deny Peter's defense. They recognized the reality of a Class-A miracle. But in their pride, they did not humble themselves and confess Jesus as Messiah.

And they called them and commanded them not to speak at all nor teach in the name of Jesus. Acts 4:18 KJV

You may not be aware of it but to this day, all over the world, powerful leaders are imposing the same restrictions on Christians—to not teach in the name of Jesus.

> But Peter and John replied, "Judge for yourselves whether it is right in God's sight to obey you rather than God. For we cannot help speaking about what we have seen and heard."
>
> Acts 4:19-20 NIV

WHAT COURAGE!

> After threatening them further, they released them, for they could not find how to punish them on account of the people, because they were all praising God for what had happened. For the man, on whom this miraculous sign of healing had been performed, was over forty years old.
>
> When they were released, Peter and John went to their fellow believers and reported everything the high priests and the elders had said to them. When they heard this, they raised their voices to God with one mind and said, "Master of all, you who made the heaven, the earth, the sea, and everything that is in them, who said by the Holy Spirit through your servant David our forefather,
>
> "'Why do the nations rage, and the peoples plot foolish things? The kings of the earth stood together, and the rulers assembled together, against the Lord and against his Christ.'
>
> "For indeed both Herod and Pontius Pilate, with the Gentiles and the people of Israel, assembled together in this city against your holy servant Jesus, whom you anointed, to do as much as your power and your plan had decided beforehand would happen. And now, Lord, pay attention to their threats, and grant to your servants to speak your message with great courage."
>
> Acts 4:21-29 NET

I like the focus of their prayer—the need for courage! And God answered their request.

> And they were all filled with the Holy Spirit, and they spoke the word of God with boldness.
>
> Acts 4:31 NKJV

Repentance

Peter had told the Jewish leaders to...

> *"Repent therefore, and turn back, that your sins may be blotted out."*
> Acts 3:19 ESV

A dictionary[1] definition for repentance reads like this: *Repentance: deep sorrow, compunction, or contrition for a past sin, wrongdoing, or the like.*

But according to the Bible, you can have deep sorrow for your sin and still not be repentant. To understand biblical repentance, it is helpful to make a distinction between the root of repentance and its fruit.

The Root	The Fruit
Thoughts that are unseen	Actions that are seen
The New Testament, which was written in Greek, uses a word for *repent* that means "to have a change of mind." The Old Testament, which was written in Hebrew, uses a word that carries the idea of "returning" as in "returning home." (The Israelites were to *repent* or spiritually *return home* to God.)	A person who once opposed the truth, now embraces the truth. In contrast to before, he or she now talks differently about Scripture, Christ, God, sin, death and the afterlife. This change in perspective can and should result in godly behaviour. It can also include regret and deep sorrow.

The essence of repentance is a change of mind—that is the *root*. When you read the context—the story surrounding the word—you understand just what the change of mind was all about and how it affected the person involved—that being the *fruit*. It is very important that any claim of repentance be driven by the root, as many people can adjust their behaviour to look "righteous" but have never experienced true biblical repentance. Many religious people live exemplary lives, but they have never changed their minds about who Jesus is and what he has done for them. They are just extra good at changing their behaviour.

As one of the disciples, Judas Iscariot lived such a good life that the other eleven did not know it was he who would betray Jesus. The fruit of his life looked good, but most Bible scholars would say Judas' root thinking never changed — he never trusted in Jesus. One might say he showed fruit that would normally have been consistent with repentance, but he never experienced the root.

It is also helpful to remember that fruit is something that is accomplished by God, not something we conjure up within ourselves. Sometimes it is evident immediately; other times seen a little later, but always something of God's doing. Peter was initially a coward, but then went on to have great courage. It was God who effected the change.

It is always right to have a change of mind about sin, even if we don't feel bad about it. We may actually have enjoyed the sin, but when confronted in our hearts about the sin, we need to have a change of heart and line our minds up with God's point of view. This is sanctification.

3 THE LIE

The Bible does not command or encourage living with all things held in common, such as in a commune. That being said, in the early days after Pentecost…

> …those who believed were of one heart and mind, and no one said that any of his possessions was his own, but everything was held in common. With great power the apostles were giving testimony to the resurrection of the Lord Jesus, and great grace was on them all. For there was no one needy among them, because those who were owners of land or houses were selling them and bringing the proceeds from the sales and placing them at the apostles' feet. The proceeds were distributed to each, as anyone had need.
>
> Now a man named Ananias, together with Sapphira his wife, sold a piece of property. He kept back for himself part of the proceeds with his wife's knowledge; he brought only part of it and placed it at the apostles' feet.   Acts 4:32-35, 5:1-2 NET

Ananias let on that he was giving all the money to the church. It wasn't true. He had only given a part, but who would know? What mattered to Ananias and Sapphira was appearances—that they "look good" before the church. After all, they had been generous too!

> Then Peter said, "Ananias, how is it that Satan has so filled your heart that you have lied to the Holy Spirit and have kept for yourself some of the money you received for the land? Didn't it belong to you before it was sold? And after it was sold, wasn't the money at your disposal? What made you think of doing such a thing? You have not lied to men but to God." Acts 5:3-4 NIV

The proceeds from the land sale were not coerced out of Ananias. As Peter said, he was free to keep all of it and was under no obligation to give money to the apostles. This is important because some "pastors" pressure you to give money. If you find yourself in such a church, I would look elsewhere. The Bible teaches that giving is to be voluntary.

> You must each decide in your heart how much to give. And don't give reluctantly or in response to pressure. "For God loves a person who gives cheerfully." 2 Corinthians 9:7 NLT

Ananias went astray when he pretended to give all, when he had only given a part. This lie was a form of blasphemy.

When we think of blasphemy we think of someone swearing and cursing, but it is much more than that. The word *blasphemy* means to injure the reputation of another. When we ruin God's reputation—when we bring shame on his name—we are guilty of blasphemy. By lying, Ananias created a bad name for the church and ultimately for the Lord. This was not good. As believers, we are told:

> Do not grieve the Holy Spirit of God. Ephesians 4:30 NASB

When we ruin the good name of someone who loves us dearly, we grieve that person. We are not to do that.

Peter confronted Ananias. He pointed out his lie to him.

> And as he heard these words, Ananias fell down and breathed his last; and great fear came over all who heard of it. The young men got up and covered him up, and after carrying him out, they buried him.
>
> Now there elapsed an interval of about three hours, and his wife came in, not knowing what had happened. And Peter

responded to her, "Tell me whether you sold the land for such and such a price?" And she said, "Yes, that was the price."

Acts 5:5-8 NASB

DISHONEST

This was a lie. Sapphira had conspired with her husband in order to "look good."

Peter then told her, "Why have you agreed together to test the Spirit of the Lord? Look! The feet of those who have buried your husband are at the door, and they will carry you out!" At once she collapsed at his feet and died.

So when the young men came in, they found her dead, and they carried her out and buried her beside her husband. Great fear gripped the whole church and all who heard about these things.

Acts 5:9-11 NET

CREDIBLE

Obviously, not every deceptive Christian dies, or we would all be dead. But I believe God brought this judgment as a warning to all who would be part of the church over the coming centuries. It shows just how seriously we must regard honesty in the body of Christ. As Christians we must be credible and maintain a good name before unbelievers. Sadly, this is often not true.

QUENCH NOT

There are many ways we can bring shame upon the body of Christ. It would seem the two most common involve business dealings and immorality. Let's look at immorality as an example. The Scriptures tell us to…

Flee sexual immorality. Every sin that a man does is outside the body, but he who commits sexual immorality sins against his own body. Or do you not know that your body is the temple of the Holy Spirit who is in you, whom you have from God, and you are not your own? For you were bought at a price; therefore glorify God in your body and in your spirit, which are God's.

1 Corinthians 6:18-20 NKJV

When we participate in immoral behavior, we are dragging the pure and perfect Spirit with us. Believe me, he doesn't go quietly. He makes no end of effort to remind us that what we are doing is wrong. But to persist is to reject his guidance.

So, he who rejects this is not rejecting man but the God who gives His Holy Spirit to you.

1 Thessalonians 4:8 NASB

The Bible says:

> *Quench not the Spirit.*   *1 Thessalonians 5:19 KJV*

The word *quench* is used in Scripture in the sense of "suppressing fire." This is poignant since, as we have already seen, fire is a symbol of God's presence. To quench is to suppress or stifle the lesson God is trying to teach us. It may be God is speaking to us about an area of sin. Or it could be he is asking us to do something we don't want to do. In both cases, to quench the Spirit is to suppress his voice.

As believers we are all guilty of this from time to time. Certainly Ananias and Sapphira would have known they were wrong. Scripture has strong words for those who persistently quench the Spirit.

> *You stubborn people! You are heathen at heart and deaf to the truth. Must you forever resist the Holy Spirit?*   *Acts 7:51 NLT*

When we are tempted to run from God's guiding Spirit, we need to remember Ananias and Sapphira. We need to remember that God disciplines his children.

> *And have you forgotten the encouraging words God spoke to you as his children? He said, "My child, don't make light of the Lord's discipline, and don't give up when he corrects you.*
>
> *"For the Lord disciplines those he loves, and he punishes each one he accepts as his child."*   *Hebrews 12:5-6 NLT*

God doesn't punish us to "get even" with us for sinning. He doesn't lose his temper and hit us. He disciplines us to bring us back in line with what is right and safe. Now a child may feel "punished" because Dad says "no" to another chocolate, but Dad knows best. The same applies to God — he knows what is best for us. He disciplines us to restore us to fellowship with him.

> *As you endure this divine discipline, remember that God is treating you as his own children. Who ever heard of a child who is never disciplined by its father? If God doesn't discipline you as he does all of his children, it means that you are illegitimate and are not really his children at all. Since we respected our earthly fathers who disciplined us, shouldn't we submit even more to the discipline of the Father of our spirits, and live forever?*
>
> *For our earthly fathers disciplined us for a few years, doing the best they knew how. But God's discipline is always good for us, so that we might share in his holiness. No discipline is*

enjoyable while it is happening—it's painful! But afterward there will be a peaceful harvest of right living for those who are trained in this way.

So take a new grip with your tired hands and strengthen your weak knees. Mark out a straight path for your feet so that those who are weak and lame will not fall but become strong.

Hebrew 12:7-13 NLT

Ananias and Sapphira, as genuine believers, went to Heaven when they died. The death they experienced was God's chastening hand, the ultimate in discipline for those he loves. Although they may have been upright in every other way, they nonetheless serve as a reminder that God does not allow his children to run wild.

4 THE MIRACLES

The apostles performed many miraculous signs and wonders among the people. And all the believers used to meet together in Solomon's Colonnade. No one else dared join them, even though they were highly regarded by the people. Nevertheless, more and more men and women believed in the Lord and were added to their number. As a result, people brought the sick into the streets and laid them on beds and mats so that at least Peter's shadow might fall on some of them as he passed by. Crowds gathered also from the towns around Jerusalem, bringing their sick and those tormented by evil spirits, and all of them were healed.   *Acts 5:12-16 NIV*

Notice for a moment that all who sought healing were healed. Nothing was "hit and miss." These miracles clearly overruled the natural laws and processes that govern the universe—they were without question supernatural.

CLASS-A MIRACLES

In an earlier chapter, I proposed the classification of miracles. Class-A miracles were the type Jesus performed. If it involved food, it was feeding 5000 men with a boy's lunch. If it involved healing, it was a person verifiably crippled for a long time, and the healing was instant—he jumped to his feet—no tentative steps, nothing dragging on over weeks or months. We saw that only fools would debate Class-A miracles.

We see this when the apostles also performed Class-A miracles. When Peter healed the beggar, even a skeptical court acknowledged:

> *"Everybody living in Jerusalem knows they have done an outstanding miracle, and we cannot deny it."*   Acts 4:16 NIV

In all my years as a believer, I don't know that I have ever witnessed a Class-A miracle. I am sure I would have remembered it, as it would have left an impression.

Class-B Miracles

Most miracles in the Bible would be Class-A, but there are some that could be given a different label. We will call them Class-B miracles, though some scholars call them "interventions." In my way of thinking they are still miracles, still supernatural events orchestrated by God, but they're not so obvious—certainly not so sensational.

I believe I have witnessed Class-B miracles, perhaps many of them. I say "perhaps," because the nature of Class-B miracles is such that they could have a non-supernatural explanation.

This class of miracles takes many forms, but let me relate two stories that involve miraculous power and miraculous timing:

Power: It is not unusual to hear Christians say, "I did not do that in my own power." It usually means that they believe God enhanced their limited ability beyond that which is normal.

Many years ago I directed a video production of four missionaries who had been taken hostage by rebels.[2] We were filming the escape of Paul Dye, the missionary pilot. The escape happened at night and involved the use of a single-engine bush plane. Before the engine could be started, the plane had to be turned to face the airstrip. The aircraft was a taildragger, and turning the plane in the jungle involved lifting the tailwheel over a tree stump. When it came time to film it, Paul was replaying the role. However, this time he lacked strength to lift the plane.[3] Knowing the possible effects of an adrenalin rush on the escape night, I assigned a couple of fellows outside the picture frame to help him hoist the plane. It was only when we had three men added to the task that we were able to get a shot of the plane actually being heaved up and over the stump. Paul is a strong man, but it certainly appeared that his natural strength was greatly enhanced the night he escaped.

Now personally, I think God gave Paul that extra strength, but a skeptic could argue that he had a rush of adrenalin that gave him the ability to do the work of four men. Because of that, I would call this a Class-B miracle—there is a possible natural explanation.

Timing: Our second story begins in the very place where I am sitting writing this book—a room known as the Prophet's Chamber. It is located on the fourth floor of the Carrubbers Christian Centre in Edinburgh, Scotland. The "miracle" involved a well-known local Bible teacher named Jock Troop.

"On this particular occasion, Jock Troop was living in the small flat in the top of the building known as the Prophet's Chamber. One evening he found it impossible to sleep, so he got up, dressed and walked down the Royal Mile to the Queen's Park. He stopped in front of the rocky outcrop known as Salisbury Crags and at the top of his voice, proclaimed the well-known text, John 3:16:

> For God so loved the world, that He gave His only begotten Son that whosoever believeth in Him should not perish but have everlasting life.

"Mr. Troop then walked back to the mission premises and reported that following the incident, he had a good night's sleep. The following evening after the Gospel rally, one of the enquirers, a lady in her 30s, asked to speak to the evangelist. She related that the previous night it had been her intention to commit suicide and she had stood at the top of Salisbury Crags with the intention of leaping to her death. When she was about to do this, she heard the voice of an angel proclaiming a message of God's love. Mr. Troop, with a wry smile, informed the lady that it was no angel that gave the message. He explained to this distraught woman how he had been constrained to visit the park that evening and proclaim the Gospel text. That woman trusted Christ and discovered the peace that passeth understanding."[4]

In referring to situations like this, you will hear Christians talk about God's timing. As incredible as this story is, I think it is still a Class-B miracle. A skeptic could argue that Jock and the unhappy lady conspired together to make a "miracle."

This brings us to another reason why these miracles are Class-B—often they have no witnesses. They are low-key, out-of-sight events, quietly providing assistance to members of the body of Christ. They are no less genuine, but it does mean they can be called into question.

The defining point between Class-A and Class-B miracles is that a skeptic can plausibly debate Class-B miracles in a court of public opinion, something very hard to do with a Class-A miracle. We need to recognize Class-B miracles for what they are and not assign them the same degree of credibility as Class-A miracles. They won't stand up in court.

MORE CERTAIN

In the early years after Pentecost, Peter performed many Class-A miracles, but when it came time to authenticate the truthfulness of Scripture, he wrote these words:

> We did not follow cleverly invented stories when we told you about the power and coming of our Lord Jesus Christ, but we were eyewitnesses of his majesty. For he received honor and glory from God the Father when the voice came to him from the Majestic Glory, saying, "This is my Son, whom I love; with him I am well pleased." We ourselves heard this voice that came from heaven when we were with him on the sacred mountain.   2 Peter 1:16-18 NIV

Peter was referring to the time when he, James and John had witnessed Jesus' miraculous transfiguration on the mountain. It was a true Class-A miracle. Peter then went on to say that in spite of the incredible nature of a Class-A miracle in authenticating God at work, we have something more sure. It is the Word of God—and it is better than a miracle.

> And we have the prophetic word more fully confirmed, to which you will do well to pay attention as to a lamp shining in a dark place…knowing this first of all, that no prophecy of Scripture comes from someone's own interpretation. For no prophecy was ever produced by the will of man, but men spoke from God as they were carried along by the Holy Spirit.
>   2 Peter 1:19-21 ESV

We base our faith upon the Word of God, not upon a miracle.

HIGHLY DEBATABLE

It seems that some Christians, perhaps in their zeal to support the Bible as true, create a third category: Class-C Miracles. These miracles are certainly not Class-A, nor are they really Class-B. Some of them are downright corny—even frivolous. Class-C miracles are highly debatable and certifiably weak. For example, the healing of an internal complaint that occurs over days or months cannot be easily verified. Such miracles, when scrutinized, have often been shown to be non-existent to the point that civil rulers have labeled the miracle workers as frauds.

This is not good. It brings shame on the body of Christ and the name of Jesus. It ruins the credible reputation of the church and makes us the laughingstock of unbelievers. The Lord Jesus never performed Class-C miracles—such "miracles" were beneath him, an embarrassment to his awesome nature. Indeed, nowhere does the Bible record such "miracles" as true miracles, and we would do well to not claim them either.

IN SUMMARY

We do not need to resort to claims of debatable miracles to prove the reality of a risen Saviour. As Peter said, we have something more sure—we have the written Word of God.

To those who feel they are missing out because they have never witnessed a physical miracle, you should know your Christian experience lacks nothing. The Bible is clear. It is the Lord's desire that…

> …we walk by faith, not by sight.   *2 Corinthians 5:7 KJV*

We need not seek miracles. Whether they happen in our lifetime or not is God's choosing, not ours. It is far more important to the Lord to live a pure and honest life by which you…

> …glorify God in your body.   *1 Corinthians 6:20 KJV*

Class of Miracles	**A**	**B**	**C** Not biblical
Nature of Miracle	Highly visible, a number of witnesses	Often quiet; may be no witnesses	Unclear to witnesses, may be no witnesses
Response of Unsaved	Not debatable, cannot deny the miracle	Debatable, may give it a natural explanation	Highly debatable, may be fraudulent
Source of Miracle	Clearly performed by Jesus or the Apostles	Most likely God, but can not be stated with absolute certainty	Unknown, often appears to exalt the miracle worker

5 The Persecution

The fact that Peter and the other apostles had a growing church created problems.

> Then the high priest and all his associates, who were members of the party of the Sadducees, were filled with jealousy. They arrested the apostles and put them in the public jail.
>
> Acts 5:17-18 NIV

Persecution comes in many forms. It may be an insult, the mocking tone in a voice. It may be silence, ostracization or being cut off from friends. It may involve physical suffering. When faced with such trials, Peter wrote:

> "Do not fear their threats; do not be frightened." But in your hearts set apart Christ as Lord. Always be prepared to give an answer to everyone who asks you to give the reason for the hope that you have. But do this with gentleness and respect, keeping a clear conscience, so that those who speak maliciously against your good behavior in Christ may be ashamed of their slander.
>
> 1 Peter 3:14-16 NIV

Having heard from many who have read my previous books, I have no doubt that some of you right now are facing persecution. If you are, you are in the company of a long, distinguished band of believers who have suffered for the Lord.

Remember

The night the apostles were jailed you can see them in discussion, recalling the words of Jesus. He had told them:

> "Remember the word that I said to you: 'A servant is not greater than his master.' If they persecuted me, they will also persecute you."
>
> John 15:20 ESV

But sometimes — every now and then — miracles happen. In this case it was a Class-A!

> But during the night an angel of the Lord opened the doors of the jail and brought them out. "Go, stand in the temple courts," he said, "and tell the people the full message of this new life."
>
> Acts 5:19-20 NIV

God has a sense of humour. It was the Sadducees who had thrown the apostles in jail. The Sadducees believed in neither angels nor the resurrection. But here God used an angel to release the apostles so they could tell others about the resurrection.

At daybreak they entered the temple courts, as they had been told, and began to teach the people. Acts 5:21 NIV

PUZZLED

Somehow the Jewish leaders did not get word of the "jailbreak." They showed up for work as usual, called together the court and prepared to enact judgment on the apostles.

When the high priest and his associates arrived, they called together the Sanhedrin—the full assembly of the elders of Israel—and sent to the jail for the apostles. But on arriving at the jail, the officers did not find them there. So they went back and reported, "We found the jail securely locked, with the guards standing at the doors; but when we opened them, we found no one inside." On hearing this report, the captain of the temple guard and the chief priests were puzzled, wondering what would come of this.

Then someone came and said, "Look! The men you put in jail are standing in the temple courts teaching the people." Acts 5:21-25 NIV

The escapees were "hiding" right under their noses, in the Temple court, teaching.

Then the captain with the officers went and brought them, but not by force, for they were afraid of being stoned by the people. Acts 5:26 ESV

Notice how, at times, even the godless are forced to show respect, if for no other reason than fear for their own skin.

And when they had brought them, they set them before the council. And the high priest questioned them. Acts 5:27 ESV

LOSING FACE

"We gave you strict orders not to teach in this name," he said. "Yet you have filled Jerusalem with your teaching and are determined to make us guilty of this man's blood." Acts 5:28 NIV

Ahhh, so that was it. It was an image thing. The Sanhedrin was looking bad—guilty. The apostles were told to stop their teaching. What should they say?

Jesus had told them:

"You will stand trial before governors and kings because you are my followers. But this will be your opportunity to tell

the rulers and other unbelievers about me. When you are arrested, don't worry about how to respond or what to say. God will give you the right words at the right time. For it is not you who will be speaking—it will be the Spirit of your Father speaking through you."   Matthew 10:18-20 NLT

So when faced with the Sanhedrin and their questions, the apostles had in their minds an answer, placed there by the Holy Spirit.

Peter and the apostles answered, "We must obey God rather than men. The God of our fathers raised up Jesus, whom you had put to death by hanging Him on a cross. He is the one whom God exalted to His right hand as a Prince and a Savior, to grant repentance to Israel, and forgiveness of sins."   Acts 5:29-31 NASB

Note for a moment that since Pentecost, the gospel and the coming of the Holy Spirit had been solely focused on the nation of Israel. In a few pages we will see that change.

Continuing with the story, Peter said,

"And we are His witnesses to these things, and so also is the Holy Spirit whom God has given to those who obey Him."

When they heard this, they were furious and plotted to kill them.   Acts 5:32-33 NKJV

DEATH

As the apostles listened to the Sanhedrin debate, once again they must have recalled the words of Jesus.

"A time is coming when the one who kills you will think he is offering service to God."   John 16:2 NET

It looked like the apostles were facing execution. But then a miracle happened—possibly a Class-B.

Then one in the council stood up, a Pharisee named Gamaliel, a teacher of the law held in respect by all the people, and commanded them to put the apostles outside for a little while. And he said to them: "Men of Israel, take heed to yourselves what you intend to do regarding these men. For some time ago Theudas rose up, claiming to be somebody. A number of men, about four hundred, joined him. He was slain, and all who obeyed him were scattered and came to nothing. After this man, Judas of Galilee rose up in the days of the census, and drew away many people after him. He also perished, and all who obeyed him were dispersed. And now I say to you, keep away from these men and let them alone; for if this plan or this work is of men, it will come to nothing; but if it is of God, you cannot overthrow it—lest you even be found to fight against God."

And they agreed with him. Acts 5:34-40 NKJV

Whew! That was close. It seems God had moved Gamaliel to defend the apostles. But then it could be asked, "Why didn't God cause the Sanhedrin to skip their next decision?" The Sanhedrin...

...called the apostles in and had them flogged. Acts 5:40 NIV

The night before the Lord had delivered his followers from jail by an angel. Now he allowed them to be flogged. Why did he not extend his deliverance to the flogging as well? We really don't know. We can only have confidence in God's goodness and allow God to be God. Whether delivered or not, the Lord is still Lord and worthy to be praised.

COUNTED WORTHY

The Sanhedrin...

... ordered them not to speak in the name of Jesus, and let them go.

The apostles left the Sanhedrin, rejoicing because they had been counted worthy of suffering disgrace for the Name. Day after day, in the temple courts and from house to house, they never stopped teaching and proclaiming the good news that Jesus is the Christ. Acts 5:40-42 NIV

Peter, who obviously knew what it was like to suffer for the Lord, wrote these words near the end of his life:

Dear friends, do not be surprised at the painful trial you are suffering, as though something strange were happening to you. But rejoice that you participate in the sufferings of Christ, so that you may be overjoyed when his glory is revealed. If you are insulted because of the name of Christ, you are blessed, for the Spirit of glory and of God rests on you. If you suffer, it should not be as a murderer or thief or any other kind of criminal, or even as a meddler. However, if you suffer as a Christian, do not be ashamed, but praise God that you bear that name. 1 Peter 4:12-16 NIV

So then, those who suffer according to God's will [that is, the King's will] should commit themselves to their faithful Creator and continue to do good. 1 Peter 4:19 NIV

6 THE SAMARITANS

Historically, persecution is part of the church experience. In the last couple of centuries, the church in the West has been relatively free of physical persecution, but that seems to be changing. On a global basis, the twentieth century saw more Christian martyrs than in any other century. The Bible says:

> Indeed, all who desire to live godly in Christ Jesus will be persecuted. 2 Timothy 3:12 NASB

The biblical book of Acts records the acts or actions of the apostles and the early church. It is somewhat of a transitional book, showing how life changed for believers with the ascension of the Lord and the arrival of the Holy Spirit.

Early on in the book, it records:

> Now on that day a great persecution began against the church in Jerusalem, and all except the apostles were forced to scatter throughout the regions of Judea and Samaria.
>
> Now those who had been forced to scatter went around proclaiming the good news of the word. Philip went down to the main city of Samaria and began proclaiming the Christ to them. Acts 8:1,4-5 NET

Philip was a deacon, a leader in the church in Jerusalem. The role of deacons included caring for the physical welfare of the local believers. We find Philip in Samaria fleeing persecution. It was not the place one would expect to find a Jew.

NEW MEMBERS

The Samaritans were not a large ethnic group. Undoubtedly, they had heard about the Messiah from the leper who was healed and the woman who met Jesus at Jacob's well. They were a people with prepared hearts.

> When they believed Philip as he preached the things concerning the kingdom of God and the name of Jesus Christ, both men and women were baptized. Acts 8:12 NKJV

The Samaritans believed the gospel! As an outward sign of their inner belief, both men and women identified themselves with Christ by water baptism.

An age-old bias was toppling. This must have created quite a stir in Jerusalem. Was God concerned about the Samaritans? Could they really be part of the body of Christ? This needed to be checked out by an apostle, by a couple of them.

> Now when the apostles in Jerusalem heard that Samaria had accepted the word of God, they sent Peter and John to them. These two went down and prayed for them so that they would receive the Holy Spirit. (For the Spirit had not yet come upon any of them, but they had only been baptized in the name of the Lord Jesus.) Acts 8:14-16 NET

We need to stop for a moment and think about what had happened up to this point. On the day of Pentecost, the Lord Jesus inaugurated the body of Christ and then placed the Holy Spirit into this new group of believers. This marked the time when the Holy Spirit officially arrived on earth. From that point on, whenever individuals became believers, the Holy Spirit immediately indwelt or took up residence within them. But until now[5] that had only applied to Jews, which is exactly what they would have expected. After all, they were Yahweh's chosen people.

But now the Samaritans had also believed the gospel. This was unforeseen and was quite likely thought impossible. Was it really true that God intended the despised Samaritans to be members of his body too?

> Then Peter and John placed their hands on them, and they received the Holy Spirit. Acts 8:17 NIV

This was no transfer of the Holy Spirit through the apostles' hands. The laying on of hands was well-recognized by Jew and Samaritan alike, originating in the Jewish Temple. When one brought a lamb sacrifice, he would place his hands on the head of the lamb to show identification, that the lamb was dying in his place. When the apostles laid hands on the Samaritans they identified the Samaritans as fellow believers. Immediately God endorsed that action by indwelling the Samaritans with the Holy Spirit.

When the Spirit arrived on the day of Pentecost, there were both visual and audible signs—a sound like wind, the appearance of flames and words spoken in foreign tongues. But none of this is recorded here with the Samaritans and yet somehow all who were present knew that the Samaritans were now part of the body.

The Samaritans were part-Jews, the first national group after full Jews to enter the body of Christ. The Lord made this a special event—a marked point in time when he officially overthrew centuries of bias against anyone outside of the Chosen People. It was a singular statement to everyone present...

> ...that God was in Christ reconciling the world to Himself, not counting their trespasses against them. 2 Corinthians 5:19 NASB

It was God in Christ reconciling the *world* to himself, not just *one nation*.

7 THE FALSE TEACHER

The world has many who claim to be teachers of spiritual truth. In the Bible, teachers are often referred to as prophets. The word *prophet* can be used in a couple of different ways:

- It can refer to a person who foretells the future.
- It can apply to someone who teaches things of a spiritual nature.

Of course, the Bible speaks of many true prophets, but since this section is on false prophets, I will define four different kinds of false teachers.

RELIGIOUS BELIEFS

First of all, there are those who proclaim a system of beliefs entirely independent of the Bible. When Peter and John were in Samaria they crossed paths with such a prophet.

> Now for some time a man named Simon had practiced sorcery in the city and amazed all the people of Samaria. He boasted that he was someone great, and all the people, both high and low, gave him their attention and exclaimed, "This man is the divine power known as the Great Power." They followed him because he had amazed them for a long time with his magic. Acts 8:9-11 NIV

Simon's sorcery and magic were empowered by Satan. As believers, we need to be alert to the fact that Satan can impress with signs and wonders. Supernatural miracles are not necessarily evidence of God. They can be Satanic.

> The coming of the lawless one will be in accordance with the work of Satan displayed in all kinds of counterfeit miracles, signs and wonders. 2 Thessalonians 2:9 NIV

Every religion has its prophets and gurus. This may not be politically correct, but the Bible calls them false prophets. We need to be courteous when talking about other religions, but not compromise what the Bible teaches. We need to graciously point out that Jesus was different. As Peter said:

> *"Salvation is found in no one else, for there is no other name under heaven given to men by which we must be saved."*
>
> Acts 4:12 NIV

NON-RELIGIOUS BELIEFS

A second group of false prophets would be the outspoken proponents of **secularism**. The word *secular* comes from a Latin word meaning "of this age, belonging to the world." Secularists deny any sort of immaterial or spiritual dimension. The Bible warns us:

> *Above all, understand this: In the last days blatant scoffers will come, being propelled by their own evil urges and saying, "Where is his promised return?"*   2 Peter 3:3-4 NET

Not only do these people scoff at how things will end when the Lord returns, they scoff at God being the Creator in the beginning. They hold exclusively to **gradualism**, the belief that the world evolved over billions of years, and that…

> *…all things have continued as they were from the beginning of creation.*   2 Peter 3:4 NET

They deny catastrophism, the belief in Noah's flood.

> *For they deliberately suppress this fact, that by the word of God heavens existed long ago and an earth was formed out of water and by means of water. …the world existing at that time was destroyed when it was deluged with water. But by the same word the present heavens and earth have been reserved for fire, by being kept for the day of judgment and destruction of the ungodly.*   2 Peter 3:5-7 NET

They reject the Bible as a whole, considering it a fairy tale. Those who teach secularism are identified in Scripture as false prophets.

SOME BIBLE

Then there is another category of false prophets who proclaim a system of beliefs supposedly based on the Bible. Though these teachers may claim to be Christians, they are unbelievers and deny key elements of the gospel. With a little bit of research you can spot them, as they tend to believe one or the other of the following:

- The Bible has significant mistakes in it.

- Jesus is not God, certainly not Yahweh.

- To go to Heaven we must do good works. It takes both Jesus and us. We must do righteous acts to be saved.

Once again, we need to make a distinction in our minds between true Christianity and religious Christianity. Religious Christianity walks the same path as all the other religions of the world with very little difference in the way they view salvation. The religions of this world, including religious Christianity, emphasize what man must *do* to be saved, while true Christianity emphasizes what God has *done* to save us. It is a critical distinction to understand.

Often the false prophets who teach these things will surround themselves with an aura of academia, uttering scholarly platitudes. Peter warned:

> *These men are springs without water and mists driven by a storm. Blackest darkness is reserved for them. For they mouth empty, boastful words and, by appealing to the lustful desires of sinful human nature, they entice people who are just escaping from those who live in error. They promise them freedom, while they themselves are slaves of depravity—for a man is a slave to whatever has mastered him.* 2 Peter 2:17-19 NIV

We need to be on guard against those who masquerade as Christians, but teach error.

Confused Bible

The fourth category of false prophets is comprised of true believers who badly misunderstand the Bible and teach serious error. While Peter and John were in Samaria...

> *Simon himself believed and was baptized.* Acts 8:13 NIV

Apparently, the sorcerer became a Christian. He latched onto the deacon and...

> *...followed Philip everywhere, astonished by the great signs and miracles he saw.* Acts 8:13 NIV

> *Now Simon, when he saw that the Spirit was given through the laying on of the apostles' hands, offered them money, saying, "Give me this power too, so that everyone I place my hands on may receive the Holy Spirit." But Peter said to him, "May your silver perish with you, because you thought you*

> *could acquire God's gift with money! You have no share or*
> *part in this matter because your heart is not right before God!"*
>
> Acts 8:18-21 NET

Just because people call themselves Christians, take the role of teachers, or do marvellous things does not mean they are legitimate. Peter warned us:

> *But there were also false prophets among the people, even as*
> *there will be false teachers among you, who will secretly bring*
> *in destructive heresies, even denying the Lord who bought*
> *them, and bring on themselves swift destruction. And many*
> *will follow their destructive ways, because of whom the way*
> *of truth will be blasphemed.*
> 2 Peter 2:1-2 NKJV

Watch out for those who claim to work miracles, but when the miracles are scrutinized they are definitely Class-C. These "miracle workers" bring the way of truth into disrepute, causing the unbelieving world to laugh and mock.

> *In their greed these teachers will exploit you with stories they*
> *have made up.*
> 2 Peter 2:3 NIV

Watch out for those who ask for money in return for "spiritual" favours, who aggrandize themselves with stories that cannot be verified. Simon, the converted sorcerer, was such a man. Peter told him that he needed to have a serious change of mind about his craving for the limelight. Peter told him:

> *"Repent of this wickedness and pray to the Lord. Perhaps he*
> *will forgive you for having such a thought in your heart. For*
> *I see that you are full of bitterness and captive to sin." Then*
> *Simon answered, "Pray to the Lord for me so that nothing*
> *you have said may happen to me."*
> Acts 8:22-24 NIV

BE ON GUARD

Jesus said:

> *"Beware of false prophets who come disguised as harmless*
> *sheep but are really vicious wolves. You can identify them*
> *by their fruit."*
> Matthew 7:15-16 NLT

The fruit of their lives, both their teaching and actions, will reveal them as false teachers. The written Word of God is our measuring stick. We must always compare what we see and hear with what the Bible teaches. Only then will we know if one is a true or false prophet.

Chapter Ten

1 THE UNCLEAN

As persecution swept across the local church in Jerusalem, the believers fled for their lives. As they travelled, news of the resurrection went with them. In the process Peter moved to Joppa, now part of modern-day Tel Aviv. We pick up the story in Caesarea, a city about 55 kilometres (35 miles) north of Joppa.

> Now there was a man in Caesarea named Cornelius, a centurion of what was known as the Italian Cohort.   Acts 10:1 NET

Cornelius was a Gentile and most likely from Italy. He was a non-commissioned officer in the Roman army, part of the Italian cohort, a group of 600 soldiers. As a centurion, he was responsible for 100 of those men.

> He and all his family were devout and God-fearing; he gave generously to those in need and prayed to God regularly.
> Acts 10:2 NIV

Cornelius knew about Yahweh and respected him as the true God. To the best of his knowledge, he followed the Old Testament Scriptures.

> One day at about three in the afternoon he had a vision. He distinctly saw an angel of God, who came to him and said, "Cornelius!" Cornelius stared at him in fear.   Acts 10:3-4 NIV

This was not a normal experience for Cornelius. He was "in fear," or as another translation puts it, he was "terrified."

> "What is it, Lord?" he asked. The angel answered, "Your prayers and gifts to the poor have come up as a memorial offering before God. Now send men to Joppa to bring back a man named Simon who is called Peter. He is staying with Simon the tanner, whose house is by the sea."
>
> When the angel who spoke to him had gone, Cornelius called two of his servants and a devout soldier who was one of his attendants. He told them everything that had happened and sent them to Joppa.
>
> About noon the following day as they were on their journey and approaching the city, Peter went up on the roof to pray. He became hungry and wanted something to eat, and while the meal was being prepared, he fell into a trance. Acts 10:4-10 NIV

The word *trance* is used to denote a state of mind where one experiences both fear and wonderment at some novel event.

Peter was witnessing something he had never seen before.

> He saw the sky opened up, and an object like a great sheet coming down, lowered by four corners to the ground, and there were in it all kinds of four-footed animals and crawling creatures of the earth and birds of the air.
>
> A voice came to him, "Get up, Peter, kill and eat!"
>
> But Peter said, "By no means, Lord, for I have never eaten anything unholy and unclean."   Acts 10:11-14 NASB

The Ceremonial Law forbids the Jews from eating certain foods—pork being the best known. Peter was being offered a whole spectrum of "impure" animals to eat. He refused, calling them unclean.

> The voice spoke to him again, a second time, "What God has made clean, you must not consider ritually unclean!"
>
>   Acts 10:15 NET

God had given the rules in the first place and if he wanted to expand them that was his prerogative. Something previously unclean was now being considered clean.

> This happened three times, and immediately the object was taken up into heaven.
>
> Now while Peter was puzzling over what the vision he had seen could signify, the men sent by Cornelius had learned where Simon's house was and approached the gate. They called out to ask if Simon, known as Peter, was staying there as a guest. While Peter was still thinking seriously about the vision, the Spirit said to him, "Look! Three men are looking for you. But get up, go down, and accompany them without hesitation, because I have sent them."
>
> So Peter went down to the men and said, "Here I am, the person you're looking for. Why have you come?" They said, "Cornelius the centurion, a righteous and God-fearing man, well spoken of by the whole Jewish nation, was directed by a holy angel to summon you to his house and to hear a message from you."   Acts 10:16-22 NET

As Peter stood at the gate listening to these three men relay their message, he must have sensed that God was educating him to something new.

> So Peter invited them in and entertained them as guests.
>
>   Acts 10:23 NET

DREAMS AND VISIONS

As you read through the Bible, you find stories of men and women who had dreams or visions. Is this still happening today?

There is a universal principle in God's Word that we as believers are to…

… walk by faith, not by sight.   *2 Corinthians 5:7 NJKV*

Dreams and visions fit under the "sight" side of things. And yet in the past, God did use dreams and visions to capture people's attention for a specific purpose. There certainly is a biblical precedent for such a phenomenon.

Whatever one's personal belief on this matter, it is difficult to minister to Muslim background believers (MBBs) without crossing paths with those who have had a dream or vision. One survey showed that up to 25% of MBBs have had these experiences.[1] It seems one can categorize them in two areas:

- **Pre-salvation Confrontation**: One might say these dreams or visions are similar to what Cornelius experienced in Acts 10:3. They usually take the form of someone or something pointing to Jesus as the way to true life.

- **Post-salvation Strengthening**: In this case the believer is often facing extreme persecution. The vision or dream encourages them in the midst of suffering. Once again, the Bible records dreams of such a nature.

On one occasion I asked a former Muslim, now a believer in Jesus, if he had experienced a vision or dream. He affirmed he had, but was reluctant to mention it as he did not want it viewed as something all believers should experience. He felt that the frequency of visions among MBBs was due to persecution and their difficulty in coming to Christ.

Dreams and visions would be Class-B miracles. They are private and cannot be attested to or proven in any way. I would view with caution those who use a dream or vision for the purpose of drawing attention or soliciting money. Because Class-B miracles can be claimed by anyone, such can be used to defraud or deceive the body of Christ.

continued next page

We must be careful that we don't assign these visions or dreams the same weight as Class-A miracles, as they would be unwitnessed.

We also need to recognize that Satan can be the source of visions as well. The apostle John wrote:

> Dear friends, do not believe every spirit, but test the spirits to determine if they are from God, because many false prophets have gone out into the world. 1 John 4:1 NET

Any vision or dream needs to remain consistent with what we see in Scripture. It would not be for entertainment and would have a very specific purpose. If the message in the dream goes beyond what we find in the Bible, then it is called extra-biblical revelation. It is highly debatable that such a message is from God and should be viewed with great caution. We need to be clear that the Bible is complete, and God is not continuing to add to Scripture through dreams or visions.

2 The Centurion

As a result of the vision given to Cornelius, he sent men to Joppa to seek out Peter. After they found him and relayed their message, they spent the night with Peter.

> The next day Peter started out with them, and some of the brothers from Joppa went along. The following day he arrived in Caesarea. Cornelius was expecting them and had called together his relatives and close friends.
>
> As Peter entered the house, Cornelius met him and fell at his feet in reverence. But Peter made him get up. "Stand up," he said, "I am only a man myself." Acts 10: 23-26 NIV

Peter made the point that he was not divine—he wasn't a god of some sort. Peter was just a man like Cornelius.

> Peter continued talking with him as he went in, and he found many people gathered together. He said to them, "You know that it is unlawful for a Jew to associate with or visit a Gentile, yet God has shown me that I should call no person defiled or ritually unclean. Acts 10:27-28 NET

BUT GOD

The "unclean animal" lesson had clicked in Peter's mind. As the Chosen People, the Jews tended to look down on the Gentiles as a race that was ceremonially unclean. Samaritans were despised, but Gentiles were at the bottom of the pile. However, the Lord was making it clear that this was not the way he viewed it and it was the divine point of view that mattered. Peter continued:

> "Therefore when you sent for me, I came without any objection. Now may I ask why you sent for me?"
>
> Cornelius replied, "Four days ago at this very hour, at three o'clock in the afternoon, I was praying in my house, and suddenly a man in shining clothing stood before me and said, 'Cornelius, your prayer has been heard and your [gifts to the poor] have been remembered before God. Therefore send to Joppa and summon Simon, who is called Peter. This man is staying as a guest in the house of Simon the tanner, by the sea.'
>
> "Therefore I sent for you at once, and you were kind enough to come. So now we are all here in the presence of God to listen to everything the Lord has commanded you to say to us."
>
> Acts 10:29-33 NET

Cornelius and his family were there to listen. It really was a God-engineered moment.

> Then Peter began to speak: "I now realize how true it is that God does not show favoritism but accepts men from every nation who fear him and do what is right. You know the message God sent to the people of Israel, telling the good news of peace through Jesus Christ, who is Lord of all.
>
> Acts 10:34-36 NIV

The news of Jesus was public knowledge which Cornelius and his family would have heard, if not understood.

> "You know what has happened throughout Judea, beginning in Galilee after the baptism that John preached—how God anointed Jesus of Nazareth with the Holy Spirit and power, and how he went around doing good and healing all who were under the power of the devil, because God was with him. We are witnesses of everything he did in the country of the Jews and in Jerusalem. They killed him by hanging him on a tree, but God raised him from the dead on the third day and caused him to be seen." Acts 10:37-40 NIV

THE GOSPEL

The crux of the gospel is found in the story of the empty cross and the empty tomb—the death, burial and resurrection of Jesus. Peter was explaining the gospel to his Gentile audience. He told them that after the resurrection, Jesus…

> "…was not seen by all the people, but by witnesses whom God had already chosen—by us who ate and drank with him after he rose from the dead. He commanded us to preach to the people and to testify that he is the one whom God appointed as judge of the living and the dead." Acts 10:41-42 NIV

At the Great White Throne Judgment, it would be Jesus behind the courtroom bench, holding the gavel. To escape that judgment, Peter said:

> "About him all the prophets testify, that everyone who believes in him receives forgiveness of sins through his name."
>
> Acts 10:43 NET

As Peter taught the good news about Jesus, the mind of each listener was processing the information as true or false. If they accepted it as true, then they believed the message.

> While Peter was still speaking these words, the Holy Spirit fell upon all those who were listening to the message.
>
> Acts 10:44 NASB

BELIEVE

Peter's whole audience believed the message to be true. Instantly, God the Holy Spirit indwelt these new believers. But he did it in a way that had potent implications to all who witnessed the event.

> All the [Jewish] believers who came with Peter were amazed, because the gift of the Holy Spirit had been poured out on the Gentiles also. For they were hearing them speaking with tongues and exalting God. Acts 10:45-46 NASB

The same signs occurred with the Gentiles as had transpired with the Jews on the day of Pentecost. They spoke in a foreign language previously unknown to them. These were not empty syllables, but meaningful phrases understood by those present. The Scriptures say that the Gentiles were speaking in tongues "exalting God." The Jews understood clearly what they were saying. As we saw before:

> The Jews require a sign. 1 Corinthians 1:22 KJV

The Jewish believers present could not have had a clearer statement that God had accepted the Gentiles as full members in the body of Christ. Centuries of bias and misunderstanding fell by the wayside. It all happened in a most gracious way, engineered by a loving and caring God.

Then Peter said, "Can anyone keep these people from being baptized with water? They have received the Holy Spirit just as we have." Acts 10:46-47 NIV

JUST AS WE HAVE

Peter recognized the similarity between what happened at Pentecost ten years[2] before and what was happening here in Caesarea.

And he commanded them to be baptized in the name of the Lord. Acts 10:48 KJV

This was water baptism. Water baptism publicly identified these new believers with the body of Christ.

Then they asked Peter to stay with them for a few days. Acts 10:48 NIV

This would have been unthinkable before the "unclean animals" lesson, but now with that in mind and the evidence of the Holy Spirit present in the lives of these Gentiles, Peter did stay on, probably to instruct Cornelius and his family more fully in their new-found faith.

3 THE SIGN

In a previous chapter I addressed the whole issue of miracles. There is no doubt that miracles catch our attention and in some cultures people become almost obsessed with them. To help bring perspective and clarity, I mentioned different classes of miracles—Class-A and Class-B. As far as I am aware, we don't see too many Class-A miracles in this day and age, not at this time of writing anyway. Now why is this?

Some Bible scholars would say that Class-A miracles were largely reserved for Jesus and the apostles as signs to validate their message. After the message was established, the frequency of these miracles tapered off. It is true that miracles were concentrated earlier on in the ministries of Jesus and the apostles. Indeed, you see very few Class-A miracles recorded near the end of the apostles' lives.

Faith

The rarity of Class-A miracles is consistent with what we understand about the nature of being a follower of Jesus. Miracles are visible signs, seen with the eyes, but the Bible says…

> …the righteous will live by his faith.　　Habakkuk 2:4 NASB

> But my righteous one will live by faith, and if he shrinks back, I take no pleasure in him.　　Hebrews 10:38 NET

God wants us to follow him because we trust him, not because of miracles we see or wonders we experience. Christians sometimes call this the *faith principle*.

When we first received Jesus, we did so by faith. Now as believers, each day we are to walk step by step with him, also by faith.

> Therefore, as you received Christ Jesus the Lord, so walk in him.　　Colossians 2:6 ESV

One's initial salvation from the penalty of sin and then living daily as a follower of Jesus both involve faith. At the human level we may crave demonstrations of the supernatural, but the Lord says, "Walk with me by faith."

That being said, if God wants to perform Class-A miracles he can do so at any time, and we have the privilege of giving him all the glory. In no way is he dependent on us.

What's the fuss?

The issue of "tongues" is probably the most controversial miracle in churches today. There are basically three views:

1. First, there are those who would say "tongues," as seen at Pentecost, are Class-A miracles that have ceased. These are people who love the Lord and do not deny that God can do the miraculous. However, they would see tongues as a sign:

> For Jews demand miraculous signs.　　1 Corinthians 1:22 NET

When it comes to the *gift* of tongues they see it as being the same as what we saw in the Old Testament—a sign of impending judgment. They point out that the apostle Paul drew this parallel:

> In the Law it is written, "By people of strange tongues and by the lips of foreigners will I speak to this people, and even then they will not listen to me, says the Lord." Thus tongues are a sign not for believers but for unbelievers [Jews specifically].
> 　　1 Corinthians 14:21-22 ESV

They would teach that this sign disappeared around AD 70 after Titus, the Roman general, overthrew Jerusalem and destroyed the nation of Israel.

2. Next, there are believers who say the miracle of tongues has not ceased but it is uncommon, rarely seen today.

3. Then there is a third group who believe that tongues are evidence of "a second blessing" — a blessing beyond the initial indwelling of the Holy Spirit. They would seek to see and experience events like we have been reading about in the book of Acts.

These three groups represent large spectrums of the church. You cannot be a believer without crossing paths with sincere folks who believe one of these three interpretations.

COMMON GROUND

Is there any common ground between these groups? First of all, it is important to understand that these divergent groups would agree on most, if not all, of the Core Essentials. The differences come in understanding the way the Holy Spirit works. As a young believer, it is best to approach this issue as a Berean. Remember how they…

> …*received the word with all eagerness, examining the Scriptures daily to see if these things were so.* Acts 17:11 ESV

BIBLICAL GUIDELINES

As Christ-ones, whatever we believe about this subject needs to be firmly rooted in the Bible. Here are three points upon which the Scriptures are quite clear:

1. In the Bible, the Greek word translated *tongues* is the same word used for "language." Every instance of tongues mentioned in the Bible uses that word. The miracle of tongues can be summarized as follows: It was an actual language being spoken fluently by one who had never learned or studied the language. It was a Class-A miracle.

You may hear at times about those who speak in an *unknown* tongue, or an *ecstatic* or *angelic* tongue.

The concept of an unknown tongue comes from a translation of the Bible called the King James Version. In the text the word *unknown* was inserted to help make the English text clear. The word does not appear in the original Koine Greek. You can tell it is inserted as it is italicized. There is no basis for an "unknown tongue" either in biblical times or now.

The idea of "ecstatic" or "angelic" tongues also rests on a very weak foundation. In the Bible, any time an angel spoke, he spoke in a known language. Claims to speak in these forms of tongues need to be viewed with genuine caution as ecstatic tongues are practised in other religions.

For a number of years I lived in a part of the world where the people knew very little about the Bible. Some of the tribal villagers spoke "in tongues" but it would be safe to say they were not believers. The "tongues" they spoke were ecstatic—seemingly brought about by some sort of psychological phenomenon with possible demonic influence in certain situations.

2. In the Scriptures whenever tongues were spoken, if there were those present who did not understand the language, an interpreter was to translate the message. This was to be done one at a time.

> If anyone speaks in a tongue, two—or at the most three—should speak, one at a time, and someone must interpret. If there is no interpreter, the speaker should keep quiet in the church and speak to himself and God.   1 Corinthians 14:27-28 NIV

This was not optional. It was a must.

3. Any meeting where this miraculous gift was evident, the believers were instructed to...

> ...not forbid speaking in tongues. But all things should be done decently and in order.   1 Corinthians 14:39-40 ESV

The service was not to be chaotic, for the simple reason that...

> ...if the whole church comes together and all speak in tongues, and unbelievers or uninformed people enter, will they not say that you have lost your minds?   1 Corinthians 14:23 NET

The same rules applied here as to other miracles.[3] There is no room for Class-C manifestations. We must not make the body of Christ a laughingstock before unbelievers, for will they not say, you...

> ...are out of your mind?   1 Corinthians 14:23 NKJV

What the Bible teaches and what we practise must be consistent. May the Lord help us be good Bereans.

4 THE LOAVES

Now the apostles and the brothers who were throughout Judea heard that the Gentiles too had accepted the word of God.

Acts 11:1 NET

We cannot imagine the buzz this created in the largely Jewish Christian community at that time. Peter immediately set out to give a report to the rest of the apostles.

So when Peter went up to Jerusalem, the circumcised [or Jewish] believers took issue with him, saying, "You went to uncircumcised [or Gentile] men and shared a meal with them."

Acts 11:2-3 NET

They were aghast. Peter had done the unthinkable. But Peter had been given a special sign from God in the "unclean animal" lesson.

Peter began and explained it to them point by point, saying, "I was in the city of Joppa praying, and in a trance I saw a vision, an object something like a large sheet descending, being let down from heaven by its four corners, and it came to me. As I stared I looked into it and saw four-footed animals of the earth, wild animals, reptiles, and wild birds. I also heard a voice saying to me, 'Get up, Peter; slaughter and eat!' But I said, 'Certainly not, Lord, for nothing defiled or ritually unclean has ever entered my mouth!' But the voice replied a second time from heaven, 'What God has made clean, you must not consider ritually unclean!' This happened three times, and then everything was pulled up to heaven again.

*"At that very moment, three men sent to me from Caesarea approached the house where we were staying. The Spirit told me to accompany them without hesitation. These six brothers also went with me, and we entered the man's house. He informed us how he had seen an angel standing in his house and saying, 'Send to Joppa and summon Simon, who is called Peter, who will speak a message to you by which you and your entire household will be saved.' Then as I began to speak, **the Holy Spirit fell on them just as he did on us at the beginning**."*

Acts 11:4-15 NET

Peter did not say, "just as he has come upon *every* believer since Pentecost." No, he said "just as he did on *us* at the beginning." Peter referred to an event ten years before when the Holy Spirit had originally come upon the Jews at Pentecost.

JUST AS WE HAVE

Peter recognized the similarity between what had happened at Pentecost and what was happening in Caesarea. These were singular, history-making events. The Holy Spirit had not been baptized or placed into two bodies of Christ. There was only one.

> For by one Spirit are we all baptized into one body, whether we be Jews or Gentiles.　　1 Corinthians 12:13 KJV

Pentecost was a one-time historical event, first to the Jews, then extended to the Samaritans and now to the Gentiles — two groups that the Jews would not have expected to receive such honour. God knew this and had overwhelmed their bias with a sign that tied them all together in one body.

ANCIENT PREJUDICES

Earlier in this book, we saw three stories in which Jesus interacted first with a Jewish Nicodemus, then with a Samaritan woman and finally with a Gentile royal official. These stories appear sequentially in the gospel of John, an unlikely coincidence, since Jew, Samaritan and Gentile had huge barriers to overcome. When on earth, Jesus had persistently broken down these walls and now, with the coming of the Holy Spirit, the process had continued — in the same sequence — now recorded in the book of Acts. The point was clear. *All* were included in the body of Christ.

> For Christ himself has brought peace to us. He united Jews and Gentiles into one people when, in his own body on the cross, he broke down the wall of hostility that separated us.
> 　　Ephesians 2:14 NLT

PROPHECY FULFILLED

Pentecost itself was laden with symbolism that pointed in this direction. As we saw before, Pentecost was just another word for the Feast of Weeks. For centuries the Jews had celebrated this significant feast, which followed 50 days after three previous feasts: the Feasts of Passover, Unleavened Bread and Firstfruits.

We saw that the Feast of Passover spoke of Jesus, the perfect Lamb slain in our place, just as the lamb died in the place of the firstborn. Then with the Feast of Unleavened Bread, we saw that it pointed to the sinless Jesus whose body was broken on the cross, just as the bread without yeast was broken in the feast. Finally, with the Feast of Firstfruits which was celebrated on the very day Jesus was resurrected, we learned it was an apt reminder that Jesus was the first one resurrected from the grave. It was a poignant reminder of the harvest to follow when all believers will be resurrected with new bodies.

Now 50 days later, Pentecost would remind us all of another great event on God's calendar. During that feast two loaves of bread were presented in the Tabernacle. This bread was unlike the bread that pictured Jesus. These loaves were baked with yeast—yeast being a picture of sin. Could it be that these loaves represented the population of the world—one being the Jews, the other the Gentiles—both not perfect, still with sin? Could it be that the loaves represented an ingathering of people from all nations of the world even as the physical bread represented a harvest to come from all the fields? The Bible does not specifically say, but it seems a reasonable interpretation.

The Prophetic Significance of Pentecost (the Feast of Weeks)	
Pictured by: —Type—	**Fulfilled by:** —Antitype—
50 days after the Feast of Fruits	50 days after the Resurrection
New grain gathered	A new group of people, known as the body of Christ, being gathered from the harvest fields of the world
Two loaves	The Jews and the Gentiles
Baked with yeast	Believers, but still with sin

Perhaps the apostles recalled words written 600 years before Pentecost. Speaking of the Messiah, Isaiah had written to the Jews:

"I, the LORD, have called you in righteousness; I will take hold of your hand. I will keep you and will make you to be a covenant for the people and a light for the Gentiles, to open eyes that are blind, to free captives from prison and to release from the dungeon those who sit in darkness." Isaiah 42:6-7 NIV

THEN I REMEMBERED

As Peter spoke, he reminded the believers in Jerusalem of the words of Jesus—words all the apostles had personally witnessed.

> *"And I remembered the word of the Lord, as he used to say, 'John baptized with water, but you will be baptized with the Holy Spirit.' Therefore if God gave them the same gift as he also gave us after believing in the Lord Jesus Christ, who was I to hinder God?"*   Acts 11:16-17 NET

The gift of the Holy Spirit had been given equally to Jew and Gentile alike. What could be said? God had made it clear to everyone.

> *When they heard this, they ceased their objections and praised God, saying, "So then, God has granted the repentance that leads to life even to the Gentiles."*   Acts 11:18 NET

HIS PRESENCE IN TWO WAYS

Before Pentecost: Throughout the Old Testament, it seems the Holy Spirit came *upon* believers for a specific purpose. The person may have been a believer for some time before this happened. In the Old Testament, there was no promise of the Spirit remaining forever and not every believer had the presence of the Holy Spirit in the same way.

As we come into the New Testament, we see anticipation of a change in the way the Holy Spirit works. John the Baptist and Jesus stated that the Holy Spirit would soon come in a unique way. Jesus said:

"John baptized with water, but you will be baptized with the Holy Spirit." Matthew 3:11; Mark 1:7,8; Luke 3:16; John 1:30-34; Acts 1:1-9

At Pentecost: On the day of Pentecost, the Holy Spirit arrived as prophesied and was baptized, or placed, into the body of Christ which at that time consisted of the disciples and other Jewish believers, 120 in total (Acts 2:1-4). This was a one-time historical event, first to the Jews, then extended to the Samaritans (Acts 8:15-17) and the Gentiles (Acts 10:44-48). The final group included was an isolated band of disciples who were followers of John the Baptist (Acts 19:3-7).

CHAPTER ELEVEN

1 The Person and Work

The express goal of my former books was to communicate the identity and life purpose of the Messiah. It is helpful to understand that this is expressed in theological terms as "the person and work of Jesus Christ." It is what you learned as you read one of these books:

- The Stranger on the Road to Emmaus
- All that the Prophets have Spoken
- By This Name

These books carried essentially the same message but were written to different worldviews. They all discuss:

1. **His Person (Identity)**: Jesus is Yahweh
2. **His Work (What he was known for)**: Jesus came into the world to take care of our sin problem—a message built around the empty cross and the empty tomb.

This Book

The purpose of this sequel is to understand the Holy Spirit.

1. **His Person (Identity)**: The Holy Spirit is Yahweh. We have seen in Scripture that the Spirit possesses all the attributes of God—his intellect, feelings and will.

2. **His Work (What he is known for)**: We have seen how the Holy Spirit worked before and after Pentecost. We saw that it was the Holy Spirit who was the power behind the scenes in all that God accomplished. It is for this reason that after he ascended, Jesus sent the Spirit into the world to continue his work through the body of Christ.

As we progressed through the Bible, we saw that the Holy Spirit had a broad effect on this world, from the energizing power behind creation to the conviction of sin in the life of an individual. In this chapter we want to focus on five works of the Holy Spirit, each a critical concept to understand as it pertains to our spiritual growth.

At Salvation

When a person is "saved," the Holy Spirit comes to live within the body of the new believer (Indwelling). With the arrival of the Spirit, this new believer becomes spiritually alive—born again (Regeneration).

The Holy Spirit places the new believer into the body of Christ whereby he is now fully identified as a Christ-one—part of the universal Church (Baptism). There is also a fourth work of the Spirit that we will be looking at called the Sealing. These four "works of the Holy Spirit" are accomplished instantaneously at the moment of salvation and can be remembered with the acronym RIBS.[1]

- R— Regeneration
- I — Indwelling
- B— Baptism
- S — Sealing

} Happens only once, at the point of salvation

In the next four sections, we will dedicate our time to briefly review and enlarge on the first three (RIB), and take a quick look at the last one (S). Then we will discuss two other important aspects related to the work of the Spirit in our lives.

It is very important to understand these concepts clearly. This is not a chapter you can read quickly. You may need to stop many times and ponder what you are reading. Study the charts carefully. Once you understand these concepts well, vast areas of Scripture will fall into place and make sense to you. We will begin with:

- **R— Regeneration**
- I — Indwelling
- B— Baptism
- S— Sealing

2 THE REGENERATION

Earlier on in the book we read the story about Nicodemus.

> He came to Jesus at night and said, "Rabbi, we know you are a teacher who has come from God. For no one could perform the miraculous signs you are doing if God were not with him."

> In reply Jesus declared, "I tell you the truth, no one can see the kingdom of God unless he is **born again**." *John 3:2-3 NIV*

We saw that to be born again was to be regenerated. When the Holy Spirit takes up residence in the new believer, he brings with him spiritual life. It is that simple, nothing more.

> He saved us, not because of righteous things we had done, but because of his mercy. He saved us through the washing of **rebirth** and renewal by the Holy Spirit. *Titus 3:5 NIV*

Here is how the same verse reads in another translation:

> *He saved us, not on the basis of deeds which we have done in righteousness, but according to His mercy, by the washing of* **regeneration** *and renewing by the Holy Spirit.*   Titus 3:5 NASB

Regeneration or rebirth happens instantaneously at the moment of salvation, when one is born again. It is no coincidence that the Bible uses the word *birth* to describe regeneration.

Physical Birth	Spiritual Birth
Pictured by:[2] — Type —	**Fulfilled by:** — Antitype —
Happens when you leave the womb to enter the world.	Happens at the moment you put your trust in Jesus Christ.
It happens only once.	Happens only once. The Bible does not speak of being born again, then unborn, then reborn again and again—of being regenerated and then un-regenerated. Nor does it talk of re-regeneration. It is a one-time event that occurs at the moment of faith.
Physical birth has its beginnings at the moment of conception, when the "perishable" seed and egg come together.	Spiritual life began when you were "***born again*** *not of seed which is perishable but imperishable, that is, through the living and enduring word of God."* 1 Peter 1:23 NASB
No matter how fragile, all the components for adult life are present at birth—you cannot reverse the process.	The beginnings of spiritual life can be very fragile, but once started, it cannot be undone.
Physical life begins in a moment and continues till death.	Spiritual life begins in a moment and continues into eternity.

Many years after Jesus walked the face of the earth, Peter wrote of this new birth. I am going to include the whole passage, so that you can sense the energy and excitement of this man—this one who went from being a common coward to one of immense courage. This is what he wrote:

> Praise be to the God and Father of our Lord Jesus Christ! In his great mercy he **has given us new birth** into a living hope through the resurrection of Jesus Christ from the dead, and into an inheritance that can never perish, spoil or fade—kept in heaven for you, who through faith are shielded by God's power until the coming of the salvation that is ready to be revealed in the last time [when Jesus returns].
>
> In this you greatly rejoice, though now for a little while you may have had to suffer grief in all kinds of trials. These have come so that your faith—of greater worth than gold, which perishes even though refined by fire—may be proved genuine and may result in praise, glory and honor when Jesus Christ is revealed.
>
> Though you have not seen him, you love him; and even though you do not see him now, you believe in him and are filled with an inexpressible and glorious joy, for you are receiving the goal of your faith, the salvation of your souls.
>
> 1 Peter 1:3-9 NIV

Peter's enthusiasm for all that the Lord had done for him spills out of his heart in abundant praise to the Lord. In so doing, Peter recognizes that this new life brings with it "all kinds of trials." Peter was obviously a realist. But he looked to the future hope, the return of Christ.

GRACE

Regeneration is always a work of the Holy Spirit as a result of a person's individual response to God's Word.

> He chose to **give us birth** through the word of truth, that we might be a kind of firstfruits of all he created.   James 1:18 NIV

No one can be "saved" on our behalf. We must trust in Jesus individually as we understand the truth of his Word. At that moment we move from death to life. It is all possible because of the Lord's love for us—an underserved love called *grace*.

> *But because of his great love for us, God, who is rich in mercy, **made us alive** with Christ even when we were dead in transgressions—it is by grace you have been saved.*
> *Ephesians 2:4-5 NIV*

It was a love fully expressed on the cross when Jesus died in our place, paying our sin-debt.

> *When you were dead in your sins…God **made you alive** with Christ. He forgave us all our sins, having canceled the written code, with its regulations, that was against us and that stood opposed to us; he took it away, nailing it to the cross. And having disarmed the powers and authorities [Satan and his demons], he made a public spectacle of them, triumphing over them by the cross.*
> *Colossians 2:13-15 NIV*

FOUR WORKS

Once again, we have just touched on this subject, but let's move on to the next work of the Holy Spirit—the Indwelling.

- R— Regeneration
- **I — Indwelling**
- B— Baptism
- S — Sealing

3 THE INDWELLING

At the beginning of time when Yahweh created the world…

> *…the LORD God formed man of the dust of the ground, and breathed into his nostrils the breath of life; and man became a living soul.*
> *Genesis 2:7 KJV*

We saw that in Scripture, a breath of air and wind are used as pictures of the Holy Spirit. When Adam stood on his feet, he was not just alive physically but he had a spiritual dimension that was alive to the Lord. As we saw, some conclude that God the Holy Spirit was present within Adam, giving him spiritual life.

> *So God created man in his own image, in the image of God created he him; male and female created he them.*
> *Genesis 1:27 KJV*

Only human beings possessed the image of God. As image-bearers, we were distinct from all other parts of God's creation. We were not some higher form of an animal.

Role	Category	Personal Name
Creator	God	Yahweh
Created	Spirit Beings	Gabriel, Michael
Created in the image of God	Humans	Kumar, James, Ali, Susan, etc.
Created	Animals, Birds, Fish, Reptiles, Insects, etc	Arabian Horse, Bald Eagle, Bluefin Tuna, etc.

FALLEN

But then Adam and Eve sinned. When this occurred two significant things happened to the human race:

- We lost the "family" presence of God, and
- The image was badly marred.

Thankfully, God provided a way for us to be right with him.

RESTORED

As we put our trust in the Lord Jesus, we are once again restored to the presence of Yahweh. God, in the person of the Holy Spirit, comes and lives inside us. It is not something to be spooky about. Probably most new believers are unaware that this has happened, but nonetheless the Bible says the Holy Spirit has moved within.

Once again, we are image-bearers. This is so true that…

> …if anyone does not have the Spirit of Christ, he does not belong to Him.　　　　　　　Romans 8:9 NASB

TEMPLE

This has personal and practical implications that are important to understand. Think of it this way.

Just as Jesus, the Son of God, needed to have a physical body to accomplish his work on earth, so the Spirit of God uses physical bodies to accomplish his work.

> Do you not know that you are the temple of God and that the Spirit of God dwells in you?　　1 Corinthians 3:16 NKJV

The Jewish Temple had an outer courtyard and an inner sanctuary. In a sense, the physical side of us—our material bodies—are like the outer courtyard. They are what everyone can see. But the Holy Spirit takes up residence in the inner sanctuary, our immaterial side — the part the Bible refers to as spirit, soul, heart and so forth. In a sense, he creates within us our own personal Holy of Holies. And there he lives — his sacred presence within.

This does away with the idea of the Spirit "floating" around our house or church building in some mystical, ghostly sort of way. The Holy Spirit does not minister in a vacuum. Rather, he works through those in whom he lives.

> *Your body is a temple of the Holy Spirit, who is in you...*
> *Therefore honor God with your body.* 1 Corinthians 6:19-20 NIV

As "temples" of the Holy Spirit, our bodies become tools in his hands to honour the Lord Jesus Christ. But how can that be since we are still in our marred condition — we are still sinful people?

The good news is this: the moment you trust in Jesus, God not only indwells you by his Holy Spirit but he begins to conform you back into his image. And he will continue that process until you enter Heaven (see chart on page 252). This is so certain, God says that all believers have been...

> *...predestined to be conformed to the image of His Son.*
> Romans 8:29 NKJV

As image-bearers, the indwelling Spirit affects how we look at life. We may find we do not have so much in common with old friends. It is not that we "dump" them — indeed, we may be more concerned for them than ever before. But we may begin to seek new friendships with believers. The Holy Spirit may begin to affect where we go. Places we once felt comfortable in may now seem "out of place." Others may notice changes in our lives — some big, some small — changes affecting the way we talk, what we wear[3] and how we treat others. These are good things. They are all part of being conformed into the image of Christ.

PERMANENT FRIEND

Until Pentecost, it seems the Holy Spirit only came upon certain believers to empower them for certain tasks. As we saw with King David, he was a believer for some time before this happened. The Holy Spirit would come, and in some cases, go; there was no promise of him remaining forever. And not every believer had the presence of the Holy Spirit, nor in the same way. But now all that has changed.

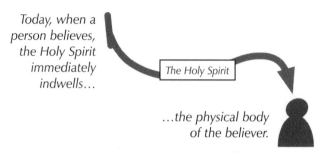

Today, when a person believes, the Holy Spirit immediately indwells…

The Holy Spirit

…the physical body of the believer.

From Pentecost on, whenever one became a believer, the Holy Spirit would take up immediate residence within that person's body, never to leave. For that reason there is no mention of a believer losing the Spirit and then being re-indwelt again and again.

Now, this is very significant! This means that where we go, he goes; and what we do, he's a part of too! Of course this has very down-to-earth, practical implications. As an example, consider the following verses:

> You say, "I am allowed to do anything"—but not everything is good for you. And even though "I am allowed to do anything," I must not become a slave to anything.
>
> But you can't say that our bodies were made for sexual immorality. They were made for the Lord, and the Lord cares about our bodies.
>
> Don't you realize that your bodies are actually parts of Christ? Should a man take his body, which is part of Christ, and join it to a prostitute? Never! And don't you realize that if a man joins himself to a prostitute, he becomes one body with her?
>
> Run from sexual sin! No other sin so clearly affects the body as this one does. For sexual immorality is a sin against your own body. Don't you realize that **your body is the temple of the Holy Spirit**, who lives in you and was given to you by God? You do not belong to yourself, for God bought you with a high price. So you must honor God with your body.
>
> 1 Corinthians 6:12-16, 18-20 NLT

There is a lot of food for thought in these verses. As with any close friend, we must not embarrass the Holy Spirit, taking him places where he would not feel comfortable—indeed, where we should not feel comfortable. We must not involve ourselves in those things in which he would not participate. When we respect his sacred presence, we will find a great strength within—the power of the Holy Spirit.

UP TILL NOW

Centuries before, Yahweh told Moses to celebrate Pentecost, marking a notable day in history when the Holy Spirit would expand his role and work in the world. Some Bible scholars would say that before Pentecost the Holy Spirit came *upon* a believer, but after Pentecost the Holy Spirit *indwelt* a believer.

The chart below summarizes all of history, showing the correlation between the indwelling Holy Spirit and having spiritual life.

		At Creation	After the Fall	Born Again	Future Hope
Material	**Physical Body**	Perfect Without blemish; perfect health	Dying Marred, subject to suffering and death	Dying Still suffering and death, but now with hope	Glorified Body Same type of body Jesus had after his resurrection
Immaterial* (unseen by eyes)	**Soul**	Innocent Able to sin	Corrupted Dominated by sin	Corrupted Able to be free from sin's domination	Perfect Unable to sin
	Spirit	Man spiritually ALIVE by the sacred presence of God	Man spiritually DEAD separated from…	Man spiritually ALIVE reunited with God by the indwelling Holy Spirit	Man spiritually ALIVE dwelling as family in the presence of God forever
		*The Bible uses words such as *breath of life, heart, mind, conscience, spirit* and *soul*.	…God's "family" presence		

FOUR WORKS

So much more could be said, but let's continue to look at the four works of the Holy Spirit performed at the moment of salvation. Next is the topic of baptism.

- R— Regeneration
- I — Indwelling
- **B— Baptism**
- S — Sealing

4 THE BAPTISM

We have mentioned this a number of times before, however, the repetition is needed for clarity. Of the four works of the Spirit, this is the one that people tend to confuse the most, and not without reason—the Bible speaks of a number of "baptisms."[4] For the purpose of this section, you only need to understand two. Neither of these baptisms involves water, though water baptism is given to illustrate the second one. Read carefully. This may seem technical, but it will help you greatly in interpreting the Bible accurately.

1. Baptism by Jesus Christ

> **a. Prophecy Given**: Both John the Baptist and Jesus foretold the official arrival of the Holy Spirit on earth. Since believers lacked both ability and strength for the journey, Jesus said he would send the Holy Spirit.
>
> > *"You will receive power when the Holy Spirit comes on you; and you will be my witnesses in Jerusalem, and in all Judea and Samaria, and to the ends of the earth."* Acts 1:8 NIV
>
> **b. Prophecy Fulfilled**: On the day of Pentecost, the Holy Spirit arrived. He was baptized or placed into the body of Christ. The Lord Jesus did this—it was he who sent the Spirit.
>
> - Who: The Holy Spirit...
> - What: ...was baptized or placed into...
> - Where: ...the body of Christ...
> - By: ... Jesus Christ...
> - When: ...on the day of Pentecost.[5]

2000 years ago, on the day of Pentecost, the Holy Spirit was sent from Heaven by Jesus, to be placed in the 120 believers gathered in the city of Jerusalem. It could be said that this was the offical arrival of the Holy Spirit on earth.

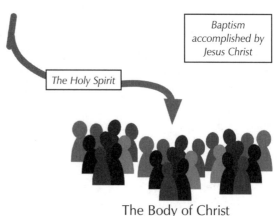

Baptism accomplished by Jesus Christ

The Holy Spirit

The Body of Christ

With the Holy Spirit's arrival on earth, believers were equipped with both the gifts and the power to complete the job left to us by Jesus.

2. Baptism by the Holy Spirit

Since the day of Pentecost, the moment people trust in Jesus, they are baptized or placed into the body of Christ by the Holy Spirit. Notice, in this case, the Holy Spirit does the placing or baptizing, not Jesus.

> *For by one Spirit are we all baptized into one body, whether we be Jews or Gentiles.* 1 Corinthians 12:13 KJV

- Who: Every new believer…
- What: …is baptized or placed into…
- Where: …the body of Christ…
- By: …the Holy Spirit…
- When: …the moment a person trusts in Jesus.

When a person is baptized by water, this is the baptism that is being illustrated. As a visual aid, water baptism illustrates our identification with Christ in his death, burial and resurrection, and is a public statement of the new believer having been moved from the multitude who are "in Adam" to the body of believers who are "in Christ."

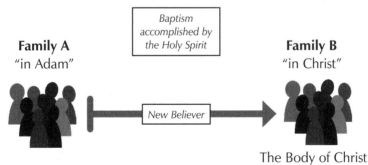

Believers have a new identity. They belong to the "in Christ" group, otherwise known as the body of Christ.

As you study the difference between the baptism by Jesus and the baptism by the Holy Spirit, note specifically the *who, by* and *when* for each event. These distinctions are the key to being clear on the differences. The blurring of these distinctions has led to a lot of confusion.

THE BODY

Just as the hand, ear, eye and so forth, have a role in the total function of the human body, so each believer has a role in the ministry of the entire body of Christ.

> Now you are the body of Christ, and each one of you is a part of it.
> 1 Corinthians 12:27 NIV

GIFTS

When we were placed into the Body, the Holy Spirit gave each of us a particular gift or gifts, which are abilities to help other believers and equip us as we reach out to a hurting world.

These are not necessarily gifts that we use, but rather what the Spirit uses to serve others. It is the Holy Spirit *in us* who does the serving *through us*, using our physical bodies as we submit to him. This is how the job that Jesus left us to do is accomplished.

The Power	The Tool	The Means	The Purpose
The Holy Spirit...	...through the believers' bodies, as we offer ourselves to him...	...uses the gifts he has given each one of us...	...to take care of others in the body of Christ ...to reach out to a needy world

It is all done by the Holy Spirit's power, using our physical bodies. Peter wrote to all believers when he said:

> Each one should use whatever gift he has received to serve others, faithfully administering God's grace in its various forms. If anyone **speaks**, he should do it as one speaking the very words of God. If anyone **serves**, he should do it with the strength God provides, so that in all things God may be praised through Jesus Christ. To him be the glory and the power for ever and ever. Amen.
> 1 Peter 4:10-11 NIV

Peter wrote that these "gifts" are for the purpose of God's glory, not man's praise. He defined two major spheres of engiftment:

1. The *speaking* gifts are for those believers who are given the ability to teach the Bible to young and old.

2. The *service* gifts are for those with abilites in business, hospitality, organizational or creative areas, to support the various ministries performed by the body of Christ.

This is all God's doing. We don't have a say in what gifts we receive.

But in fact God has arranged the parts in the body, every one of them, just as he wanted them to be. 1 Corinthians 12:18 NIV

The purpose of these gifts are…

…to prepare God's people for works of service, so that the body of Christ may be built up until we all reach unity in the faith and in the knowledge of the Son of God and become mature, attaining to the whole measure of the fullness of Christ. Ephesians 4:12-13 NIV

In addition to these gifts, everyone is encouraged to be hospitable, to give of their financial resources, to look for ways to be good ambassadors of the gospel. Peter wrote:

Above all, love each other deeply, because love covers over a multitude of sins. Offer hospitality to one another without grumbling. 1 Peter 4:8-9 NIV

This is a trustworthy saying. And I want you to stress these things, so that those who have trusted in God may be careful to devote themselves to doing what is good. These things are excellent and profitable for everyone. Titus 3:8 NIV

SUMMARY

As new believers, baptized into the body of Christ, we have a new identity. We are now Christ-ones—we are image-bearers. Whatever we were known for previously shrinks in significance to what we have now become. This is an identity we can never lose, a truth we can delight in every new day.

5 THE SEALING

We will now continue our overview of the works of the Holy Spirit by taking a look at the fourth concept.

- R— Regeneration
- I — Indwelling
- B— Baptism
- **S— Sealing**

The moment we put our trust in Christ, God placed a seal on us—a mark of ownership that says we belong to him. This seal will remain in place until the Lord returns and gives us new bodies on the day of redemption.

> *And do not grieve the Holy Spirit of God, by whom you were sealed for the day of redemption.* Ephesians 4:30 NKJV

The Greek word translated *sealed* literally means "to mark a person or a thing; to prove, to confirm or authenticate, to place beyond doubt something as genuine." The Bible tells us that the Holy Spirit himself is the seal.

> *Having believed, you were marked in him with a seal, the promised Holy Spirit.* Ephesians 1:13 NIV

Ownership

> *Nevertheless the solid foundation of God stands, having this seal: "The Lord knows those who are His."* 2 Timothy 2:19 NKJV

This seal is God's mark of ownership on us as believers and nobody can remove it. Personally, this makes me very, very grateful.

> *Who shall separate us from the love of Christ? Shall trouble or hardship or persecution or famine or nakedness or danger or sword? As it is written: "For your sake we face death all day long; we are considered as sheep to be slaughtered."*

> *No, in all these things we are more than conquerors through him who loved us. For I am convinced that neither death nor life, neither angels nor demons, neither the present nor the future, nor any powers, neither height nor depth, nor anything else in all creation, will be able to separate us from the love of God that is in Christ Jesus our Lord.* Romans 8:35-39 NIV

Every possible circumstance is covered. Nothing and no one can break God's seal of ownership on our lives. As we have seen, the New Testament Scripture does not talk about the believer...

- being indwelt only to later lose the Spirit;
- being born again, then unborn, and then being re-born again, and again;
- being placed into the body of Christ only to be removed and then perhaps later placed back into his body.

We now add to that list by saying the Bible does not speak of...

- being sealed and then losing the seal only to be sealed again later.

As with the other works of the Spirit, the sealing is permanent. Oh, the grace of God that makes this so! If I had to live a good enough life to keep me "born again," to keep me "indwelt," then I would be without hope. But that is not the way it is. I am sealed.

I have a permanent standing with God. Now I pray, "Lord, help me live a life worthy of such a great and loving God! Help me to honour you, to bring you pleasure, just as a good son honours his father and seeks to please him."

GUARANTEE

The portions of the Bible that talk about the sealing also mention the indwelling presence of the Holy Spirit functioning like a down payment. He is our guarantee that we will receive a future inheritance in Heaven.

> *Having believed, you were marked in him with a seal, the promised Holy Spirit, who is a deposit guaranteeing our inheritance until the redemption of those who are God's possession—to the praise of his glory.*   Ephesians 1:13-14 NIV

> *And it is God who establishes us with you in Christ, and has anointed us, and who has also put his seal on us and given us his Spirit in our hearts as a guarantee.* 2 Corinthians 1:21-22 ESV

The seal and deposit are God's guarantee that we will make it Home. All of this is cause for us to praise him for his wonderful love and grace. No matter how "good" we may live life here on earth, we don't deserve what God has set aside for us—what he guarantees. Only by his grace is this extended to us as believers, with the result that it is…

> *…to the praise of his glory.*   Ephesians 1:14 NKJV

TO HIS PRAISE

In summary, we know a little bit more about:

- R— Regeneration
- I — Indwelling
- B— Baptism
- S — Sealing

These are called the works of the Holy Spirit—what he has done for us as believers. When you stop and consider them it is really quite wonderful. And we have only been touching on these truths—there is so much more we could say. Peter wrote that such knowledge should cause us to crave a deeper understanding of God's Word.

> *For you know that it was not with perishable things such as silver or gold that you were redeemed from the empty way of life handed down to you from your forefathers, but with the precious blood of Christ, a lamb without blemish or defect.*

*He was chosen before the creation of the world, but was
revealed in these last times for your sake. Through him you
believe in God, who raised him from the dead and glorified
him, and so your faith and hope are in God.*

*Now that you have purified yourselves by obeying the truth so
that you have sincere love for your brothers, love one another
deeply, from the heart. For you have been born again, not of
perishable seed, but of imperishable, through the living and
enduring word of God. For, "All men are like grass, and all
their glory is like the flowers of the field; the grass withers
and the flowers fall, but the word of the Lord stands forever."
And this is the word that was preached to you.*

*Therefore, rid yourselves of all malice and all deceit, hypocrisy,
envy, and slander of every kind. Like newborn babies, crave
pure spiritual milk, so that by it you may grow up in your
salvation, now that you have tasted that the Lord is good.*

1 Peter 1:18 - 2:3 NIV

6 THE ASSURANCE

As a new believer you need to understand that there is a debate
in the church. Some feel that you can be saved and then lose your
salvation, and then get saved again. Others would say that once
you are saved, you are always saved. Why the confusion? There
are a number of contributing factors.

THE WORD SIN

If we believe that somehow good deeds keep us saved, then
we have to ask ourselves—just how bad does a bad deed have
to be to cause us to lose our salvation? And how many of these
sins would we need to commit before salvation would be lost?
Of course, the Bible tells us that sin is sin, and although some
sin carries with it greater consequences, the truth of the matter
is that any sin, no matter how little, still separates us from God.

Intrinsic to our human nature is an inability to comprehend the
sinfulness of any sin, and as such, we think we can live good
enough lives to keep ourselves saved. I believe this thinking is
one reason for the confusion. Here is another.

SALVATION, SAVED

Earlier in the book I mentioned that it is common for Christians
to refer to their moment of salvation as the time they were
"saved." Because this vocabulary is so common, some assume that

whenever you see the word *salvation* in Scripture, it is referring to the moment one is saved from the eternal penalty of sin. This is not so. It is common in language to use one word with many different definitions. As an example, consider the word *face*.

- The face of a person
- The face of a coin
- The face of a cliff
- The face value of an item

One word can have many meanings. The context reveals what definition is in question. As we have seen, this applies to the words *salvation* and *saved*. Here are the most common usages:

- To be saved from Hell, the eternal penalty of sin
- To be saved from the daily power of sin
- To be saved from the presence of sin when we go to Heaven
- To be saved from physical death
- To be saved from a catastrophe

These sentences all use the word *saved*, but with very different meanings. If you get the wrong meaning attached to the word *salvation*, you may think that a person must do good works to be saved from Hell, or if you don't do enough good works, you will lose your salvation. For this and other reasons, we need to be good Bereans and study Scripture in light of the context. It will be slow at first, but soon it will make more and more sense.

CAN'T BE BOTH

It is important to understand that any form of salvation from sin cannot be partly by grace and partly by works—it cannot be both.

> *But if it is by grace, it is no longer on the basis of works, otherwise grace is no longer grace.* Romans 11:6 NASB

Grace is God's love shown to undeserving sinners. If we could do anything to deserve it—such as good works—then it would cease to be grace. You can't mix the two.

It is clear that salvation from the eternal *penalty* of sin is the result of God's grace. Scripture says:

> *For by grace you have been **saved** through faith. And this is not your own doing; it is the gift of God, not a result of works, so that no one may boast.* Ephesians 2:8-9 ESV

But this also applies to being saved from the daily *power* of sin. Not only do we trust in Jesus to save us from Hell, but we also trust him to save us from sinful thoughts and actions. As we go to him daily, we seek his counsel and strength to experience salvation from the everyday dominion of sin.

> So then, my beloved, just as you have always obeyed, not as in my presence only, but now much more in my absence, work out your **salvation** with fear and trembling; for it is God who is at work in you, both to will and to work for His good pleasure. *Philippians 2:12-13 NASB*

When all is said and done, only God will be worthy of credit for our salvation from sin. If it were possible for us to maintain salvation from the Second Death by doing good works, then one day, standing before the Lord in Heaven, we could say, "Lord, you may have died for me but I kept myself saved with good works." That will not happen. We will only be in Heaven because of God's mercy and grace. Of that, there will be no debate.

Double Grip

Our eternal destiny rests solely in God's underserved love—a love that refuses to let go. As the great Shepherd, Jesus said:

> "My sheep hear my voice, and I know them, and they follow me." *John 10:27 ESV*

Jesus was speaking of believers—the sheep he cares for. He then continued on with both a positive and negative declaration.

> "I give them eternal life, and they will never perish…" *John 10:28a ESV*

Eternal means eternal, and never means never. The word translated *never* in English is actually two words in the original Greek. They form a double negative. Loosely put it means, "No, not ever, absolutely no possibility of perishing." That is what Jesus said. But he didn't stop there. He adds:

> "…and no one will snatch them out of my hand." *John 10:28b ESV*

We are kept firmly in the hand of Jesus; it is he who is holding onto us. Just as a father holds tightly to his child's hand as they cross a busy street, so Jesus has a tight grip on us. The verse carries on:

> "My Father, who has given them to me, is greater than all, and no one is able to snatch them out of the Father's hand. I and the Father are one." *John 10:29-30 ESV*

Not only are we in the hand of Jesus, but we are also in the hand of the Father. God has a double grip on us! That is a pretty secure place to be.

PRESENT POSSESSION

We can count on eternal life now. We don't need to wait until we die to see if it's eternal or not.

> And this is the testimony, that God gave us eternal life, and this life is in his Son. Whoever has the Son has life; whoever does not have the Son of God does not have life.
>
> I write these things to you who believe in the name of the Son of God, that you may know that you have eternal life.
>
> 1 John 5:11-13 NKJV

It says we can *know* that we have eternal life. It is a present possession. Such knowledge moves us from serving the Lord out of fear of losing our salvation, to serving him out of love for his boundless grace.

WHAT IF...?

As we go through life we will stumble often—we will sin. But that is why Jesus sent the Holy Spirit to be our Guide. It is he...

> ...who is able to keep you from falling and to present you before his glorious presence without fault and with great joy.
>
> Jude 24 NIV

The word *keep* means "to be kept under a military guard for safe conduct." While we as believers may "fall" in our spiritual lives, we will never fall to the point of losing our salvation. This is not because the keeping of our salvation is in any way dependent upon ourselves, but rather because our salvation is entirely dependent upon God's power to "keep" us. His keeping power will bring us into his very presence one day, where we will see him with our own eyes. Now that is true love—it is grace—and something we can be quite assured about.

7 THE MOTIVATION

Some concerned Christians quite rightly ask, "If good works are not necessary for salvation to stay saved, then does it not encourage people to live any way they wish—in sin?" This is a good question. First of all, we must be careful that we don't fix one error (the error of sinful living), with another error (the error of adding good works to salvation). Here then is the same question right out of the pages of the Bible.

> *Well then, should we keep on sinning so that God can show us more and more of his wonderful grace? Of course not!*
> Romans 6:1-2 NLT

The answer to this question is very strong in the original Greek. Never! To take advantage of God's love should be unthinkable.

As for those who go ahead and trample on God's grace anyway, they need to be reminded that God does not let his children run wild. As we mentioned earlier, there are consequences for sin, even for believers. God disciplines his children right here on earth. That being said, any deterrent that smacks of threats, fear or guilt is a terrible motivator for righteous living.

There is a much better motivation for not sinning. It is God's undeserved love—his grace. It is a known fact that we go much further and work much harder when motivated by love and respect than by fear or threats. Threats create rebellion; love motivates service. And in this case, great love is in the picture.

> *For Christ's love compels us, because we are convinced that one died for all, and therefore all died. And he died for all, that those who live should no longer live for themselves but for him who died for them and was raised again.* 2 Corinthians 5:14-15 NIV

Love is a more effective motivation to live a good life than fear of losing one's salvation. The Bible says:

> *My dear children, I write this to you so that you will not sin. But if anybody does sin, we have one who speaks to the Father in our defense—Jesus Christ, the Righteous One.* 1 John 2:1 NIV

There are verses in the Bible that would seem to indicate that believers can lose their salvation. There are good answers for each of those verses. Whether on this or any other subject difficult to understand, we need to be good students of the Bible and apply these principles of Bible interpretation:

- Do not build a major interpretation around isolated Bible verses that godly scholars debate as to their meaning.

- Always interpret difficult verses in light of those that are plain and clear. Not the other way around.

- Always keep the Bible's "big picture" in mind when reading a single verse. Never change the big picture to accommodate a single verse. For example, when the Lord Jesus died on the cross, the curtain in the Temple was torn. On that basis…

…we have confidence to enter the holy places by the blood of Jesus, by the new and living way that he opened for us through the curtain.   Hebrews 10:19-20 ESV

I enter into God's "family" presence through the torn curtain because of Christ. That is the big picture. But if I could lose that salvation, God would have to cast me out of his presence and stitch up the torn curtain. We do not see that in Scripture. We have no stories that give a corresponding type/antitype to that idea. This would be true of a multitude of salvation types and antitypes.

RESPECT

As believers we should welcome careful, respectful discussion on this subject. If we disagree, we must disagree without being disagreeable.

WHAT IF…?

There are those who claim to be Christians, but:

- show no interest in the Bible;
- live their lives following the values of the world;
- take part in overtly sinful behaviour;
- show no signs of guilt for bringing shame to the Lord's name.

Some of these people may go to church on Sunday, but the rest of the week live as hypocrites.

We need to be careful that we don't confuse Christian religiosity with true Christianity. God does not accept "church-ianity" as an acceptable basis for salvation. Some will tell stories of how they "went forward" or "prayed a prayer" and that was when they became Christians. But their lives tell another story. There are warnings in the Bible for such people.

I feel there is the possibility that many of these individuals have never understood the gospel in the first place—there has never been a true "change of mind" (repentance). My first step with such people is to encourage them to take a hard look at what they understand of the gospel. See pages 286 and 287 for tools to help explain the message clearly.

8 The Filling

As we mentioned at the beginning of the chapter, these four works of the Holy Spirit are accomplished instantaneously at salvation.

- R— Regeneration
- I — Indwelling
- B— Baptism
- S — Sealing

} This happens only *once*—at the point of salvation

There is another work of the Holy Spirit that we must touch on, called the *filling*.

- **Filling** } This happens *often*—after salvation

As I said before, to be filled with the Spirit has no similarity to filling a glass with water. Also, do not confuse the filling with any other work of the Holy Spirit. It is not the same as baptism. To understand the filling we must go back to the fact that...

> ...God created man in his own image.   *Genesis 1:27 KJV*

That image was badly marred when man sinned in the garden. But we also learned that the moment we trusted in Jesus, God began to conform us back into his image and this will continue until we enter his presence in Heaven.

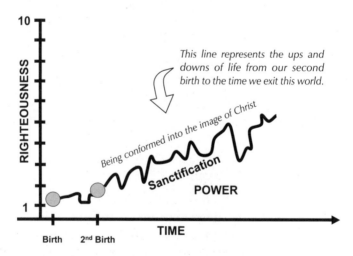

This line represents the ups and downs of life from our second birth to the time we exit this world.

RIGHTEOUSNESS

10

1

Being conformed into the image of Christ

Sanctification

POWER

TIME

Birth   2nd Birth

This process of *being conformed into the image of Christ* is sometimes called "walking with God" since it occurs one step at a time, each day. It is the same as "walking by faith," a concept we discussed when we read about Abraham and Sarah. Christians also refer to this as "walking in the light," "walking in the Spirit," of being "in fellowship with the Lord." They all mean the same thing. It has to do with being set apart for God's use—our sanctification.

WISE CHOICES

The concept of walking with God is simple to understand. It is the process of learning to make wise choices in life.

> Look carefully then how you walk, not as unwise but as wise, making the best use of the time, because the days are evil. Therefore do not be foolish, but understand what the will of the Lord is. And do not get drunk with wine, for that is debauchery, but be filled with the Spirit. Ephesians 5:15-18 ESV

How does making wise choices fit with being filled by the Spirit? What does it mean to be "filled"? The key to understanding this concept is seen in the context. Note the comparison between alcohol and the Holy Spirit.

When people are drunk with wine, they display certain characteristics: slurred speech, clumsy feet, impaired judgment. Just as there are characteristics which distinguish someone who is controlled by alcohol, there are also characteristics that identify someone who is controlled by the Holy Spirit. Those characteristics are the fruit of the Spirit.

> But the fruit of the Spirit is love, joy, peace, patience, kindness, goodness, faithfulness, gentleness, [and] self-control.
>
> Galatians 5:22-23 NASB

As we go through each day, we face choices. As we make wise choices, the Holy Spirit will be guiding us—controlling us—not in the sense of a robot, but rather in the way we make our choices.

As we make wise choices, others will see the image of Christ shining through our lives. They will see the personality of Jesus—the fruit of the Spirit. It is not me or you in the driver's seat, but the power of Christ at work within us.

I just talked with a man who, ten weeks previously, had become a believer through reading *The Stranger on the Road to Emmaus*. He had lived a tough life, but now God was at work in him. The day before we met, he had sworn at one of his co-workers. Although this was commonplace before he was saved, it now bothered him greatly. After he got home from work, he could not wait to call his co-worker on the phone and apologize. In his own words he told his coworker, *"You may not understand why I am doing this, but I know I will feel a lot better for saying it. I should not have been angry with you and sworn. It was not right. Please accept my apology."* No one told him to do this. The Spirit of God put it in his heart and he responded. You can be sure his co-worker saw something different—the fruit of the Spirit in his life. This new believer had stumbled in his "walk," but he made the right choice. He got back on his feet and kept going. This is why we say that walking with God is a day-by-day, hour-by-hour, minute-by-minute "walk of faith."

Now remember, this is all a result of *knowing* Christ, and in knowing him we *trust, love* and *respect* him. And in the process it works its way out in our lives as service to him and to others. It's our daily walk.

Also remember, just as we originally put our trust in the Lord for salvation—a step of faith—so each choice we make in our walk with the Lord is a step of faith.

> *Therefore as you have received Christ Jesus the Lord, so walk in Him, having been firmly rooted and now being built up in Him and established in your faith, just as you were instructed, and overflowing with gratitude.* Colossians 2:6-7 NASB

When I was learning to fly, I gained experience in an aircraft by "logging time"—putting in the flying hours needed to master the plane. In the same way, the Lord Jesus is pleased when we "log time" in fellowship with him, for as he said:

> *"This is to my Father's glory, that you bear much fruit, showing yourselves to be my disciples."* John 15:8 NIV

We only "bear much fruit" when we demonstrate obedience in the same direction over a long period of time. To say it again, walking with God is the process of making wise choices over an extended period of time. That is what it means to be "filled by the Spirit."

Foolish Choices

If, however, we make foolish choices, those choices will reveal what is called the works or "acts of the sinful nature." It is as though we are being controlled by wine—our judgment is impaired.

> *The acts of the sinful nature are obvious: sexual immorality, impurity and debauchery; idolatry and witchcraft; hatred, discord, jealousy, fits of rage, selfish ambition, dissensions, factions and envy; drunkenness, orgies, and the like.* Galatians 5:19-21 NIV

Christians speak of this as "walking in the flesh," or as being "out of fellowship" with the Lord. Once again, they all refer to the same thing—a Christian making foolish choices. It is the opposite of being "filled with the Spirit."

> You, however, did not come to know Christ that way. Surely you heard of him and were taught in him in accordance with the truth that is in Jesus.
>
> Therefore each of you must put off falsehood and speak truthfully to his neighbor, for we are all members of one body. "In your anger do not sin": Do not let the sun go down while you are still angry, and do not give the devil a foothold.
>
> He who has been stealing must steal no longer, but must work, doing something useful with his own hands, that he may have something to share with those in need.
>
> Do not let any unwholesome talk come out of your mouths, but only what is helpful for building others up according to their needs, that it may benefit those who listen.
>
> And do not grieve the Holy Spirit of God, with whom you were sealed for the day of redemption. Get rid of all bitterness, rage and anger, brawling and slander, along with every form of malice. Be kind and compassionate to one another, forgiving each other, just as in Christ God forgave you.
>
> Ephesians 4:20-21, 25-32 NIV

As believers, we are reliant on Scripture to know the difference between a wise and a foolish choice. It is why I call the Bible our Map—it points out the various directions we can take in life. But then the Holy Spirit sensitizes us to those directions—good and bad—and guides us toward the right choice as we are strengthened by the Lord himself.

> And we pray this in order that you may live a life worthy of the Lord and may please him in every way: bearing fruit in every good work, growing in the knowledge of God, being strengthened with all power according to his glorious might so that you may have great endurance and patience, and joyfully giving thanks to the Father, who has qualified you to share in the inheritance of the saints in the kingdom of light.
>
> Colossians 1:10-12 NIV

And remember, when we do fail, when we do make foolish choices, the Lord is there to "wash our dirty feet."

CHAPTER TWELVE

1 THE REQUEST

2 THE ANSWER

3 THE GOSPEL

4 THE LAW VERSUS GRACE

5 THE MARTYR

6 THE SAINTS

7 THE LAST ORDER

1 The Request

The events surrounding Peter's meeting with Cornelius, the Gentile from Caesarea, happened about ten years after Pentecost.

> It was about this time that King Herod arrested some who belonged to the church, intending to persecute them.
>
> Acts 12:1 NIV

This was Herod Agrippa I, the grandson of Herod the Great, who had ruled at the time of Jesus' birth. This Herod was following in the footsteps of his grandfather by persecuting the Lord and his people.

> He had James, the brother of John, executed with a sword. When he saw that this pleased the Jews, he proceeded to arrest Peter too. (This took place during the feast of Unleavened Bread.)
>
> Acts 12:2-3 NET

Herod Agrippa was a crowd-pleaser. He jailed Peter.

> And when he had seized him, he put him in prison, delivering him over to four squads of soldiers to guard him, intending after the Passover to bring him out to the people. So Peter was kept in prison, but earnest prayer for him was made to God by the church.
>
> Acts 12:4-5 ESV

Prayer

Though collective prayer has a role in the church, it is essentially an individual matter. Prayer is a believer communicating with God.

- We listen to him as we read his Word, and…
- We talk to him with thoughts expressed in the silence of our minds and spoken by the words of our mouths.

Our prayers do not need to be planned or written out. We can pray from the heart, freely and spontaneously. If prayer is difficult for you, open to the book of Psalms and read the words to the Lord. If you identify with what the Psalmist wrote then you can say amen to it. Amen means "so be it" or "it is true."

If your situation is desperate, pray through Psalm 121.

> I lift up my eyes to the hills. From where does my help come? My help comes from the LORD, who made heaven and earth.
>
> Psalm 121:1-2 ESV

If your heart is broken, you can draw strength from the Lord as you read and pray through Psalm 147.

He heals the brokenhearted and binds up their wounds.
Psalm 147:3 NKJV

What is true of the Psalms is true of the rest of Scripture. If you are sensing opposition from Satan, you can pray, thanking the Lord that…

…greater is He who is in you than he who is in the world.
1 John 4:4 NASB

When you are worried, read the words of Jesus to his disciples:

"Do not let your hearts be troubled. Trust in God; trust also in me."
John 14:1 NIV

When sick, we can pray in the words of the two blind men who called out to Jesus from the side of the road:

"Lord, Son of David, have mercy on us!"   *Matthew 20:31 NASB*

And, at any time, we can know that we have a God who cares, for the same story tells us that…

Moved with compassion, Jesus touched their eyes; and immediately they regained their sight and followed Him.
Matthew 20:34 NASB

When facing death, we can read the story surrounding Mary, Martha and Lazarus. We can take hope in the fact that Jesus said:

"I am the resurrection and the life. Whoever believes in me, though he die, yet shall he live, and everyone who lives and believes in me shall never die. Do you believe this?" *John 11:25-26 ESV*

When death does come as it surely will, and we mourn, we can then be comforted with these words:

Blessed are they that mourn: for they shall be comforted.
Matthew 5:4 KJV

When we are in doubt, perplexed and don't know what to pray, we can draw courage from knowing…

…the Spirit helps us in our weakness. We do not know what we ought to pray for, but the Spirit himself intercedes for us with groans that words cannot express. And he who searches our hearts knows the mind of the Spirit, because the Spirit intercedes for the saints in accordance with God's will.
Romans 8:26-27 NIV

As we read the Bible, it is helpful to underline the verses that speak to the concerns we all face. As we journey through life we can return to those verses over and over again as a way to pray.

HOW TO PRAY

We need not pray with eloquent words. We are to be honest with what is on our minds. Our prayers should not be wordy.

> Do not be hasty in word or impulsive in thought to bring up a matter in the presence of God. For God is in heaven and you are on the earth; therefore let your words be few.
>
> Ecclesiastes 5:2 NASB

Neither should prayer be a mindless, repetitive ritual.

> When you pray, don't babble on and on as people of other religions do. They think their prayers are answered merely by repeating their words again and again.   Matthew 6:7 NLT

We can pray anywhere at any time, quietly or out loud, with our eyes open or closed. The purpose for closing our eyes is to minimize distraction. There is no one correct posture. In the Bible people are recorded as praying with uplifted hands, faces up, heads down, on their knees, standing, bowing or prostrate—literally, on their faces. Prayer is not about technique and outward posture. It is all about the condition of our hearts—are we humble and sincere in our prayers, or arrogant and demanding? That being said, I find that when I pray, I am conscious of who I am speaking to and something inside me says, "Be respectful. Don't slouch."

WHY PRAY?

Some may wonder why we should pray. If God is in control, will he not do what is right? I am not sure that any Bible scholar can adequately answer our questions when it comes to prayer. In many ways prayer remains a mystery. And yet we are repeatedly told to pray. It is God who says that prayer makes a difference.

> Then Jesus told his disciples a parable to show them that they should always pray and not give up.   Luke 18:1 NIV

> "Ask, and it will be given to you; seek, and you will find; knock, and it will be opened to you."   Matthew 7:7 NKJV

> And pray in the Spirit on all occasions with all kinds of prayers and requests. With this in mind, be alert and always keep on praying for all the saints [or believers].   Ephesians 6:18 NIV

One thing is clear—prayer deepens our friendship with the Lord. As a married man, if I don't speak to my wife, our marriage relationship will deteriorate. In the same way, prayer in some unexplainable way draws us closer to the Lord.

We must have this in mind as we read the story of Peter's arrest and imprisonment. Everyone knew what Herod had in mind. Peter had the sentence of death hanging over his head.

> *So Peter was kept in prison, but those in the church were earnestly praying to God for him.* Acts 12:5 NET

2 The Answer

When we pray we are instructed to humbly and clearly express our thoughts to the Lord. If it is a request, we can honestly state what we would like to see happen in the situation and then trust him to do what is right. We can approach God in the same manner as Jesus did in the garden of Gethsemane when he prayed:

> *"Yet not as I will, but as you will."* Matthew 26:39 NIV

We can be honest about what we desire—our will—but then be prepared to humbly submit to what he desires—his will. Only then can we find rest in the Lord. If the Lord chooses to answer our prayers differently from what we requested, then we can be assured he will give us his supernatural strength to endure what is before us. Such was the situation facing Peter.

Herod had executed the apostle James and was certainly planning the same fate for Peter, yet Peter found his heart resting in the Lord, confident that the Lord would accomplish his will. Though Peter was in chains, he was fast asleep.

> *The night before Herod was to bring him to trial, Peter was sleeping between two soldiers, bound with two chains, and sentries stood guard at the entrance. Suddenly an angel of the Lord appeared and a light shone in the cell. He struck Peter on the side and woke him up. "Quick, get up!" he said, and the chains fell off Peter's wrists.*

> *Then the angel said to him, "Put on your clothes and sandals." And Peter did so. "Wrap your cloak around you and follow me," the angel told him. Peter followed him out of the prison, but he had no idea that what the angel was doing was really happening; he thought he was seeing a vision.* Acts 12:6-9 NIV

This was so unreal that Peter thought he was dreaming.

> *When they had passed the first and second guard, they came to the iron gate that leads into the city, which opened for them by itself; and they went out and went along one street, and immediately the angel departed from him.* Acts 12:10 NASB

It seems the Lord doesn't go beyond what is necessary to accomplish a miracle. He could have freed Peter and destroyed the prison as well as Herod, but that is not what happened.

> When Peter came to himself, he said, "Now I am sure that the Lord has sent his angel and rescued me from the hand of Herod and from all that the Jewish people were expecting."
>
> Acts 12:11 ESV

You can be sure Peter made short work of putting space between the prison and himself.

> He went to the house of Mary, the mother of John Mark, where many people had gathered together and were praying. When he knocked at the door of the outer gate, a slave girl named Rhoda answered. When she recognized Peter's voice, she was so overjoyed she did not open the gate, but ran back in and told them that Peter was standing at the gate. Acts 12:12-14 NET

DOUBTERS

In the culture of that day, a woman's word was not considered reliable—no one believed Rhoda.

> "You're out of your mind," they told her. When she kept insisting that it was so, they said, "It must be his angel."
>
> Acts 12:15 NIV

It was so unlikely that Peter would be released that the "prayer warriors" figured seeing an angel was more believable! And yet God had answered their prayers, feeble as they were. We need to remember this story when we are prone to doubt God's willingness to answer one of our prayers.

> But Peter continued knocking: and when they had opened the door, and saw him, they were astonished. Acts 12:16 KJV

In the last section I mentioned how we can pray when in certain situations—when desperate, broken, worried, anxious, sick, facing death, mourning, doubting, perplexed and when we don't know what to pray. But what are we to pray when we are thankful? No doubt, Peter and his friends were very grateful. Once again we can turn to the Psalms.

> Oh give thanks to the LORD, for he is good, for his steadfast love endures forever! Psalm 107:1 ESV

Praying when we are thankful is not so hard. As to Peter and his friends, their praises to God must have raised quite a commotion.

> *Peter motioned with his hand for them to be quiet and described how the Lord had brought him out of prison. "Tell James and the brothers about this," he said, and then he left for another place.*
>
> Acts 12:17 NIV

Seeing no use in inconveniencing the Lord to perform another miracle, Peter went into hiding.

NEXT DAY

> *Now when day came, there was no little disturbance among the soldiers over what had become of Peter. And after Herod searched for him and did not find him, he examined the sentries and ordered that they should be put to death.*
>
> Acts 12:18-19 ESV

A similar situation happened with the soldiers guarding the tomb of Jesus. The officials paid the guards a huge sum of money to spread a lie, saying the body of Jesus had been stolen while the guards slept. But now with Peter, the guards were not politically useful, so they were executed. That would effectively smother any stories the guards might relate about the miraculous disappearance of a prisoner under their watch. After executing the guards…

> *…Herod went down from Judea to Caesarea and stayed there.*
>
> *On a day determined in advance, Herod put on his royal robes, sat down on the judgment seat, and made a speech to them. But the crowd began to shout, "The voice of a god, and not of a man!"*
>
> Acts 12:19, 21-22 NET

Herod, though a king, was just a man. Yet he allowed the crowd to worship him as though he was divine. Herod knew better.

> *Immediately an angel of the Lord struck him down, because he did not give God the glory, and he was eaten by worms and breathed his last.*
>
> Acts 12:23 ESV

The secular historian, Josephus, recorded this event.[1] He wrote that it was morning when Herod walked onto the stage, clothed in a silver cloak, prepared to give his speech. At that moment the sun peeked above the lip of the coliseum and shone on Herod, setting his clothing ablaze with light. Josephus recorded the adulation he received and his subsequent horrible death. It is notable that the story ends with these words:

> *But the word of God kept on increasing and multiplying.*
>
> Acts 12:24 NET

3 THE GOSPEL

The fact that a Gentile audience had accepted a Jewish message created a crisis in the early church. It boiled down to the nature of the gospel.

> Now some men came down from Judea and began to teach the brothers, "Unless you are circumcised according to the custom of Moses, you cannot be saved."   Acts 15:1 NET

The Law of Moses clearly prescribed the rite of circumcision for all Jewish males—the cutting off of the foreskin on all male babies. Some of the new Jewish believers were stating that in order to be saved, all male Gentiles needed this procedure too, in addition to trusting in Christ. A counsel was called in Jerusalem to settle the controversy. Those involved in the discussion headed to the city, and...

> When they arrived in Jerusalem, they were received by the church and the apostles and the elders, and they reported all the things God had done with them. But some from the religious party of the Pharisees who had believed stood up and said, "It is necessary to circumcise the Gentiles and to order them to observe the law of Moses."   Acts 15:4-5 NET

These new Jewish believers were not only calling for circumcision, but obedience to all 613 laws of Moses. They felt this was necessary to be saved.

> Both the apostles and the elders met together to deliberate about this matter. After there had been much debate, Peter stood up and said to them, "Brothers, you know that some time ago God chose me to preach to the Gentiles so they would hear the message of the gospel and believe. And God, who knows the heart, has testified to them by giving them the Holy Spirit just as he did to us, and he made no distinction between them and us, cleansing their hearts by faith.
>
> "So now why are you putting God to the test by placing on the neck of the disciples a yoke that neither our ancestors nor we have been able to bear? On the contrary, we believe that we are saved through the grace of the Lord Jesus, in the same way as they are."   Acts 15:6-11 NET

The counsel concluded that requiring anyone to keep the Law of Moses was adding to the gospel. As that first counsel affirmed—we are saved simply by faith in Jesus.

Two Events

Part of the confusion came as a result of not understanding the difference between *law* and *grace*. There is a big difference, not only as it relates to being saved, but also in regards to our daily walk as a believer. Here is a little background.

According to Jewish calculations, the day the Lord gave Moses the 613 laws on Mount Sinai was the same day of the year later celebrated as the Feast of Pentecost. Almost 1400 years after Mount Sinai, on that same day of the year, the Holy Spirit arrived and was placed into the body of Christ. Now whether the Jewish calculations are correct or not, you still end up with quite a contrast—the coming of the Law and the coming of the Spirit.

	Two events that happened on the same day of the year	
What	The Law of Moses given	The Holy Spirit indwells church
Source	Jewish Calculations[2]	The Scriptures
Where	Mount Sinai	Mount Zion (Jerusalem)
When	Circa 1440 BC	AD 33 - on the day of Pentecost
Focus	LAW	GRACE

The Bible is clear that keeping the Law, or any other list of good deeds, will not make a person right with God. The Law shows us that we are sinners, that it is impossible to keep the Law perfectly. The good news is that...

> ...*now a righteousness from God, apart from law, has been made known, to which the [entire Old Testament testifies]. This righteousness from God comes through faith in Jesus Christ to all who believe. There is no difference, for all have sinned and fall short of the glory of God, and are **justified freely** by his grace through the redemption that came by Christ Jesus.*
> Romans 3:21-24 NIV

Jesus never sinned, yet **God chose to treat Jesus as if he had sinned, so that he would be able to treat us as if we were righteous**. This is the concept of justification. It is critical to everything you have been learning—it is the foundation. Let me say it again: God chose to treat Jesus as if he had sinned, so that he would be able to treat us as if we were righteous.

*So we, too, have put our faith in Christ Jesus that we may be **justified by faith** in Christ and not by observing the law, because by observing the law no one will be justified.*

Galatians 2:16 NIV

As we trust in Jesus, the Lord takes our sin and gives us his righteousness. It is a great exchange. From that point on, God makes a judicial decision to look upon us as perfect in his sight. We are justified—declared righteous, fit for God's presence—all as a result of faith in Christ.

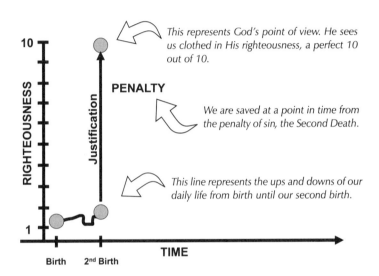

This represents God's point of view. He sees us clothed in His righteousness, a perfect 10 out of 10.

We are saved at a point in time from the penalty of sin, the Second Death.

This line represents the ups and downs of our daily life from birth until our second birth.

PREPARED BY THE LAW

Now that faith has come, we are no longer under the supervision of the law.

Galatians 3:25 NIV

What does "no longer under the supervision of the law" mean? Think of the Law as though it were a stern schoolmaster. Professor Law was put in charge of us to give us a good dose of his thinking. He ruled with an iron rod to keep us out of trouble, all the while teaching us the Moral Law, God's standard of righteousness. That lesson left us feeling lost, as helpless sinners. He also schooled us in the Ceremonial Law and we found out we needed a substitute to deliver us from sin. But Professor Law did not discuss the Saviour.

Once we had learned our lessons in the school of Law,[3] the professor took us by the arm and led us to another school—the school of Grace. It was here we learned that Jesus was our perfect substitute; our sin could be forgiven and we could be declared righteous by faith in Christ. As we saw in an earlier chapter...

...the law was our schoolmaster to bring us unto Christ.

Galatians 3:24 KJV

Once we put our faith in Christ, we graduated from the school of Law and were set completely free from the professor's iron clad authority—his supervision.

But we weren't set free to be "above the law." We did not graduate into the school of Grace to forget everything we had learned in the school of Law. The Law prepared us for grace. You see, we couldn't really understand grace until we had experienced Law.

Think of it this way. A traffic policeman pulls you over for speeding. He writes out a ticket that hits you with the full penalty of the law. You realize you are out of pocket a significant sum of money. But then he writes "WARNING" across the ticket and says that you don't have to pay the fine. At that moment he has shown you something you didn't deserve—he has shown you grace. As you drive off, a little slower (keeping the law), you sense in your being a profound relief. You have experienced both law and grace. As I said before, you can't really understand grace until you have experienced law. The biblical Law prepared us for the grace that was shown in Christ. To be saved from sin, we rely on his grace alone.

4 The Law versus Grace

I mentioned in an earlier chapter, a question often asked by new believers is, "As a Christian, do I need to keep the Ten Commandments?" This was a question faced by the early church. Once again, the answer lies in a story involving Peter. Peter was visiting with believers in a city called Antioch, located in the country of Lebanon. While there he faced a situation later recorded by another apostle, called Paul:

But when Peter came to Antioch, I had to oppose him to his face, for what he did was very wrong. When he first arrived, he ate with the Gentile believers, who were not circumcised.

Galatians 2:11-12 NLT

Antioch was essentially a Gentile church. As long as Gentiles surrounded Peter, he ate the diet of a Gentile.

But afterward, when some friends of James came, Peter wouldn't eat with the Gentiles anymore.   Galatians 2:12 NLT

James was part of the local church in Jerusalem, so his friends were Jewish. When they showed up in Antioch, Peter changed his diet, making a beeline back to the school of Law. He began to follow the part of the 613 laws that governed what a Jew ate and did not eat. James' Jewish friends hadn't said this was necessary, but Peter wasn't taking a chance. Peter was...

...afraid of criticism from these people who insisted on the necessity of circumcision. As a result, other Jewish Christians followed Peter's hypocrisy, and even Barnabas was led astray by their hypocrisy.   Galatians 2:12-13 NLT

Poor Peter. There he was, denying everything he had learned in the school of grace. He was afraid of what the Jews—the circumcision group—would think of him. The apostle Paul confronted Peter.

When I saw that they were not following the truth of the gospel message, I said to Peter in front of all the others, "Since you, a Jew by birth, have discarded the Jewish laws and are living like a Gentile, why are you now trying to make these Gentiles follow the Jewish traditions?"   Galatians 2:12-14 NLT

Paul wasn't speaking of what Peter needed to do to be saved. Rather, he was confronting Peter about how he should live as a believer.

"You and I are Jews by birth, not 'sinners' like the Gentiles. Yet we know that a person is made right with God by faith in Jesus Christ, not by obeying the law. And we have believed in Christ Jesus, so that we might be made right with God because of our faith in Christ, not because we have obeyed the law. For no one will ever be made right with God by obeying the law."   Galatians 2:15-16 NLT

"If, while we seek to be justified in Christ, it becomes evident that we ourselves are [living like the Gentiles], does that mean that Christ promotes sin?"   Galatians 2:17 NIV

To rephrase the question, "If we are saved by grace, then do we need to keep the Law to walk with the Lord?" Paul said:

"Absolutely not! Rather, I am a sinner if I rebuild the old system of law I already tore down."   Galatians 2:17-18 NLT

Paul said that it was sin to enforce the 613 laws on believers. To do so was to put them back in the school of Law, under the iron fist of a professor who knew nothing of grace. Paul said the reason for this was that...

> ...when I tried to keep the law, it condemned me.
>
> Galatians 2:19 NLT

The Law didn't make Paul righteous; it just condemned him.

Although for studying purposes it may be helpful to distinguish between the Moral, Civil and Ceremonial Law, from a practical viewpoint, the Bible makes no such distinction. If you are going to try keeping the laws of Moses, whether for salvation or in your daily walk as a believer, then you need to obey all 613 laws, not just the Moral Code.[4] If you are feeling a huge weight descend upon your shoulders, you should, for you are back in the school of Law.

But then, let go of your heavy burden, for Jesus said:

> "Do not think that I have come to abolish the Law or the Prophets; I have not come to abolish them but to fulfill them."
>
> Matthew 5:17 NIV

Jesus fulfilled the demands of the Mosaic Law which called for perfect obedience. You could say he wrapped things up for all 613 laws. Now we are not...

> ...under law but under grace.
>
> Romans 6:14 NKJV

In other words, we no longer live under the strict supervision of Professor Law, but we live in the school of Grace.

Does that mean we don't have to obey any laws anymore? Well, not really. In fact, the New Testament has far more laws than the 613 found in the Old Testament. We are now told to...

> ...obey the law of Christ.
>
> Galatians 6:2 NLT

The "law of Christ" is different than the "law of Moses," and yet on moral issues, they are essentially the same.

But it isn't about a list of rules anyway; it is about the purpose and motivation behind it all. You see, he who fulfilled the Law also works in us to obey the spirit of the Law—not the letter, but the spirit.

We are not saved by grace from the eternal penalty of sin, only to find ourselves needing to keep the Ten Commandments to be delivered from the daily power of sin. That is impossible. No, it is all grace, a love that is undeserved, yet abundant and free.

> I do not set aside the grace of God, for if righteousness could be gained through the law, Christ died for nothing! Galatians 2:21 NIV

School of Law	School of Grace
Condemned me as unable to please the Lord	Sets me free to please the Lord as I trust in him
Put me on the treadmill of performance to be accepted	Teaches me that I am accepted because of Christ's performance
Life lived as a promissory IOU note	Life lived as a thank you note
Letter of the Law—legalism	Spirit of the Law—liberty
Performance-driven—I get the glory for my efforts to be good.	Love-driven—God gets the glory for his grace to sinners
The Law says, "Run, John, run," but then gives my feet no strength to run.	Grace says, "Run, John, run," and then the Holy Spirit empowers my feet to run.
Written on stone	Written on the human heart
Called the Mosaic Law, or the Law of Moses	Called the "law of Christ" (1 Corinthians 9:21; Galatians 6:2)
For the law was given through Moses... John 1:17a ESV	*...grace and truth came through Jesus Christ.* John 1:17b ESV

I was discussing the Law versus Grace dynamic with a lawyer friend. He gave a helpful illustration. He said, "I don't go home from work determined to not take up with the lady next door because the Law says it is wrong. I go home to dwell with my wife because she is the one I love. My behaviour is not ruled by the Law, but constrained by my love."

The difference is huge! It is the love of Christ that motivates us, and in motivating us, he controls our behaviour.

> *For the love of Christ constraineth us.* 2 Corinthians 5:14 KJV

Another translation of the same verse reads:

> *For the love of Christ controls us.* 2 Corinthians 5:14 ESV

As believers, we want to please the Lord by the way we live. But that is only possible as the life of Christ is lived out in us moment by moment, as we are "constrained" or "controlled" by his love. Grace does not do away with obedience to God. In fact, the grace of God is the only means whereby I can obey God. Why? Because grace does not just motivate me to do righteous works; it works in me to become an obedient person. He died to set me free to love him, and in loving him I serve him. It is all part of being conformed to his image.

5 The Martyr

After the events surrounding Cornelius in Caesarea and Peter's subsequent escape from King Herod, we don't hear much more about him. The Bible does not record Peter's death. The early church fathers or leaders—those who came immediately after the apostles—recorded Peter as having been martyred.

In the original biblical sense of the word, martyrs voluntarily suffered or died as the punishment for refusing to renounce their faith. In the process of dying, a martyr did not destroy property or someone else's life. Martyrs were killed because someone despised what they stood for.

It is quite certain that Peter died for his faith. Late in the first century, Clement of Rome, who was said to have had direct connections with the apostles, wrote of Peter:

"The greatest and most just pillars of the Church were persecuted, and came even unto death... Peter, through unjust envy...having delivered his testimony, departed unto the place of glory due to him."[5]

Beyond That

Details of Peter's martyrdom are sketchy, but tradition has it that Peter was crucified in Rome at the time of the great fire under Emperor Nero. It is said that Peter requested that he be crucified upside down so as not to die in the same manner as his Saviour.

There may be a kernel of truth about Peter being martyred in Rome, for no source describes Peter's death as being in any other place. Beyond that, additional information seems to come from a second century book called *The Acts of Peter*.[6] In this book, Peter is recorded as saying, *"I beseech you the executioners, crucify me thus, with the head downward and not otherwise."*

Consider the Source

The only problem is that *The Acts of Peter* is a highly questionable source for reliable information.[7] During this time there was a heightened interest in all things related to Jesus and the apostles. A number of spurious books were written, no doubt, for monetary gain or sensational value.

Some of these counterfeit books have been dragged to the forefront in recent years. Of these, the Gnostic Gospels are best known with *The Gospel According to Thomas* at the forefront. These "gospels" read very differently from the Gospels in your Bible. The early church leaders called *The Gospel of Thomas* and other similar books a false gospel, not only bogus, but "the fictions of heretics," irreverent and bizarre, "to be cast aside as absurd and impious."[8]

So to put much stock in *The Acts of Peter* and what it had to say about Simon Peter being crucified upside down is questionable. That being said, the idea of Peter requesting such a death so as not to distract from his Lord's sacrifice, is certainly consistent with his character. Peter was a humble man. It is also consistent with history. Josephus, a first-century historian, recorded Roman soldiers amusing themselves by crucifying criminals in different positions. Jesus had told Peter:

> "Truly, truly, I say to you, when you were young, you used to dress yourself and walk wherever you wanted, but when you are old, you will stretch out your hands, and another will dress you and carry you where you do not want to go." (This he said to show by what kind of death he was to glorify God.)
>
> John 21:18-19 ESV

Whether the stretching out of the hands implied crucifixion or not we don't really know. It is best to leave it at that.

Peter knew what it was like to face hard times. He wrote the following about being ill-treated:

> But if you suffer for doing good and you endure it, this is commendable before God. To this you were called, because Christ suffered for you, leaving you an example, that you should follow in his steps. "He committed no sin, and no deceit was found in his mouth." When they hurled their insults at him, he did not retaliate; when he suffered, he made no threats. Instead, he entrusted himself to him who judges justly. He himself bore our sins in his body on the tree, so that we might die to sins and live for righteousness; by his wounds you have been healed. For you were like sheep going astray, but now you have returned to the Shepherd and Overseer of your souls.
>
> 1 Peter 2:20-25 NIV

Glorification

The Lord has not promised us a "bed of roses," but he does say he will be with us through the dark times in life. And when the day comes to face death, whether by ill health, old age or martyrdom, the Bible says we will be delivered from the very **presence** of sin.

> *For we know that when this earthly tent we live in is taken down (that is, when we die and leave this earthly body), we will have a house in heaven, an eternal body made for us by God himself and not by human hands. We grow weary in our present bodies, and we long to put on our heavenly bodies like new clothing. For we will put on heavenly bodies; we will not be spirits without bodies.*
>
> *While we live in these earthly bodies, we groan and sigh, but it's not that we want to die and get rid of these bodies that clothe us. Rather, we want to put on our new bodies so that these dying bodies will be swallowed up by life. God himself has prepared us for this, and as a guarantee he has given us his Holy Spirit.*
>
> *So we are always confident, even though we know that as long as we live in these bodies we are not at home with the Lord. For we live by believing and not by seeing. Yes, we are fully confident, and we would rather be away from these earthly bodies, for then we will be at home with the Lord.* 2 Corinthians 5:1-8 NLT
>
> *Therefore we make it our aim, whether present or absent, to be well pleasing to Him. For we must all appear before the judgment seat of Christ, that each one may receive the things done in the body, according to what he has done, whether good or bad.* 2 Corinthians 5:9-10 NKJV

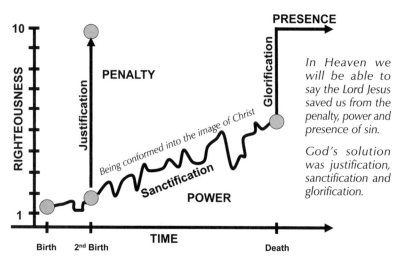

In Heaven we will be able to say the Lord Jesus saved us from the penalty, power and presence of sin.

God's solution was justification, sanctification and glorification.

6 THE SAINTS

Death is never a pleasant subject to talk about. But for believers the sting of death is gone. When we die the Lord is waiting for us.

> *Precious in the sight of the LORD is the death of his saints.*
> Psalm 116:15 KJV

In the Bible, the designation of *saint* does not apply to just a few select individuals. Rather, it is a synonym for all genuine believers.

> *As Peter traveled about the country, he went to visit the saints in Lydda.*
> Acts 9:32 NIV

It simply means that Peter visited the Christians in Lydda. The same was said of Christians in other cities—the saints in Jerusalem, the saints in Rome, and so forth. It is a collective term.

> *As in all the congregations of the saints...* 1 Corinthians 14:33 NIV
>
> *To all [not just a select few] that be in Rome, beloved of God, called to be saints.*
> Romans 1:7 KJV

The idea of labelling a few as saints and venerating them to the point of worship and prayers, is completely out of step with the entire tenor of Scripture. Peter refused to be so honoured. Remember how Cornelius fell on his face before Peter?

> *But Peter made him get up. "Stand up," he said, "I am only a man myself."*
> Acts 10:26 NIV

Only Yahweh, the Creator God, is to be held in such regard.

UNIQUE ONES

So if all believers are called *saints*, then what does the word mean? The word is actually related in meaning to the words *sanctify* and *holy*.

We saw before that the word *holy* carries the idea of being "separated from, being unique, one-of-a-kind." In a similar way, the word *saint* means "to be set apart or sanctified." As believers, God has separated us from the masses of the world and placed us into the body of Christ as his holy ones—as his saints.

> *Therefore, prepare your minds for action; be self-controlled; set your hope fully on the grace to be given you when Jesus Christ is revealed. As obedient children, do not conform to the evil desires you had when you lived in ignorance. But just as he who called you is holy, so be holy in all you do; for it is written: "Be holy, because I am holy."*

Since you call on a Father who judges each man's work impartially, live your lives as strangers here in reverent fear.

1 Peter 1:13-17 NIV

As saints, we are not to be weird or bizarre, but we are to be unique in the sense of having integrity and honour. Jesus prayed:

"I do not ask that you take them out of the world, but that you keep them from the evil one. They are not of the world, just as I am not of the world. Sanctify them [or set them apart] in the truth; your word is truth."   *John 17:15-17 ESV*

As "set apart ones" we are to follow in the footsteps of those who have gone before. Peter wrote:

Humble yourselves, therefore, under God's mighty hand, that he may lift you up in due time. Cast all your anxiety on him because he cares for you.

Be self-controlled and alert. Your enemy the devil prowls around like a roaring lion looking for someone to devour. Resist him, standing firm in the faith, because you know that your brothers throughout the world are undergoing the same kind of sufferings.

And the God of all grace, who called you to his eternal glory in Christ, after you have suffered a little while, will himself restore you and make you strong, firm and steadfast. To him be the power for ever and ever. Amen.   *1 Peter 5:6-11 NIV*

God has given us a Map and a Guide that we can count on. As we take steps of faith each day, relying on the Lord Jesus to strengthen us for the journey, we will be growing up in him. We will be maturing spiritually. Remember to "log time" in fellowship with the Lord. It will not always be easy or comfortable, however, God has not left us here to be comfortable, but to be comforters. We need to press on, determined to follow the Lord at all cost, knowing the truthfulness of what Peter wrote, when he said:

But in keeping with his promise we are looking forward to a new heaven and a new earth, the home of righteousness.

2 Peter 3:13 NIV

7 The Last Order

As I close this book, I want to take you back to the seven Jewish Feasts. First, there were the Feasts of Passover, Unleavened Bread and Firstfruits. We saw that these Feasts prophetically pictured the death and resurrection of our Lord.

Then 50 days after the resurrection came Pentecost. This feast illustrated the coming of the Holy Spirit to live in all believers. It completed the four spring feasts. We haven't considered the three fall feasts since they concern the Lord's return.

However, sandwiched between the instructions related to the spring and fall feasts were four months linking the two seasons. In a very real sense, prophetically, we are living in this time period. Pentecost is past, but the events surrounding the fall feasts are yet to come. It is perhaps significant that when God gave the instructions to Moses, he had this to say about that interval:

> *"When you reap the harvest of your land, do not reap to the very edges of your field or gather the gleanings of your harvest. Leave them for the poor and the alien. I am the LORD your God."*
>
> Leviticus 23:22 NIV

In this context, an alien was a non-Jew—a Gentile. God gave Moses instructions as to who could participate in the harvest. Simply put, when the Israelites went out to gather their crops, the Gentiles should be allowed to harvest as well.

Earlier on, we saw that Jesus compared the people of the world to a huge field of ripe grain needing the gospel. He said:

> *"Do you not say, 'Four months more and then the harvest'? I tell you, open your eyes and look at the fields! They are ripe for harvest."*
>
> John 4:35 NIV

Based on God's prophetic instruction to Moses, all believing Gentiles have now been included in the harvest.

> *For you are all sons of God through faith in Christ Jesus. For all of you who were baptized into Christ have clothed yourselves with Christ.*
>
> *There is neither Jew nor [Gentile], there is neither slave nor free man, there is neither male nor female; for you are all one in Christ Jesus.*
>
> Galatians 3:26-28 NASB

Both Jew and Gentile are part of the harvest.

However, God instructed the Jews to include not only the Gentiles, but also the poor. What does this mean? I think it refers to the kind of people the Lord often uses to accomplish his work.

> *Think about the circumstances of your call, brothers and sisters. Not many were wise by human standards, not many were powerful, not many were born to a privileged position. But God chose what the world thinks foolish to shame the*

wise, and God chose what the world thinks weak to shame the strong. God chose what is low and despised in the world, what is regarded as nothing, to set aside what is regarded as something, so that no one can boast in his presence.

He is the reason you have a relationship with Christ Jesus, who became for us wisdom from God, and righteousness and sanctification and redemption, so that, as it is written, "Let the one who boasts, boast in the Lord." 1 Corinthians 1:26-31 NET

Jews, Gentiles, even the "poor in spirit" are included in the harvest. None can boast in their abilities. They can only boast in the Lord.

Last Order

A strange story emerged from the Pacific long after the blood and gore of World War II had washed away. As the Japanese army retreated before the advancing Allies, they left behind highly-disciplined soldiers with orders to delay the advance and provide intelligence. One such man was Second Lieutenant Hiroo Onoda. He was assigned to Lubang Island in the Philippines.

As Onoda prepared for his mission, his commander told him, *"You are absolutely forbidden to die by your own hand. It may take three years, it may take five, but whatever happens, we'll come back for you. Until then, so long as you have one soldier, you are to continue to lead him. You may have to live on coconuts. If that's the case, live on coconuts! Under no circumstances are you to give up your life voluntarily."*[9]

Within a short time of landing on Lubang, all but Onoda and three other soldiers had either died or surrendered. Onoda ordered the men to hide in the hills. In 1945, when the war ended with the surrender of the Japanese army, Onoda kept on fighting. Any efforts to convince him and his fellow soldiers that the war was over was seen as an enemy ruse. Twenty-nine years later, after the deaths of his fellow soldiers and many innocent civilians, Onoda was still fighting.

Finally in 1974, Onoda was found by Norio Suzuki, a Japanese college student travelling the world. Suzuki gained Onoda's trust to the point where he was able to talk to him about surrendering. Onoda said he would only surrender if a superior officer ordered him to do so.

Suzuki returned to Japan with photos of himself and Onoda. He sufficiently convinced the Japanese government to locate Onoda's former commanding officer, Major Taniguchi. Together with Norio

Suzuki , Major Taniguchi flew to Lubang on the ninth of March, 1974. They were able to connect with Onoda whereupon Major Taniguchi gave Onoda new orders. He was to surrender.

Very little in this story parallels the Church. The Imperial Japanese Army of WWII was often brutal to its enemies, whereas the Church is told to love its enemies. Onoda lived for years under a delusion that cost people their lives, whereas the Church is committed to sharing the truth that sets people free. But Onoda had one thing right. He knew that an order was to be obeyed. And he kept right on obeying that order even though months stretched into many years.

As believers we have been given our order. Jesus said:

> *"All authority in heaven and on earth has been given to me. Therefore go and make disciples of all nations, baptizing them in the name of the Father and of the Son and of the Holy Spirit, and teaching them to obey everything I have commanded you. And surely I am with you always, to the very end of the age."*   Matthew 28:18-20 NIV

It has been a long time since Jesus gave that command—almost 2000 years. It is an order that has not changed. We need to keep on obeying it, as a lifelong lifestyle. We have the promise that his sacred presence is with us.

For centuries God spoke to the world through his Chosen People, the Israelites. But now, the task belongs to both Jews and Gentiles—all are included. It is harvest time.

I leave you with the final words written by Peter. Notice how it talks about growing in love and knowing Jesus better, all necessary for us to be conformed to his image.

> *But grow in grace, and in the knowledge of our Lord and Saviour Jesus Christ. To him be glory both now and for ever. Amen.*   2 Peter 3:18 KJV.

GLOSSARY

Antitype: a New Testament fulfillment of an Old Testament "type," *anti* being Greek or Latin for "opposite" or "corresponding to" such as in the case of two halves of a die used in casting a product. The type would be a picture or symbol, usually presented in physical form (such as a lamb), with the antitype being the actual fulfillment (such as Jesus being the Lamb of God).

Baptism: to be identified with, as when a new believer is identified with the death, burial and resurrection of Christ; to be placed into, as when the Holy Spirit is placed into a new believer.

Bereans: a group of believers in a city called Berea. Their perspective on the Word has been used as an example for other believers over the centuries. It was said that when they heard the Bible taught, *"they received the word with great eagerness, examining the Scriptures daily to see whether these things were so"* Acts 17:11 NASB.

Circumcision: the name used of the Jews in contrast to the Gentiles. In biblical times all Jewish male infants underwent a minor surgical procedure where the foreskin was removed, a physical mark reminding them they were children of the covenant between God and his people.

Grace: to show compassion, forgiveness, undeserved love.

Indwelt (Indwelling): the Holy Spirit living within the believer.

LORD (all capital letters, Old Testament): refers to Yahweh—the personal name of God in the Hebrew language. The ancient Israelites were in such awe of Yahweh that they refused to speak his name. In reading the Hebrew Scriptures out loud, whenever they came to the word *Yahweh* they would simply say "Lord" or "The Name" with everyone understanding that it was actually referring to Yahweh.

Lord (upper and lower case letters): meaning "master" or "ruler." In the New Testament, which was written in Greek, the word *Yahweh* does not appear. However, if the word *Lord* is used in quoting the Old Testament or it is a plain reference to the Old Testament LORD, then the context may determine that it is specifically referring to God's personal name, Yahweh.

Mercy: to set aside punishment, to not give what is deserved.

Omnipotent: all-powerful; *omni* meaning "all," and *potent* referring to "power."

Omniscient: all-knowing; *omni* meaning "all," and *scient* derived from the word *science* meaning "knowledge."

Omnipresent: everywhere present at one time; *omni* meaning "all," and *present* referring to "presence."

Regeneration (Regenerate): to be born again; to have new life — spiritual life.

Saint: one who has been set apart; every believer is a saint.

Sanctification (Sanctify, Sanctified): to be set apart.

Sealed (Sealing): the Holy Spirit given as a mark of ownership, placed by God.

Secular: In this book I use the word *secular* in the sense of being devoid or empty of all spiritual or religious influence. I recognize that in some regions of the world, secularism is understood as giving equal treatment to all religions.

Theophany: The word comes from the Greek language, where *theo* means "God" and *phan* means "to show" — as in *theophan* or *theophany*. Indications of a theophany are the words "the Lord came down," or "the Lord appeared"; mention of "the Angel [or literally, the Messenger] of the Lord." Theophanies in the Old Testament were probably the Lord Jesus appearing on earth before his offical "first coming" arrival in Bethlehem.

Type: an Old Testament picture or symbol, usually presented in a physical form (such as a lamb), with the antitype being the "real thing" fulfilled in the New Testament (such as Jesus being the Lamb of God).

Yahweh: the personal name of the Creator, God himself. Often spelled using only the consonants, YHWH, called "the tetragrammaton."

Yoke: a U-shaped piece of wood, placed across the neck of one or two animals (such as oxen) to harness them for pulling loads.

Uncircumcision: The name used of all Gentiles in contrast to the Jews. See **Circumcision.**

ENDNOTES

CHAPTER ONE

1. I am reluctant to talk about the life of a believer in term of "charts," "next steps" or having "keys to life." Such visuals and terms can be used beyond their intended purpose and mislead a person. However, in this book I have done so, because I have seen how helpful they are to so many. If the charts tend to confuse you, then just skip them and move on.

2. The Bible does not give us a list of "keys." I mention four, but others could be added.

3. In teaching on sanctification, my goal has been to have the reader walk away each day with a passion to "know Christ," rather than "work harder" or "do better." This is what Paul the apostle aspired to when he wrote Philippians 3:8-10.

4. We will learn the place of these concepts as we progress in the story.

5. "The 'Cockcrow' was a proverbial expression for early morning before sunrise." J. F. Walvoord and R. B. Zuck, eds., *The Bible Knowledge Commentary: An Exposition of the Scriptures* (Wheaton: Victor Books, 1983-c1985), 2:179.

6. Many scholars believe that Psalms 42 and 43 were written by King David, as they have the feel of his writing. He would have presented the psalm to sons of Korah to perform (see 2 Chronicles 20:19). On the other hand, the sons of Korah may have written them. We cannot say for sure who wrote these psalms.

7. The specific religions that subscribe to these views can be easily found on the internet.

8. Discrepancies between copies are often indicated in the footnotes or margins of your Bible, giving the variant reading.

CHAPTER TWO

1. The ancient Israelites were in such awe of Yahweh that they refused to speak his name. In reading Scriptures out loud, wherever they came to the word *Yahweh* they would simply say "Lord" or "The Name" with everyone understanding that it was actually referring to Yahweh. So, in the written text of the Bible, whenever you see the name LORD, with all the letters capitalized, you are actually reading "Yahweh."

    In contrast, when you read the word *Lord*, spelled using upper and lower case letters, it simply means "master" or "ruler." The exception to this would in be in the New Testament, where the Old is being quoted. In that case, checking the Old Testament verse will show whether it is God's personal name or simply referring to "master."

2. Jeremiah 18:1-6.

3. The soul, conscience, mind, heart and spirit are somehow interrelated. Some teach that humanity is dichotomous (two parts: body and soul/ spirit); others make the case for a trichotomous being (three parts: body and soul and spirit). There are good arguments for both views.

4. *Collins English Dictionary, 12th ed.*, s.v. "conscience."

5. On the inverse, a computer-programmer God, if true, could be blamed by man for "making me this way." A sexual deviant could say this was the way God predetermined him to be, so he cannot help it, shifting the blame for his sin on God. Such a concept is not found in Scripture, and an overall understanding of God's character places it far from such a belief system. Islam and the eastern religions do hold to a deterministic god as did some of the ancient Greek and Nordic religions, but the sovereignty of God must not be confused with such determinism.

CHAPTER THREE

1. Some create a fourth category just for the Ten Commandments, dividing them out of the Moral Law, as those inscribed in stone.
2. The Ceremonial Law, as part of the 613 laws, had a role in leading us to Christ. I focused more on this in my previous books.
3. Q.I. Hingora, *The Prophecies of the Holy Qur'an* (Lahore: Sh. Muhammad Ashraf, 1997). This book suggests 22 predictions in the Qur'an. Generally, among Qur'anic scholars, there are said to be 22 predictive prophecies in the Qur'an. (NOTE: A chapter in the Qur'an is called a *Sura*). Those 22 cited predictions are found in: Suraw 2:23-24; 3:10,106,107,144; 5:70; 8:7; 9:14; 15:9,96; 24:55; 28:85; 30:2-4; 41:42; 48:16-21, 27, 28; 54:44-48; 56:1-56; and 110:1-2.
4. Biblical scholars call illustrative prophesies *types* and their fulfillments are called *antitypes* — "anti"(Greek/Latin) being the corresponding "opposite" of a type. It was used of a die or mould, where the one side of the mould corresponds to the impression made over against or opposite the other side. The biblical *type* is a foreshadow of the real event, that being the opposite type or *antitype*.
5. Those whom Jesus brought back to life while he ministered here on earth were essentially resuscitations, not resurrections. They continued to live in sinful bodies and died again. They did not receive glorified bodies.
6. It seems quite evident that the way the Holy Spirit related to believers before Pentecost is different than after. To ignore this distinction creates problems in Bible interpretation, forcing one to make a number of unsupported assumptions.

CHAPTER FOUR

1. Exodus 13:1-2 NLT: *"Then the Lord said to Moses, 'Dedicate to me every firstborn among the Israelites. The first offspring to be born, of both humans and animals, belongs to me.'"*
2. I have been to this well a couple of times. A cup of water poured down the well took over three seconds to splash. It is thought the well may have been twice as deep during the life of Christ.
3. I am not sure where the idea of classifying miracles originated. I found one source mentioning Dr. Henry Morris, but it did not state he had originated the idea, just that he spoke of miracles having defining characteristics. Of course, Scripture makes no such distinctions. I do find it helpful in understanding the nature of miracles. The distinctions you see in this book are mine, which may differ somewhat from others.
4. The secondary purpose for these miracles was to relieve suffering, rescue the threatened, etc.

5. If Class-A miracles authenticate a message and messenger, then why are they not more common today? Surely, the need still exists for a message to be authenticated. The difference between now and then would be that we have the full body of revealed Scripture. This did not exist back then. Scripture authenticates the identity of Jesus as well as his message.

CHAPTER FIVE

1. Priests were only from the tribe of Levi and the family of Aaron. With kings, an injunction came after King Saul saying the king would be of the line of David, from the tribe of Judah (2 Samuel 7:8-16). Genesis 49:10 also says, *"The sceptre shall not depart from Judah."*

2. Scholars state that Matthew 16:18 is built around wordplay, specifically the underlying meaning of two words: Peter and rock. In Koine Greek, the name *Peter* refers to a rock that has broken off a ledge, something separate, as in a stone. In contrast, the word *rock* implies a massive boulder, or bedrock. *"And I tell you, you are Peter [stone], and on this rock [bedrock] I will build my church."* Matthew 16:18 ESV

    The Greek word *Peter* is masculine while the word *rock* is feminine. This makes it less likely that these two words are talking about the same person. It would be like saying, "You are a waiter and with this waitress I will serve a meal."

    So, if Peter was not the foundation for the church as some claim, then what was Jesus meaning? Scholars mention several possible interpretations:
    a) The rock upon which Jesus would build his church could be referring to Peter's confession of faith in Jesus, the bedrock for all spiritual growth.

    "You are the Christ, the Son of the living God." Matthew 16:16 NKJV

    Jesus would build his church upon those who confessed him as such. There is no argument over this, as many other verses in the Bible would support this idea.

    b) Others state that the verse could be applying to Jesus himself.

    "For no man can lay a foundation other than the one which is laid, which is Jesus Christ." 1 Corinthians 3:11 NASB

    "The LORD is my rock, and my fortress, and my deliverer; my God, my strength, in whom I will trust." Psalm 18:2 KJV

    "For who is God, except the LORD? And who is a rock, except our God?" Psalm 18:31 NKJV

    "They drank from the spiritual rock...and that rock [bedrock] was Christ." 1 Corinthians 10:4 NIV

    No one debates that Jesus is a rock or a foundation. Scripture teaches both.

    c) Some would say this verse teaches that God used Peter to establish believers—the church—in the first century. All would agree that this was true.

    One could say these interpretations are "safe" since other Scriptures support them. However, to extend Peter's authority beyond his lifespan, to create an ongoing power with both religious and political authority, would certainly evoke much disagreement and controversy. There are essentially no verses that would support such an interpretation.

3. Deuteronomy 19:15 NLT: *"You must not convict anyone of a crime on the testimony of only one witness. The facts of the case must be established by the testimony of two or three witnesses."*

4. Romans 1:18 NLT: *"But God shows his anger from heaven against all sinful, wicked people who suppress the truth by their wickedness."*

5. Josephus, *The Works of Josephus,* trans. W. Whiston (Peabody: Hendrickson Publishers, 1987) Wars 7.1 1-3.

CHAPTER SIX

CHAPTER SEVEN

1. Some Bible scholars see the Bema Seat Judgment and the Great White Throne Judgment as being the same. Many of these scholars are godly men who by reason of their study have come to this conclusion. Others agree with what I have presented in this book, as two unrelated judgments. In such situations, where the issue is not critical to one's eternal salvation, it is good to remember that one can disagree without being disagreeable.

2. A.W. Tozer, *Man: The Dwelling Place of God* (Camp Hill, PA: Wing Spread Pub.), 39-40.

CHAPTER EIGHT

1. A proselyte was a Gentile who had converted to Judaism.

2. Some church groups immerse a person three times.

3. I like to make sure the person being baptized clearly understands:
a) The identity of Jesus as the Creator God. NOTE: The term, *Son of God*, can be misunderstood to mean that Jesus is lesser than the Father, a sort of scaled-down God. This needs to be clarified.
b) The substitutionary work of Jesus on the cross, often expressed as, "He died for my sin."
c) Jesus is a resurrected Saviour.
I ask the person being baptized if he or she believes each one of these points to be true (Romans 10:9).

4. Having discussed infant baptism with parents and those baptized as infants, it seemed few understood the doctrinal stance of the church and simply viewed this as a form of child dedication. The meaning of the water and rite was vague. It was just "something you did."

5. Josephus, *The Works of Josephus,* Antiquities 18.3 63-64.

6. We should note that because of our sin, we are all guilty of nailing Jesus to the cross.

7. We learned in Chapter Two that when you see the name *LORD,* with all letters capitalized, you are reading *Yahweh*—the personal name of God. However, when you read the word *Lord* in the New Testament, with upper and lower case letters, it simply means "master" or "ruler" in the Greek language. (*Yahweh* is not a Greek word.) The exception to this is when the Old Testament is being quoted or referenced in the New Testament. If it is a **quote**, then checking the Old Testament verse will show whether it is God's personal name or simply referring to "master." If the God of the Old Testament is being **referenced**, it may be referring to God's personal name. In this case, context is the deciding factor.

8. This is not to be confused with the denomination called "The Local Church," associated with Witness Lee and Watchman Nee.

9. Some churches refer to this meal as Holy Communion or the Blessed Sacrament. I have used terminology that avoids overtones of liturgy that was not part of the original meal.

10. Juice is often substituted for wine.

CHAPTER NINE

1. *Dictionary.com*, s.v. "repentance," accessed Oct. 11, 2018, www.dictionary .com/browse/repentance

2. I filmed this story with rather primitive equipment in 1990. It is an incredible story of how armed guerrillas took Tim and Bunny Cain hostage in Colombia and forced them to call their base for medical help. Missionary pilots Steve Estelle and Paul Dye flew into the guerrillas' trap. God provided miraculous protection and freedom for the four hostages in this story of fear, despair, and ultimately, faith in God's ability to do the impossible. The video may be old, but it is well worth watching. It will challenge and strengthen your faith. *When Things Seem Impossible*, directed by John R. Cross (Sanford, FL: NTM, 1993).

3. In corresponding with Paul Dye on this event, he explained that although the airplane was heavy, it was also awkward. As he lifted the tail of the plane, the rudder was sticking in his face. It prevented him from using all his strength while lifting.

4. Eric Scott, *150 Years of Carrubbers Christian Centre*, (Edinburgh: Latent Publishing, 2008), 43. I have known Eric Scott as a friend for many years. He personally related this story to me. Also see www.carrubbers.org

5. There also may have been some converts to Judaism.

CHAPTER TEN

1. "We find that about one out of every three Muslim-background believers has had a dream or vision prior to their salvation experience. Some more precise surveys...suggest a little over 25 percent of Muslims had a dream or a vision before becoming disciples of Jesus. Either way, the percentage is significant. As powerful as [they]...are, though, they are just the door opener for most Muslims, the starting point for conversion." Tom Doyle, *Dreams and Visions: Is Jesus Awakening the Muslim World?*, with Greg Webster (Nashville, TN: Thomas Nelson, 2012), 127.

2. W.W. Wiersbe, *The Bible Exposition Commentary* (Wheaton: Victor Books, 1996, c1989), Acts 10:1. This event took place about ten years after Pentecost.

3. I have never seen a miracle worker perform a Class-A miracle that has met the biblical standard for both worker and miracle. Where does that leave it? It seems there is room in Scripture to acknowledge the reality of miracles without affirming individuals as miracle workers. One can say that God is still a God who heals even though he does not work through people designated as faith healers.

CHAPTER ELEVEN

1. The source of this acronym is unknown to me. I was taught "RIBS" many years ago and have found it helpful. Many thanks to the unknown individual who provided this simple way to remember the works of the Holy Spirit.

2. It could be legitimately argued that this comparison is not consistent across the entire chart as conception and birth are quite different and I have

lumped them together. For sake of space I have presented it on one chart to keep the physical-spiritual parallels of Scripture before us.

3. The Bible does not give specifics about clothing, colour or style. It does teach us to be "modest" which means we should not draw undue attention to ourselves. Some, in an attempt to be modest, dress in such a way that, although they cover their bodies, in their extreme they end up with an inappropriate focus on themselves.

4. Some Bible scholars identify as many as seven different baptisms in Scripture.

5. This is a one-time historical event, first to the Jews, then extended to the Samaritans (Acts 8:15-17) and the Gentiles (Acts 10:44-48). The final group included was an isolated group of John the Baptist's disciples (Acts 19:3-7).

CHAPTER TWELVE

1. Josephus, *The Works of Josephus*, Antiquities 19.8.2 343-350.

2. The Bible clearly states that the Holy Spirit offically arrived on the day of Pentecost, also known as the Feast of Weeks. It is not so clear regarding the giving of the Law. Jewish tradition and calculations state it so, and I have used it to make an interesting and helpful comparison, but no teaching in the Bible is reliant on it having happened on the same day.

3. The Ceremonial and Civil Law, as part of the 613 laws, had a role in leading us to Christ. One could view it as the rules in a classroom, how one should get along with others while in school. Once we moved to the school of grace, we had a different set of classroom laws, the ones that applied to the function of the body of Christ.

4. The Moral Code in the Mosaic Law actually involved more than the Ten Commandments. For example, the following verse is part of the Moral Code, but it does not appear in the Ten Commandments: "...you must love your neighbor as yourself" (Leviticus 19:18 NET). Over the centuries, God has revealed laws to govern different people at different times. That does not remove the fact that God is the same yesterday, today and forever (Hebrews 13:8), which refers to his nature, not his laws for mankind.

5. St. Clement of Rome, trans. J.B. Lightfoot, *The First Epistle of Clement to the Corinthians*, 1 Clem. 5:2,4.

6. M.R. James, trans., "The Acts of Peter," in *The Apocryphal New Testament* (Oxford: Clarendon Press, 1924), XXXVII.

7. The apocryphal book *The Acts of Peter* has Simon Peter resurrecting smoked fish and making dogs talk.

8. "*But we have nevertheless felt compelled to give a catalogue of these also, And further, the character of the style is at variance with apostolic usage, and both the thoughts and the purpose of the things that are related in them are so completely out of accord with true orthodoxy that they clearly show themselves to be the fictions of heretics. Wherefore they are not to be placed even among the rejected writings, but are all of them to be cast aside as absurd and impious.*" Eusebius, bishop of Caesarea from AD 314 to 339 and the first Church historian. Philip Schaff and Henry Wace, ed., *The Nicene and Post-Nicene Fathers*, ser. II, vol. 1 (Grand Rapids: Eerdmans), ch. 25:6-7.

9. Hiroo Onoda, *No Surrender: My Thirty-Year War*, (Japan: Naval Institute Press, 2013), 44.

TELLING THE STORY CREATION TO CHRIST

Christianized WORLDVIEW

For those influenced by Christianity—whether Protestant, Catholic or Orthodox.

Islamic WORLDVIEW

Available at www.goodseed.com

25% different than *The Stranger*.
Those influenced by Islam, but not necessarily Muslim by belief.

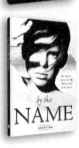

Eastern WORLDVIEW

60% different than *The Stranger*, 1593 Bible verses.

Those influenced by polytheism, pantheism, atheism, agnosticism and animism. Also those with New Age ideas. Includes those who appease ancestors and spirits.

Secular WORLDVIEW

25% shorter than *The Stranger*; 44% shorter than *By This Name*; Bible verses: 1028

For those who consume information in small bites. The core message is found in eight booklets, 40 pages per booklet, excluding appendixes. Additional booklets expand beyond the core set.

Children's WORLDVIEW

All children, ages 4 and up.

Enjoyed by many ages and backgrounds.

PUZZLED ABOUT WORLDVIEWS?

A question to ask:
"When you hear the word 'God' what do you think of?"

If the answer includes a powerful person or being, as described in the Bible, then you are facing a **Christianized Worldview.**

If the answer is Allah as explained in the Koran, then you are facing the **Islamic Worldview.**

If the answer sounds like "Let the force be with you," or includes many gods and goddesses, then you are facing the **Eastern Worldview.**

If they don't know or seem indifferent, then you are facing the **Secular Worldview**, which may include atheistic, agnostic, postmodern or Utopian ideas such as Critical Theory.

Each book answers the questions a worldview asks about the Bible. It does so without changing the message or specifically mentioning the religion or worldview.

VideoBook

This 10.4-hour, award-winning video series clearly and logically explains the Bible from creation to Christ. Following *The Stranger* book, often word for word, the greatest of stories is brought to life on screen. Using over 70 visual aids, John R. Cross leads the viewer through the story of the Bible in a way that is unforgettable.

Available on DVD or USB   Also in Spanish

Amharic	Dutch	Lao	Thai
Albanian	Faroese	Lingala	Turkish
Arabic	Farsi	Lithuanian	Ukrainian
Bangla	French	Luxembourgish	
Chechen	German	Mongolian	
Chichewa	Hebrew	Portuguese	**Books available in**
Czech	Hungarian	Romanian	**these languages**
Chinese (Traditional)	Korean	Russian	
Chinese (Simplified)	Italian	Spanish	

GOODSEED® International

P. O. Box 3704

Olds, AB T4H 1P5

CANADA

Business: 403 556-9955
Facsimile: 403 556-9950
Email: info@goodseed.com

— To Order —
www.goodseed.com

—— www.goodseed.com ——

GOODSEED® International is a not-for-profit organization that exists for the purpose of clearly communicating the contents of this book in this language and others. We invite you to contact us if you are interested in ongoing projects or translations.

'GOODSEED,' and the Book/Leaf design mark are trademarks of GOODSEED International.